Second Workshop on Pattern-based Approaches to NLP in the Age of Deep Learning (PAN-DL 2023)

Singapore
6 December 2023

ISBN: 978-1-7138-8606-8

Printed from e-media with permission by:

Curran Associates, Inc.
57 Morehouse Lane
Red Hook, NY 12571

Some format issues inherent in the e-media version may also appear in this print version.

Printed with permission by Curran Associates, Inc. (2024)

Association for Computational Linguistics
209 N. Eighth Street
Stroudsburg, Pennsylvania 18360

Phone: 1-570-476-8006
Fax: 1-570-476-0860

acl@aclweb.org

Additional copies of this publication are available from:

Curran Associates, Inc.
57 Morehouse Lane
Red Hook, NY 12571 USA
Phone: 845-758-0400
Fax: 845-758-2633
Email: curran@proceedings.com
Web: www.proceedings.com

EMNLP 2023

The Second Workshop on Pattern-based Approaches to NLP in the Age of Deep Learning (Pan-DL)

Proceedings of the Workshop

December 6, 2023

Message from the Organizers

Welcome to the second edition of the Workshop on Pattern-based Approaches to NLP in the Age of Deep Learning (Pan-DL)! Our workshop is being organized in a hybrid format on December 6, 2023, in conjunction with the 2023 Conference on Empirical Methods in Natural Language Processing (EMNLP).

In the past year, the natural language processing (NLP) field (and the world at large!) has been hit by the large language model (LLM) "tsunami." This happened for the right reasons: LLMs perform extremely well in a multitude of NLP tasks, often with minimal training and, perhaps for the first time, have made NLP technology extremely approachable to non-expert users. However, LLMs are not perfect: they are not really explainable, they are not pliable, i.e., they cannot be easily modified to correct any errors observed, and they are not efficient due to the overhead of decoding. In contrast, rule-based methods are more transparent to subject matter experts; they are amenable to having a human in the loop through intervention, manipulation and incorporation of domain knowledge; and further the resulting systems tend to be lightweight and fast. This workshop focuses on all aspects of rule-based approaches, including their application, representation, and interpretability, as well as their strengths and weaknesses relative to state-of-the-art machine learning approaches.

Considering the large number of potential directions in this neuro-symbolic space, we emphasized inclusivity in our workshop. We received 19 submissions and accepted 10 for oral presentation. This resulted in an overall acceptance rate of 52%. Our workshop also includes 6 presentations of papers that were accepted in Findings of EMNLP.

In addition to the oral presentations of the accepted papers, our workshop includes a keynote talk by Yunyao Li, who has made many important contributions to the field of symbolic approaches for natural language processing. Further, the workshop contains a panel that will discuss the merits and limitations of rules in the new LLM era. The panelists will be academics with expertise in both neural- and rule-based methods, industry experts that employ these methods for commercial products, and subject matter experts that have used rule-based methods for domain-specific applications.

We thank Yunyao Li and the panelists for their important contribution to our workshop!

Finally, we are thankful to the members of the program committee for their insightful reviews! We are confident that all submissions have benefited from their expert feedback. Their contribution was a key factor for accepting a diverse and high-quality list of papers, which we hope will make the first edition of the Pan-DL workshop a success, and will motivate many future editions.

Pan-DL 2023 Organizers
December 6, 2023

Organizing Committee

Laura Chiticariu, IBM, USA
Gus Hahn-Powell, University of Arizona, USA
Dayne Freitag, SRI International, USA
Ellen Riloff, University of Arizona, USA
Clayton T. Morrison, University of Arizona, USA
Rebecca Sharp, Lex Machina, USA
Marco Valenzuela-Escárcega, Lex Machina, USA
Mihai Surdeanu, University of Arizona, USA
Enrique Noriega-Atala, University of Arizona, USA

Program Committee

Keith Alcock, University of Arizona, USA
Dillon Mee, University of Arizona, USA
Simon Mille, Dublin City University, Ireland
Mithun Paul, University of Arizona, USA
Haris Riaz, University of Arizona, USA
Arie Sutiono, University of Arizona, USA
Zheng Tang, Samsung Research America, USA
Robert Vacareanu, University of Arizona, USA
Hoang Van, University of Colorado Boulder, USA
Vikas Yadav, Samsung Research America, USA

Table of Contents

Nearest Neighbor Search over Vectorized Lexico-Syntactic Patterns for Relation Extraction from Financial Documents
Pawan Rajpoot and Ankur Parikh 1

LEAF: Linguistically Enhanced Event Temporal Relation Framework
Stanley Lim, Da Yin and Nanyun Peng 6

A Graph-Guided Reasoning Approach for Open-ended Commonsense Question Answering
Zhen Han, Yue Feng and Mingming Sun 20

Generating Irish Text with a Flexible Plug-and-Play Architecture
Simon Mille, Elaine Uí Dhonnchadha, Lauren Cassidy, Brian Davis, Stamatia Dasiopoulou and Anya Belz 25

Symbolic Planning and Code Generation for Grounded Dialogue
Justin Chiu, Wenting Zhao, Derek Chen, Saujas Vaduguru, Alexander Rush and Daniel Fried . . . 43

Towards Zero-Shot Frame Semantic Parsing with Task Agnostic Ontologies and Simple Labels
Danilo Neves Ribeiro, Jack Goetz, Omid Abdar, Mike Ross, Annie Dong, Kenneth Forbus and Ahmed Mohamed 54

Co-evolving data-driven and NLU-driven Synthesizers for Generating Code in Domain Growth and Data Scarcity
Jiasheng Gu, Zifan Nan, Zhiyuan Peng, Xipeng Shen and Dongkuan Xu 64

Complementary Roles of Inference and Language Models in QA
Liang Cheng, Mohammad Javad Hosseini and Mark Steedman 75

Controlled Data Augmentation for Training Task-Oriented Dialog Systems with Low Resource Data
Sebastian Steindl, Ulrich Schäfer and Bernd Ludwig 92

A Hybrid of Rule-based and Transformer-based Approaches for Relation Extraction in Biodiversity Literature
Roselyn Gabud, Portia Lapitan, Vladimir Mariano, Eduardo Mendoza, Nelson Pampolina, Maria Art Antonette Clariño and Riza Batista-Navarro 103

Conference Program

Wednesday, December 6, 2023

9:00–9:15 ***Introduction***

9:15–10:30 ***Panel***

10:30–10:45 ***Coffee Break***

10:45–12:00 *Keynote*
Yunyao Li, Director of Machine Learning, Adobe Experience Platform

12:00–13:00 ***Lunch***

13:00–14:15 **Session One**

13:00–13:15 *Nearest Neighbor Search over Vectorized Lexico-Syntactic Patterns for Relation Extraction from Financial Documents*
Pawan Rajpoot and Ankur Parikh

13:15–13:30 *LEAF: Linguistically Enhanced Event Temporal Relation Framework*
Stanley Lim, Da Yin and Nanyun Peng

13:30–13:45 *A Graph-Guided Reasoning Approach for Open-ended Commonsense Question Answering*
Zhen Han, Yue Feng and Mingming Sun

13:45–14:00 *Generating Irish Text with a Flexible Plug-and-Play Architecture*
Simon Mille, Elaine Uí Dhonnchadha, Lauren Cassidy, Brian Davis, Stamatia Dasiopoulou and Anya Belz

14:00–14:15 *Findings Talk - A Lightweight Method to Generate Unanswerable Questions in English*
Vagrant Gautam

14:15–14:25 ***Short Break***

Wednesday, December 6, 2023 (continued)

14:25–15:30 Session 2

14:25–14:40 *Symbolic Planning and Code Generation for Grounded Dialogue*
Justin Chiu, Wenting Zhao, Derek Chen, Saujas Vaduguru, Alexander Rush and Daniel Fried

14:40–14:55 *Towards Zero-Shot Frame Semantic Parsing with Task Agnostic Ontologies and Simple Labels*
Danilo Neves Ribeiro, Jack Goetz, Omid Abdar, Mike Ross, Annie Dong, Kenneth Forbus and Ahmed Mohamed

14:55–15:10 *Co-evolving data-driven and NLU-driven Synthesizers for Generating Code in Domain Growth and Data Scarcity*
Jiasheng Gu, Zifan Nan, Zhiyuan Peng, Xipeng Shen and Dongkuan Xu

15:10–15:25 *Findings Talk - What Makes Chain-of-Thought Prompting Effective? A Counterfactual Study*
Aman Maadan

15:30–15:45 *Coffee Break*

15:45–17:00 Session Three

15:45–16:00 *Complementary Roles of Inference and Language Models in QA*
Liang Cheng, Mohammad Javad Hosseini and Mark Steedman

16:00–16:15 *Controlled Data Augmentation for Training Task-Oriented Dialog Systems with Low Resource Data*
Sebastian Steindl, Ulrich Schäfer and Bernd Ludwig

16:15–16:30 *A Hybrid of Rule-based and Transformer-based Approaches for Relation Extraction in Biodiversity Literature*
Roselyn Gabud, Portia Lapitan, Vladimir Mariano, Eduardo Mendoza, Nelson Pampolina, Maria Art Antonette Clariño and Riza Batista-Navarro

16:30–16:45 *Findings Talk - Solving the Right Problem is Key for Translational NLP*
Bernal Jimenez Gutierrez

16:45–17:00 *Findings Talk - TR-Rules: Rule-based Model for Link Forecasting on Temporal Knowledge Graph Considering Temporal Redundancy*
Ningyuan Li

17:00–17:10 *Short Break*

17:10–17:40 Session Four

17:10–17:25 *Findings Talk - BanLemma: A Word Formation Dependent Rule and Dictionary Based Bangla Lemmatizer*
Sadia Afrin

17:25–17:40 *Findings Talk - Evaluating Emotion Arcs Across Languages: Bridging the Global Divide in Emotion Research*
Daniela Teodorescu

17:40–17:45 ***Best Paper Award***

17:45–18:00 ***Closing***

Nearest Neighbor Search over Vectorized Lexico-Syntactic Patterns for Relation Extraction from Financial Documents

Pawan Kumar Rajpoot *
UtilizeAI Research
Bangalore, India
pawan.rajpoot2411@gmail.com

Ankur Parikh *
UtilizeAI Research
Bangalore, India
ankur.parikh85@gmail.com

Abstract

Relation extraction (RE) has achieved remarkable progress with the help of pre-trained language models. However, existing RE models are usually incapable of handling two situations: implicit expressions and long-tail relation classes, caused by language complexity and data sparsity. Further, these approaches and models are largely inaccessible to users who don't have direct access to large language models (LLMs) and/or infrastructure for supervised training or fine-tuning. Rule-based systems also struggle with implicit expressions. Apart from this, Real world financial documents such as various 10-X reports (including 10-K, 10-Q, etc.) of publicly traded companies pose another challenge to rule-based systems in terms of longer and complex sentences. In this paper, we introduce a simple approach that consults training relations at test time through a nearest-neighbor search over dense vectors of lexico-syntactic patterns and provides a simple yet effective means to tackle the above issues. We evaluate our approach on REFinD and show that our method achieves state-of-the-art performance. We further show that it can provide a good start for human in the loop setup when a small number of annotations are available and it is also beneficial when domain experts can provide high quality patterns. Our code is available at [1].

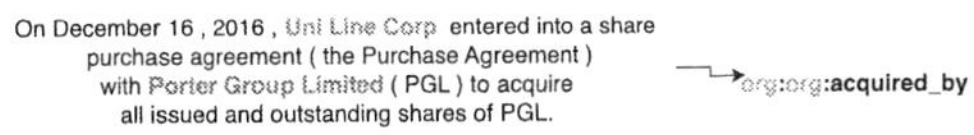

Figure 1: Relation Extraction example, here both organizations are connected with "acquired by" relation.

1 Introduction

Relation extraction (RE) from text is a fundamental problem in NLP and information retrieval, which facilitates various tasks like knowledge graph construction, question answering and semantic search. Recent studies (Zhang et al., 2020; Zeng et al., 2020; Lin et al., 2020; Wang and Lu, 2020; Cheng et al., 2020; Zhong and Chen, 2021) in supervised RE take advantage of pre-trained language models (PLMs) and achieve SOTA performances by fine-tuning PLMs with a relation classifier. However, (Wan et al., 2022) observes that existing RE models are usually incapable of handling two RE-specific situations: implicit expressions and long-tail relation types.

Implicit expression refers to the situation whereas relation is expressed as the underlying message that is not explicitly stated or shown. In Figure 1, relation "acquired_by(organization, organization)" occurs implicitly. Such underlying messages can easily confuse the relation classifier.

The other problem of long-tail relation classes is caused by data sparsity in training. For example, the REFinD dataset (Kaur et al., 2023) comprises 45.5 % of the no_relation instances. The most frequent class in the dataset - "per:title:title" has 4,468 training examples, while over 14 out of 22 classes have less than 500 examples. The majority class can easily dominate model predictions and lead to low performance on long-tail classes.

Recently, ICL (In-Context Learning) based approach (Wan et al., 2023) is utilized for RE tasks. The approach achieves improvements over not only existing GPT-3 baselines, but also on fully-supervised baselines even with only a limited number of demonstrations provided in the prompt. Specifically, it achieves SOTA performances on the Semeval and SciERC datasets, and competitive performances on the TACRED and (Zhang et al., 2017a) ACE05 datasets. (Rajpoot and Parikh, 2023) utilized the GPT-4 under ICL framework on REFinD and achieved 3rd rank in the shared task.

However, retrieval of examples to demonstrate is a key factor in the overall performance on these

[1]https://github.com/pawan2411/PAN-DL_Refind
*Equal Contribution

Proceedings of the 2nd Workshop in Pattern-based Approaches to NLP in the Age of Deep Learning , pages 1–5
December 6, 2023.

pipelines. Finding efficient demonstrates often relies on learning-based retrieval (Ye et al., 2023; Rubin et al., 2022). These learning-based retrievers use annotated data and a LLM. This type of retrieval strategy comes with the increased cost (API, infrastructure etc.), time as more experiments are required because most LLMs are black box and it also needs special expertise.

Apart from the implicit expression challenge mentioned above, REFinD poses another challenge to rule-based systems in terms of longer and complex sentences. For example, (Kaur et al., 2023) cites that the average sentence length in the REFinD dataset is 53.7 while the average sentence length in the TACRED dataset (Zhang et al., 2017b) is 36.2. Further, As per (Kaur et al., 2023), REFinD includes more complex sentences than TACRED, with an average entity-pair distance of 11, compared to 8 in TACRED. Because of this, writing rules at surface text level is a challenge. Hence, rules at lexico-syntactic level is the need of the hour. However, strict matching of these rules can yield high precision but low recall result due to accuracy of syntactic parsing. Hence, a robust fuzzy pattern matching system is required.

Inspired by recent studies (Wan et al., 2022; Khandelwal et al., 2019; Guu et al., 2020; Meng et al., 2021) using k-Nearest Neighbor to retrieve diverse expressions for language generation tasks, we introduce a simple but effective approach that consults training relations at test time through a nearest-neighbor search over dense vectors of lexico-syntactic patterns and provides a simple yet effective means to tackle the above issues. Our method achieves an improvement of 1.18% over baseline (F1-score - 0.7516). We achieved our results using commodity hardware within a day. That's why our approach is easier to deploy, lightweight and fast. We further show that our approach can provide a good start (F1-score of 0.5122) for human in the loop setup when a small number of annotations (approx. 10% of training data) are available and it is also beneficial (F1-score of 0.6939 with approx. 10% of training data) when domain experts can provide high quality patterns.

2 Preliminary Background

2.1 Task Definition

Let C denote the input context and e1 in C, e2 in C denote the pair of entity pairs. Given a set of predefined relations classes R, relation extraction

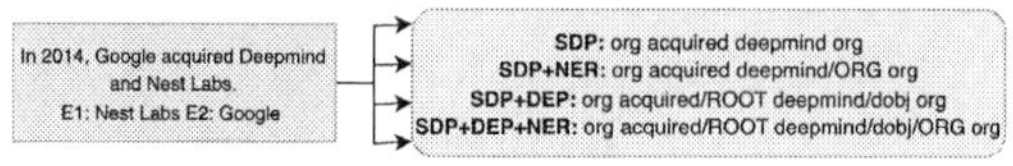

Figure 2: Patterns extracted by our pipeline

aims to predict the relation y in R between the pair of entities (e1, e2) within the context C,or if there is no predefined relation between them, predict y="no relation".

2.2 Data

The REFinD dataset (Kaur et al., 2023) is the largest relation extraction dataset for financial documents to date. Overall REFinD contains around 29K instances and 22 relations among 8 types of entity pairs. REFinD is created using raw text from various 10-X reports (including 10-K, 10-Q, etc.broadly known as 10-X) of publicly traded companies obtained from US Securities and Exchange Commission.

3 Nearest Neighbor Search over Vectorized Lexico-Syntactic Patterns

3.1 Generating Lexico-Syntactic Patterns

We replaced words representing entities of interest with their entity types given in the dataset.

Instead of conducting nearest neighbor search on a complete sentence, we applied Spacy Dependency Parser[2] and considered the shortest dependency path (henceforth SDP) between two entities to deal with long and complex sentences with the intuition that considering all sentence words can do more harm in search. SDP is essential for relationship identification in most cases.

We apply Spacy NER on REFinD sentences and replace actual named entities with their types to create higher-level patterns.

We also enriched all SDP words with their Dependency Labels to utilize structure information in our search.

For each sentence, we create 4 patterns: 1. SDP words only (SDP) 2. SDP words with named entities replaced with their types (SDP-NER) 3. SDP words enriched with their Dependency Labels (SDP-DEP) 4. SDP words with named entities replaced with their types and also enriched with their Dependency Labels (SDP-DEP-NER). Example patterns are shown in Figure 2.

[2]https://spacy.io/

3.2 Generating Dense Vectors for Lexico-Syntactic Patterns

We converted all 4 types of Lexico-Syntactic Patterns into Dense Vectors as it performs better than Sparse Vectors. To create a vector, we employed an all-mpnet-base-v2[3] sentence encoder. We also created vectors for original sentences using the encoder.

3.3 Creating Class Specific Indices

For each pattern type mentioned above, we created 21 dense vector indices each representing a relationship class except 'no_relation' class. We split 'no_relation' training data instances into 8 splits as per entity-type pairs such as "Person-Organization", "Organization-Organization" etc. and created indices for each split. In this way, there are 29 indices in total for each pattern type. Each element of the index represents a vectorized lexico-syntactic pattern for each training example. For around 11.89% of the training sentences, we faced issues in generating dependency tree and/or SDP. To deal with this, we also created another 29 indices containing dense vectors for original sentences.

3.4 Conducting Nearest Neighbor Search

After configuring lexico-syntactic pattern type and value of K, Given a test sentence and an entity-type pair, we first create a vector representing its lexico-syntactic pattern obtained using steps described above. With the entity-type pair, appropriate relation class indices are selected for search. The pattern vector is searched in every appropriate class index using cosine similarity and top K vectors from each class index are obtained. The similarity scores of each of these top K vectors are averaged and the class having the highest similarity score is selected. In the case of syntactic parsing failures, as a fallback strategy, a vector of the original sentence is created and is used against class specific sentence indices in search the same way as mentioned above.

[3]https://huggingface.co/sentence-transformers/all-mpnet-base-v2

Pattern	K	F1-score
SDP	14	0.7552
SDP-NER	12	0.7538
SDP-DEP	11	0.7610
SDP-DEP-NER	14	**0.7634**
Winner on leaderboard (baseline) [4]	-	0.7516

Table 1: Comparison on performance on REFinD dev data

Figure 3: Sensitivity Analysis

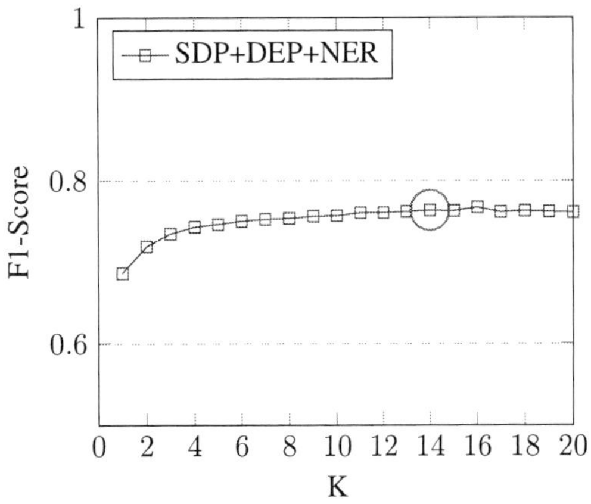

4 Experiment Settings

4.1 Dataset

The REFinD dataset (Kaur et al., 2023) released with the shared task is a part of "Knowledge Discovery from Unstructured Data in Financial Services" (KDF) workshop which is collocated with SIGIR 2023. There are 20070, 4306 and 4300 instances of training data, development data and public test data respectively. The organizers have released training data, development data and public test data with gold labels but haven't released private test data with gold labels. Because of that, we are not able to benchmark our system against the winners of the shared task. Since, leaderboard [4] and gold labels on development data is available, we have benchmarked our approach against the leaders of development data. We have used training data and public test data to create class specific indices to perform nearest neighbor search for development data sentences.

4.2 Hardware Resources

We have used a laptop with 16GB RAM and Intel® Core™ i7-7500U CPU @ 2.70GHz × 4 CPU to

[4]https://codalab.lisn.upsaclay.fr/competitions/11770

produce these results.

4.3 Efforts

Given the dataset, all setup and experiments are conducted within a day.

5 Results

We conducted experiments with 4 different pattern types. To find the best value of K, we have created a 10% split from the training data and experimented with different values of K (1 to 20). During evaluation, we faced issues in generating dependency tree and/or SDP for around 8.7% instances and for those instances, indices containing sentence vectors were used as fallback strategy. The results in Table 1 show that our best F1-score is 0.7634 for SDP-DEP-NER pattern and K=14 (Top K vectors) and our method shows improvement of 1.18% over baseline. Figure 3 shows how sensitive this approach is with respect to different values of K. This confirms our intuition that there is value in utilizing vectorized lexico-syntactic patterns to deal with long and complex sentences and implicit expressions. Further, splitting instances as per the class and performing lazy classification over these splits can help in dealing with the dataset with long-tail relation classes.

To explore the effectiveness of our approach in human in the loop situation, we conducted a few experiments as shown in Figure 4. We randomly selected N patterns per class from the training data and built indices with those patterns only. We tried different values of N. With N=100 and K=1 (derived from dev split), we achieved an F1-score of 0.5122 with around 10% of the original training data. It shows that the vectorized lexico-syntactic patterns and the cosine similarity based scoring can be a good start to label similar instances when the number of annotations are less. This method can be used in human in the loop setup to either filter out similar instances (explore) or to find similar instances (exploit) for further human review/annotation.

To explore the effectiveness of our approach when domain experts are available and can provide high quality patterns specially for the task like this which is restricted to a particular domain, types of documents, types of entities and a handful of relations, we conducted a few experiments as shown in Figure 4. To approximate this experiment, we selected N training patterns from each class which occurs frequently in Top K search when development patterns are classified correctly. We call these patterns the Most-Frequent Patterns. We built indices with those patterns only. As shown in Figure 4, with N=100 and K=4 (derived from dev split), we achieved an F1-score of 0.6939 (6.95% less than the best result) with around 10% of the original training data. It shows that it can bridge gaps quickly with a small amount of high quality patterns.

Figure 4: Training Patterns Selection

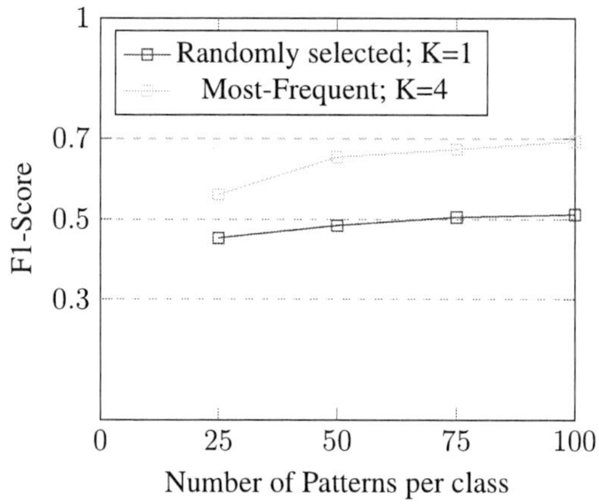

6 Conclusion

Our approach consults training relations at test time through a nearest-neighbor search over dense vectors of lexico-syntactic patterns. We evaluated our approach on REFinD and show that our method achieves state-of-the-art performance without any direct access to large language models (LLMs) or supervised training or fine-tuning or any hand-crafted rules. We achieved our results using a commodity hardware within a day. That's why our approach is easier to deploy, lightweight and fast. We further explores that our approach can provide a good start for human in the loop setup when a small number of annotations are available and it can be also beneficial when domain experts can provide high quality patterns.

7 Limitations

Since our method is based on nearest neighbors search, it's sensitive to the value of K. Furthermore, our method is also very sensitive to syntactic parsing and NER. Our vectors are not optimal representations because our syntactic patterns are not a natural fit for the sentence encoder.

References

Fei Cheng, Masayuki Asahara, Ichiro Kobayashi, and Sadao Kurohashi. 2020. Dynamically updating event representations for temporal relation classification with multi-category learning. In *Findings of the Association for Computational Linguistics: EMNLP 2020*, pages 1352–1357, Online. Association for Computational Linguistics.

Kelvin Guu, Kenton Lee, Zora Tung, Panupong Pasupat, and Mingwei Chang. 2020. Retrieval augmented language model pre-training. In *International conference on machine learning*, pages 3929–3938. PMLR.

Simerjot Kaur, Charese Smiley, Akshat Gupta, Joy Sain, Dongsheng Wang, Suchetha Siddagangappa, Toyin Aguda, and Sameena Shah. 2023. Refind: Relation extraction financial dataset. *arXiv preprint arXiv:2305.18322*.

Urvashi Khandelwal, Omer Levy, Dan Jurafsky, Luke Zettlemoyer, and Mike Lewis. 2019. Generalization through memorization: Nearest neighbor language models. *arXiv preprint arXiv:1911.00172*.

Ying Lin, Heng Ji, Fei Huang, and Lingfei Wu. 2020. A joint neural model for information extraction with global features. In *Proceedings of the 58th Annual Meeting of the Association for Computational Linguistics*, pages 7999–8009, Online. Association for Computational Linguistics.

Yuxian Meng, Shi Zong, Xiaoya Li, Xiaofei Sun, Tianwei Zhang, Fei Wu, and Jiwei Li. 2021. Gnn-lm: Language modeling based on global contexts via gnn. *arXiv preprint arXiv:2110.08743*.

Pawan Kumar Rajpoot and Ankur Parikh. 2023. Gpt-finre: In-context learning for financial relation extraction using large language models.

Ohad Rubin, Jonathan Herzig, and Jonathan Berant. 2022. Learning to retrieve prompts for in-context learning. In *Proceedings of the 2022 Conference of the North American Chapter of the Association for Computational Linguistics: Human Language Technologies*, pages 2655–2671, Seattle, United States. Association for Computational Linguistics.

Zhen Wan, Fei Cheng, Zhuoyuan Mao, Qianying Liu, Haiyue Song, Jiwei Li, and Sadao Kurohashi. 2023. Gpt-re: In-context learning for relation extraction using large language models.

Zhen Wan, Qianying Liu, Zhuoyuan Mao, Fei Cheng, Sadao Kurohashi, and Jiwei Li. 2022. Rescue implicit and long-tail cases: Nearest neighbor relation extraction. In *Proceedings of the 2022 Conference on Empirical Methods in Natural Language Processing*, pages 1731–1738, Abu Dhabi, United Arab Emirates. Association for Computational Linguistics.

Jue Wang and Wei Lu. 2020. Two are better than one: Joint entity and relation extraction with table-sequence encoders. In *Proceedings of the 2020 Conference on Empirical Methods in Natural Language Processing (EMNLP)*, pages 1706–1721, Online. Association for Computational Linguistics.

Jiacheng Ye, Zhiyong Wu, Jiangtao Feng, Tao Yu, and Lingpeng Kong. 2023. Compositional exemplars for in-context learning. *arXiv preprint arXiv:2302.05698*.

Daojian Zeng, Haoran Zhang, and Qianying Liu. 2020. Copymtl: Copy mechanism for joint extraction of entities and relations with multi-task learning. In *Proceedings of the AAAI conference on artificial intelligence*, volume 34, pages 9507–9514.

Ranran Haoran Zhang, Qianying Liu, Aysa Xuemo Fan, Heng Ji, Daojian Zeng, Fei Cheng, Daisuke Kawahara, and Sadao Kurohashi. 2020. Minimize exposure bias of Seq2Seq models in joint entity and relation extraction. In *Findings of the Association for Computational Linguistics: EMNLP 2020*, pages 236–246, Online. Association for Computational Linguistics.

Yuhao Zhang, Victor Zhong, Danqi Chen, Gabor Angeli, and Christopher D. Manning. 2017a. Position-aware attention and supervised data improve slot filling. In *Proceedings of the 2017 Conference on Empirical Methods in Natural Language Processing (EMNLP 2017)*, pages 35–45.

Yuhao Zhang, Victor Zhong, Danqi Chen, Gabor Angeli, and Christopher D. Manning. 2017b. Position-aware attention and supervised data improve slot filling. In *Proceedings of the 2017 Conference on Empirical Methods in Natural Language Processing*, pages 35–45, Copenhagen, Denmark. Association for Computational Linguistics.

Zexuan Zhong and Danqi Chen. 2021. A frustratingly easy approach for entity and relation extraction. In *Proceedings of the 2021 Conference of the North American Chapter of the Association for Computational Linguistics: Human Language Technologies*, pages 50–61, Online. Association for Computational Linguistics.

LEAF: Linguistically Enhanced Event Temporal Relation Framework

Stanley Lim Da Yin Nanyun Peng
University of California, Los Angeles
stanleylim2@g.ucla.edu {da.yin, violetpeng}@cs.ucla.edu

Abstract

Linguistic structures can implicitly imply diverse types of event relations that have been previously underexplored. For example, the sentence "John was **cooking** freshly **made** noodles for the family **gathering**" contains no explicit temporal indicators between the events, such as *before*. Despite this, it is easy for humans to conclude, based on syntax, that the noodles were **made** *before* John started **cooking**, and that the family **gathering** starts *after* John starts **cooking**. We introduce **L**inguistically enhanced **E**vent Tempor**A**l relation **F**ramework (**LEAF**), a simple and effective approach to acquiring rich temporal knowledge of events from large-scale corpora. This method improves pre-trained language models by automatically extracting temporal relation knowledge from unannotated corpora using diverse temporal knowledge patterns. We begin by manually curating a comprehensive list of atomic patterns that imply temporal relations between events. These patterns involve event pairs in which one event is contained within the argument of the other. Using transitivity, we discover compositional patterns and assign labels to event pairs involving these patterns. Finally, we make language models learn the rich knowledge by pre-training with the acquired temporal relation supervision. Experiments show that our method outperforms or rivals previous models on two event relation datasets: MATRES and TB-Dense. Our approach is also simpler from past works and excels at identifying complex compositional event relations.

1 Introduction

Event temporal relation extraction can help us better organize event flow and understand how events develop. For example, in news articles, understanding the causal relationships between events can help us better understand why certain events occurred (Tan et al., 2022; Zhang et al., 2023). In medical records, understanding the temporal relationships between events can help us better track a patient's medical history (Cheng et al., 2013; Lee et al., 2018).

Recently, there have been works focusing on first acquiring temporal relation knowledge automatically and then injecting the acquired knowledge via pre-training. For example, ECONET (Han et al., 2021b) uses explicit keyword search to retrieve the sentences that contain temporal indicators such as *before*, *after*, *during*, and *previously* as supervision. However, they do not fully exploit knowledge from sentence **linguistic structures**. While Zhou et al. 2020a make an attempt to utilize linguistic structures by extracting patterns from semantic role labeling (SRL) parses (Gardner et al., 2018; Shi and Lin, 2019), much of the linguistic information available is under-explored and they only utilize keywords found in an event's temporal argument. Moreover, previous works which utilize linguistic structure for event relation knowledge do not apply them to neural networks (D'Souza and Ng, 2013; Chambers et al., 2014).

We find that there is rich, implicit event knowledge in the **linguistic structures** that has not been explicitly leveraged in the past. For example, consider the sentence "John was **cooking** freshly **made** noodles for the family **gathering** as Adam **arrived**". Notice that in this sentence, there is only one ***explicit*** mention of the temporal relationship between any of the events, which is that John was **cooking** as Adam **arrived**. However, it is possible to extract five times the number of relations according to linguistic structures (Figure 1):

Relation 1: The noodles were **made** *before* John started **cooking**, since adjectives of event objects all occur before the event occurs.

Relation 2: John started **cooking** *before* family **gathering** began, since an event always starts before its purpose event.

Relation 3: The noodles were **made** *before* Adam **arrived**, since we know from the above relations that the noodles were made before John

Proceedings of the 2nd Workshop in Pattern-based Approaches to NLP in the Age of Deep Learning, pages 6–19
December 6, 2023.

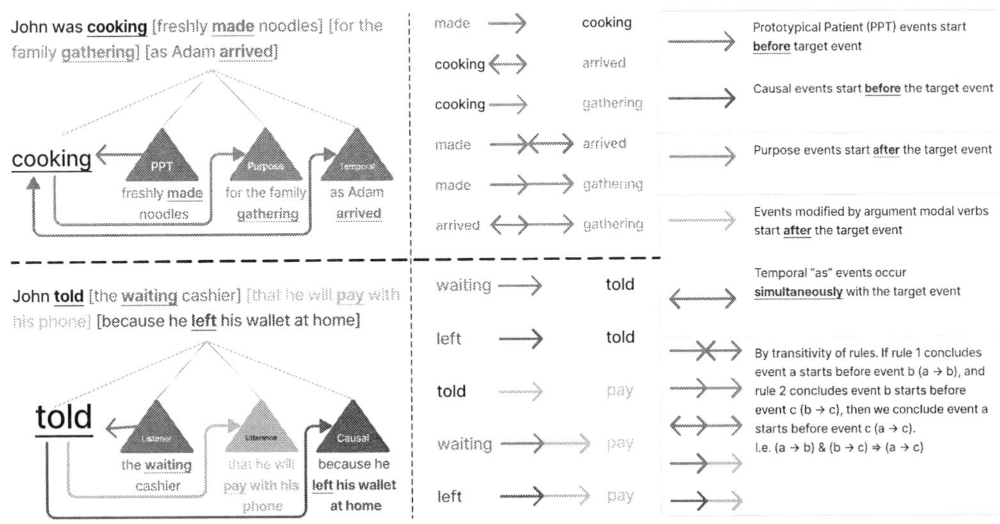

Figure 1: Process of utilizing temporal knowledge patterns to acquire temporal relation supervision for pre-training. An arrow a –> b indicates that event "a" starts before event "b". We first obtain the SRL annotations for all events (shown are the annotations for "cooking" and "told"). Then, using a list of atomic patterns, we automatically extract temporal relationships between a target event and other events in its arguments (shown by the single colored arrows). Finally, we use transitivity rules to find compositional relations (shown by the arrows with two colors). The table on the right shows the patterns corresponding to each relation. Note that this figure displays a subset of the entire set of patterns we use.

started **cooking**, and Adam **arrived** as cooking was started.

Relation 4: The noodles were **made** *before* the family **gathering**, since we know from the above relations that the noodles were **made** before John began **cooking**, and John began **cooking** before family **gathering** started.

Relation 5: Adam **arrived** *before* family **gathering**, since we know from the above relations that Adam **arrived** as John was **cooking**, and John starts **cooking** before the family **gathering**.

To this end, we propose **LEAF**, a **L**inguistically enhanced **E**vent tempor**A**l relation **F**ramework. Our method aims at capturing a diverse set of linguistic structures implicitly indicating temporal relations (a.k.a, temporal knowledge patterns), and uses them to facilitate language models to learn richer temporal knowledge. We start by manually curating a diverse list of **atomic** patterns that commonly imply certain temporal relations (Appendix A). These patterns involve pairs of events where one event is contained within the argument structure of the other. For example, a target event always starts after events in its prototypical patient (PPT) argument, and we can use this atomic pattern to find that **cooking** starts after **made** (Figure 1). Our list encompasses an extension of patterns from previous works (Zhou et al., 2020a) along with novel patterns, including the PPT pattern.

As illustrated in Figure 1, if we consider only atomic patterns, many temporal relations are still overlooked. The events **made**, **gathering**, and **arrived** are not within one another's arguments, yet they still hold temporal relations. To capture these relations, we also gather **compositional** patterns. These are connections between two events that are not directly linked in their argument structures and are derived by utilizing the transitivity of atomic patterns. From applying these temporal knowledge patterns, we are able to extract two more atomic relations (relations 1-2) and three more compositional relations (relations 3-5) from the example sentence than knowledge acquisition methods relying only on temporal indicator word searching.

To deploy temporal knowledge patterns for obtaining training supervision at scale, we use AllenNLP's SRL parser (Gardner et al., 2018; Shi and Lin, 2019) on raw text. We then search the collected patterns to determine if any patterns appear in the SRL annotations of a given sentence. Once a pattern is found, the corresponding temporal relation of the pattern can then be used as supervision to further pre-train language models. With this method, we collect millions of event relation supervisions for pre-training from the raw Gigaword headline corpus (Graff et al., 2003; Rush et al., 2015). This includes around 3.8M atomic relations and 140K compositional relations.

Our method effectively helps pre-trained language models learn rich temporal knowledge. LEAF demonstrates an improvement of up to 9 F1 over vanilla BERT$_{BASE}$ and RoBERTa$_{BASE}$ on MATRES (Ning et al., 2018) and TB-Dense (Cassidy et al., 2014). It also delivers competitive performance with previous state-of-the-art (SOTA) methods that use temporal indicators and complex fine-tuning layers. Moreover, it greatly exceeds 3-shot ChatGPT (OpenAI, 2023) by over 37 F1 points. We also perform ablation studies, which verify that both types of temporal knowledge patterns contribute to high performance. Finally, with the aid of acquired atomic and compositional relation supervision, LEAF shows an increase of up to 6.8 F1 points over baselines on challenging cases involving compositional relation prediction.

2 Related Work

In the early stages of event relation research, experts often used traditional machine learning methods to classify relations (Chklovski and Pantel, 2004; Mani et al., 2006; Pitler and Nenkova, 2009; Mirza, 2014). These methods required experts to manually identify features and use external resources, which was time-consuming and labor-intensive. Recently, there have emerged a great number of attempts to incorporate temporal relation knowledge into neural network models (Cheng and Miyao, 2017; Goyal and Durrett, 2019; Xie et al., 2022). One branch of this involves incorporating additional temporal knowledge in the fine-tuning stage on fully labeled datasets, then evaluating on the respective dataset. Some add additional parameters to train (Tan et al., 2021; Hwang et al., 2022; Lu et al., 2022; Wen and Ji, 2021), while others only add objectives during fine-tuning (Wang et al., 2022a; Zhang et al., 2022).

Another branch called weak supervision is more closely related to our work. Weak supervision does not require expensive manually labeled training data, but instead automatically labels unannotated corpora (Xie et al., 2022). This allows for greater transferability of knowledge between tasks, as well as ease of scalability. There are several popular methods for extracting event temporal relations using weakly supervised data. One approach is to perform a keyword search (Zhao et al., 2021; Han et al., 2021b). Another approach is to use a teacher model to label event relations (Ballesteros et al., 2020). The most closely related to our work is Zhou et al. 2020a, which uses keywords within a single SRL semantic tag to extract relational knowledge. However, this is only a small subset of all available syntactic knowledge. In this work, we expand the range of syntactic structures used to extract relation knowledge, enabling language models to learn more diverse and complex knowledge.

3 Method

3.1 Overview

In this section, we describe our method for extracting temporal relation knowledge from unlabeled data and continually pre-train a language model to inject this knowledge. We begin by providing background on syntactic and semantic terminology (§3.2). Next, we offer a precise definition of atomic patterns and expand on the original patterns discovered through our work (§3.3.1). We then discuss the process of culminating compositional patterns and their importance (§3.3.2). In §3.4, we detail how we obtain temporal relation supervision with our collected patterns. Finally, we show how to use the relation supervision to pre-train language models (§3.5).

3.2 Background of Syntactic and Semantic Terminology

In this section, we introduce background on syntactic and semantic terminology involved in LEAF.

An event refers to a specific occurrence of something that happens in a certain time and a certain place involving one or more participants, which can usually be described as a change of state (Li et al., 2022). Following previous works, we define the relation between two events by the occurrence of their start time (Ning et al., 2018). Consider the sentence "John was **cooking** freshly **made** noodles for the family **gathering**" and its two events e_1 = **cooking** and e_2 = **made**. In this sentence, **cooking** clearly starts after **made**, so we would label the relation between e_1 and e_2 as "after". Specifically, we consider three temporal relationships for the temporal relation supervision in pre-training stage: *before, after,* and *simultaneous*.

Verbs are elements that encode events and hold arguments. For example, in the sentence "John was **cooking** freshly **made** noodles for the family

gathering as Adam **arrived**," the verb **cooking** takes four semantic arguments: agent, prototypical patient (PPT), purpose (PRP), and temporal (TMP) (Figure 2). "John" is the agent, "freshly made noodles" is the PPT, "for the family gathering" is the PRP argument, and "as Adam arrived" is the TMP argument. Arguments are the key components of our collected temporal knowledge patterns introduced in §3.3.

3.3 Temporal Knowledge Patterns

Temporal knowledge patterns are linguistic structures which usually imply certain temporal relations. The goal in collecting patterns is to extract rich event temporal knowledge from unlabeled text, allowing for harvesting of large-scale pre-training supervision. In this section, we introduce how we curate a diverse suite of atomic and compositional patterns, covering a vast range of linguistic information.

3.3.1 Atomic Patterns

Atomic patterns involve pairs of events where one event is contained within the argument structure of the other. Take the example "John was **cooking** freshly **made** noodles for the family **gathering** as Adam **arrived**." Since **made**, **gathering**, and **arrived** are all within **cooking**'s argument, atomic patterns may underlie the linguistic structures between **cooking** and the other three events (Figure 1). To curate atomic patterns that likely indicate certain temporal relations, we analyze examples from existing temporal relation datasets (Han et al., 2021a; Ning et al., 2020; Wang et al., 2022b). A subset of the atomic pattern list can be found in Table 1, and the comprehensive list can be found in Appendix A. Our list of atomic patterns includes both extensions of patterns explored in previous works (Zhou et al., 2020a) and novel patterns with linguistic structures implicitly expressing temporal relations.

One example of an atomic pattern that does not make use of any explicit temporal indicators is the prototypical patient (PPT) modifier pattern. A PPT is an event argument that undergoes change or is affected by the target event. We find that events which modify the PPT of a target event start before the respective target event. In the sentence previously mentioned, after observing that the PPT of **cooking** is "freshly **made** noodles," we can use this pattern to extract the relation that **made** starts before **cooking** (Figure 2). As events are commonly accompanied by PPT arguments in everyday English, detecting PPT patterns help obtain abundant temporal relation supervision for further pre-training.

The general PRP tag pattern and the general CAU tag pattern are two other examples of atomic patterns which do not use explicit temporal indicators. Both of these require no keyword occurrences and we can easily detect them with SRL tools. Two examples are shown in Figure 1.

3.3.2 Compositional Patterns

As displayed in Figure 1, many event pairs do not appear in each other's arguments, and thus their relationships cannot be concluded with just atomic patterns. For example, in the sentence "John was **cooking** freshly **made** noodles for the family **gathering** as Adam **arrived**," none of **made**, **gathering**, or **arrived** are in each other's arguments, yet there still exists temporal relations between them. Compositional patterns involve pairs of such events that are not in each other's arguments. These patterns are higher in difficulty than atomic patterns, as the events are more loosely connected with each other according to the syntax. Previous works have explored only atomic relations between two events to provide supervision (Zhou et al., 2020a; Han et al., 2021b), without considering compositional patterns. We value the importance of compositional temporal relational knowledge and further leverage it as sources of additional supervision to better tackle the challenges. This allows us to not only capture more linguistically complex relations, but also inter-sentence relations.

Compositional patterns frequently appear under the following circumstance: consider three events e_1, e_2, e_3, where e_1 is not in e_3's arguments, e_3 is not in e_1's arguments, but e_2 is in both e_1 and e_3's arguments. In a scenario where atomic patterns find that e_1 occurs before e_2, and e_2 occurs before e_3, then we can also utilize transitivity to conclude e_1 occurs before e_3 without e_3 being in any of e_1's arguments and e_1 being in any of e_3's arguments.

We cumulate a comprehensive list of all possible compositional patterns that can result from transitivity between two atomic patterns. Then, we use these compositional patterns to extract compositional relations from SRL annotated text.

3.4 Creating Supervision From Patterns

In this section, we detail the algorithm we deploy in order to extract temporal relations from raw text.

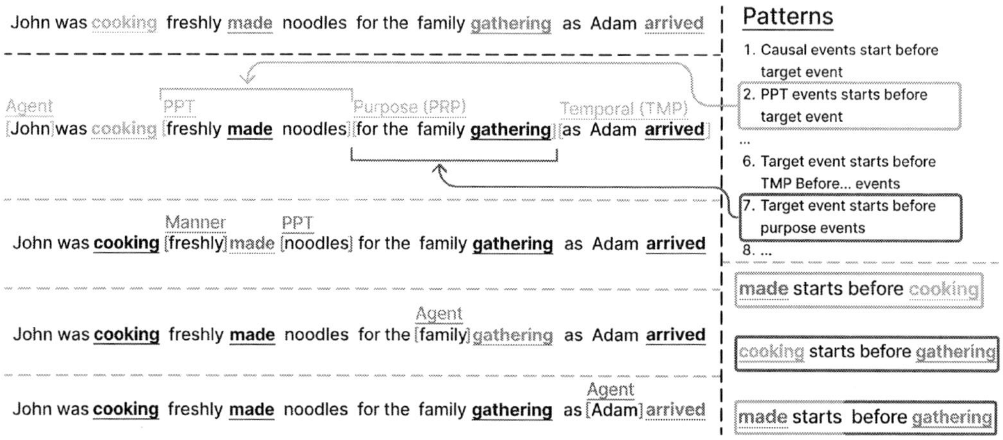

Figure 2: Examples to acquire temporal relation supervision via pattern matching. From a single sentence (top-left), we get the semantic arguments for each event using the SRL parser. The PPT pattern can help extract the relation that "made" starts before "cooking" (cyan), and the PRP pattern is used to conclude that "cooking" starts before "gathering" (purple). Finally, we use compositional patterns to gather complex relationships. We use the transitivity of the two atomic patterns to extract that "made" starts before "gathering" (cyan + purple box).

Names	Temporal Relations	Example Sentences	Explanations
CAU	After	John cooked noodles [because he was hungry].	John cooked after he was hungry
PRP	Before	John cooked noodles [for the family gathering].	John cooked before the family gathering
PPT	After	John cooked [freshly made noodles].	The noodles were made before John cooked them

Table 1: Subset of atomic patterns. CAU and PRP correspond to events in the causal and purpose tag, respectively. The PPT row refers to prototypical patient tags. These patterns indicate that all events in that tag hold the respective temporal relation to the target event.

We begin with the unannotated Gigaword headlines corpus[1] (Graff et al., 2003; Rush et al., 2015), which consists of around 3.8M news headline sentences. Then, we obtain SRL annotations of the headline sentences with SRL parser. The parser provides all arguments for each event within a headline. For example, in the sentence in Figure 2, each event **made**, **cooking**, **gathering**, and **arrived** will have its arguments labeled. Concretely, we use AllenNLP semantic role labeling (SRL) parser (Gardner et al., 2018; Shi and Lin, 2019) to obtain detailed annotation of events and the specific roles of their arguments.

With each event's arguments annotated by SRL tools, we iterate through each event and detect the existence of temporal knowledge patterns (§3.3) in each sentence. Specifically, given a target event, we first examine whether there are any atomic patterns underlying the linguistic structure of the given texts. If there is, we are able to extract relations between the target event and the events within its arguments. For example, PPT pattern is detected and helps us extract the relation that **made** starts before cooking. The PRP pattern can also be found to conclude that **cooking** starts before **gathering**. Finally, we use our list of compositional patterns to extract compositional relations between events which do not occur within each other's arguments. The process of obtaining compositional relations must also follow the principle of temporal relation transitivity. A compositional relation that we extract in the above sentence is that **made** starts before **gathering**, by transitivity of the two atomic relations above (Figure 2).

In total, we extract 3.8M atomic relations and 140K compositional relations with our collected temporal knowledge patterns. The extracted relations are all treated as the temporal relation supervision for later pre-training. To verify the accuracy of the acquired supervision, we got 2 undergraduate students to annotate 50 instances each. We observe that 86% of the sampled instances are correct. This indicates the reliability of our process

[1]https://huggingface.co/datasets/gigaword

for automatically acquiring supervision.

3.5 Pre-training LMs with Acquired Temporal Knowledge

In this section, we introduce our pre-training method to make LMs learn rich temporal knowledge with our acquired relation supervision.

Specifically, we adopt BERT (Devlin et al., 2019) and RoBERTa (Liu et al., 2019) as our base models and initialize the models with their pre-trained parameters. The masked language modeling (MLM) objective is one of our leveraged pre-training objectives. Suppose that there is an input sequence $X = [x_1, x_2, ..., x_n]$, where x_i indicates the token at the i-th index. The pre-training objective is to minimize the negative log-likelihood of predicting the masked tokens given the contexts. Thus, $\mathcal{L}_{MLM}$ is the cross-entropy loss value of predicting the masked tokens. We use the traditional BERT masking technique where 15% of tokens are either masked, replaced with a random token, or left unchanged (Devlin et al., 2019). Additionally, following previous work, we target 25% of event tokens for one of these transformations (Han et al., 2021b; Zhou et al., 2020a; Kimura et al., 2022).

Along with the traditional MLM pre-training objective, to let our models learn the acquired temporal knowledge, we utilize a temporal relation prediction objective (Ballesteros et al., 2020; Wang et al., 2020) as the other pre-training objective. Consider the contextualized embeddings $\mathcal{H} = [\mathbf{h}_1, \mathbf{h}_2, ..., \mathbf{h}_n]$ obtained from our base models. Let $\mathbf{h}_i$, $\mathbf{h}_j$ be the contextualized representations for the tokens of e_1 and e_2, respectively[2], and let $\mathbf{g}_p$, $\mathbf{g}_s$ be their element-wise Hadamard product and subtraction (Zhou et al., 2020b; Wang et al., 2020). We then feed $[\mathbf{h}_i : \mathbf{h}_j : \mathbf{g}_p : \mathbf{g}_s]$ into a multi-class classifier, where each class corresponds to one of the three considered temporal relations *before, after,* and *simultaneous*, to obtain $\hat{\mathbf{y}}$. We define the temporal relation objective $\mathcal{L}_{REL}$ as:

$$\mathcal{L}_{REL} = -\frac{1}{m}\sum_{i=1}^{m} \mathbf{y}_i \log(softmax(\hat{\mathbf{y}}_i)), \quad (1)$$

where $\mathbf{y}$ is the one-hot ground-truth vector and m is the number of training instances.

Our final loss function is thus:

$$\mathcal{L} = \mathcal{L}_{MLM} + \mathcal{L}_{REL}. \quad (2)$$

[2]For events that span multiple tokens, we simply take the first token of the event as the representation.

4 Experiments

In this section, we present experiments to demonstrate the effectiveness of LEAF for acquiring rich temporal relation knowledge. LEAF is capable of assisting LMs achieve high performance on multiple downstream event relation benchmarks. It facilitates base models to perform comparable with previous SOTA models (Section 4.2). We also verify the significance of pre-training objectives and data by conducting ablation studies (Section 4.3). Next, we reveal our method's effectiveness at predicting compositional relations (Section 4.4). Finally, we perform a case study to analyze LEAF's effectiveness at learning patterns that were seen and those that were unseen during pre-training (Section 4.5).

4.1 Experimental Setup

For our experiments, we pre-train both BERT$_{BASE}$ and RoBERTa$_{BASE}$ on our extracted data (Devlin et al., 2019; Liu et al., 2019). We train on 4 GeForce GTX 1080 Ti's for 3 epochs. For BERT$_{BASE}$, we use a 1e-4 learning rate, 0.2 dropout rate, and a batch size of 32. For RoBERTa$_{BASE}$, we use a 5e-5 learning rate, 0.3 dropout rate, and a batch size of 24.

For evaluation, we consider two temporal relation extraction datasets: MATRES (Ning et al., 2018) and TB-Dense (Cassidy et al., 2014). Details for the datasets can be found in Appendix B. For both datasets, we train a new classifier head with m output dimensions, where m is the number of labels of the respective dataset. We fine-tune for 10 epochs on both datasets, and following previous works, we report the micro-F1 score for each dataset (Wang et al., 2020).

4.2 Comparisons with Existing Systems

We compare our proposed method with two base models BERT and RoBERTa. We also demonstrate the effectiveness of LEAF in comparison with previous SOTA models.

4.2.1 Base-Models: BERT and RoBERTa

To evaluate the effectiveness of our method, we compare the performance of LEAF-enhanced BERT$_{BASE}$ and RoBERTa$_{BASE}$ with their respective vanilla counterparts. The results in Table 2 show that LEAF-enhanced models outperform the vanilla models on both datasets by a large margin. In particular, LEAF can bring 9-11 F1 improvement over vanilla RoBERTa$_{BASE}$. This demon-

	MATRES	TB-Dense
BERT$_{BASE}$	73.7	58.1
+ *LEAF*	81.3	63.2
RoBERTa$_{BASE}$	73.1	55.7
+ *LEAF*	**82.1**	66.7
ChatGPT(0-shot)	26.2	22.0
ChatGPT(3-shot)	49.2	29.1
Bi-LSTM (Cheng and Miyao, 2017)	59.5	48.4
TacoLM^{+} (Zhou et al., 2020a)	63.5	40.1
Goyal and Durrett (2019)	68.6	—
BERE-p (Hwang et al., 2022)	71.1	—
EventPlus (Ma et al., 2021)	75.5	64.5
SP+ILP (Ning et al., 2017)	76.3	58.4
Wang et al. (2020)	78.8	—
Poincaré Event Embeddings (Tan et al., 2021)	78.9	—
United-Framework (base) (Huang et al., 2023)	79.3	66.4
ECONET (Han et al., 2021b)	79.3	**66.8**
HGRU+knowledge (Tan et al., 2021)	80.5	—
Ballesteros et al. (2020)	81.6	—
Wen and Ji (2021)	81.7	—

Table 2: Overall experimental results. Following previous works, we report micro-F1 score for both datasets. $^{+}$ denotes our reproduced results. Note that ECONET is based on RoBERTa$_{LARGE}$, which is 3× bigger than our base models. We still outperform ECONET on MATRES by a large margin.

strates the benefits of pre-training with rich temporal knowledge acquired with LEAF methods.

4.2.2 Previous SOTA Models

We also compare LEAF method to 12 previous SOTA models, and find that LEAF leads to competitive performance on both datasets. Along with being simpler in design, our method requires training no additional parameters beyond a classifier, and outperforms other models with over triple the parameters. This includes outperforming EventPlus (Ma et al., 2021), a pipeline which uses twice the parameters of our model, by 6.6 F1. Wen and Ji (2021) and ECONET (Han et al., 2021b) are based on RoBERTa$_{LARGE}$, which is 3 times larger than RoBERTa$_{BASE}$. Nevertheless, RoBERTa$_{BASE}$ + LEAF surpasses both models as well.

4.2.3 Models Relying Only on Explicit Temporal Indicators

LEAF focuses on capturing richer temporal knowledge **implicitly** expressed in texts. In contrast, previous works about temporal knowledge acquisition merely utilize **explicit** indicators when gathering temporal knowledge from text. In this section, we verify the importance of implicit indicators by comparing our model to those that do not utilize this extra information when curating temporal patterns. The two models that we compare with in this section are ECONET and TacoLM.

In order to automatically gather temporal information for supervision, ECONET (Han et al., 2021b) collects a list of keywords that each imply a certain temporal relationship. For example, the words "before, until, and preceding" all imply the same temporal relation between events. However, they ignore crucial linguistic information by only doing keyword search for their patterns, limiting their scope to explicitly stated temporal relations. Results in Table 2 show that although the base model of ECONET is RoBERTa$_{LARGE}$ which is 3× bigger than our base models, LEAF can still outperform ECONET by 2.8 F1 on MATRES and achieve nearly the same performance on TB-Dense.

The major limiting factor of TacoLM discussed in §3.3.1 is that they only use a small subset of linguistic information to extract their temporal relation knowledge. In particular, they only consider the temporal arguments of events when acquiring temporal relation supervision. We conduct experiments to reproduce TacoLM based on BERT$_{BASE}$ and then evaluate the model on these two datasets. Results are shown in Table 2. Despite being trained on ~21M data, TacoLM underperforms BERT$_{BASE}$ + LEAF by a large margin.

4.2.4 ChatGPT

In this section, we analyze the performance of ChatGPT (`gpt-3.5-turbo` on 05-20-2023) on the two downstream datasets. We first design three different prompts, and for each prompt, we have a zero-shot and a three-shot variant, totalling six prompts per evaluation task (Appendix C). We then evaluate ChatGPT on TB-Dense and MATRES. Results can be found in Table 2. Aligning with past findings (Kauf et al., 2022; Yuan et al., 2023), we observe that ChatGPT does poorly at identifying event temporal relations. Both the 3-shot and the zero-shot F1 scores are significantly worse than BERT$_{BASE}$ + LEAF.

4.3 Ablations

Ablation study for pre-training objectives. To verify the significance of our pre-training objectives towards the better model performance, we conduct ablation studies to examine the effect of removing MLM and temporal relationship prediction objectives. Results can be found in Table 3. We find that for both datasets, removing either MLM or temporal relationship prediction objective leads to a worse performance than pre-training with both objectives. This indicates that both objectives are crucial in allowing the model to learn temporal

	MATRES	TB-Dense
BERT$_{BASE}$	73.7	58.1
+ ***LEAF***	**81.3**	**63.2**
- ***TMP REL***	80.2	62.0
- ***MLM***	56.6	29.7
- **Atomic**	79.6	60.7
- **Compositional**	79.9	59.9

Table 3: Ablation studies of the training objectives and patterns. The addition of LEAF improves the performance of BERT$_{BASE}$ on each dataset. The combination of the two training objectives is effective, as removing either one lowers performance on the two datasets. The combination of both types of temporal knowledge patterns also proves to be crucial, as removing either one also lowers performance on both datasets.

	MATRES-C	TB-Dense-C
BERT$_{BASE}$	72.8	53.2
+ ***LEAF***	78.5	57.0
- **Atomic**	81.0†	60.1†
- **Compositional**	75.1	53.1
RoBERTa$_{BASE}$	74.6	55.2
+ ***LEAF***	**81.1**	**62.0**

Table 4: Results on the instances involving compositional relations in MATRES and TB-Dense. -C denotes the dataset subset with only compositional relations. For both subsets, the addition of LEAF significantly increases F1 score. Although the performance marked with † is better than BERT$_{BASE}$ + LEAF, the overall performance of the corresponding baseline is lower than BERT$_{BASE}$ + LEAF 1.4 and 3.3 F1 on MATRES and TB-Dense.

knowledge and generalize to downstream tasks.

Ablation study for pre-training data. To verify the value of both atomic and compositional relations, we pre-train BERT$_{BASE}$ without atomic and compositional relations acquired by LEAF. Results can be found in the Table 3. We find that for both datasets, removing either atomic or compositional relations in the pre-training stage leads to worse performance than training with both relations. Especially, we find that although there are only 140K acquired compositional relations, training with these 140K relations performs on par with training with 3.8M atomic relations. This further emphasizes the contribution of considering compositional relations to temporal relation tasks.

4.4 Predicting Compositional Relations

It is intuitive that correctly extracting compositional relations is more challenging than identifying atomic relations. In this section, we explore the capability of our model to extract challenging compositional relations. We take the subset of MATRES and TB-Dense that contain compositional relations, and evaluate both base models BERT$_{BASE}$ and RoBERTa$_{BASE}$ and their LEAF-enhanced counterparts. Results are displayed in Table 4. We observe that further pre-training with the relation supervision derived from LEAF enhances base models at identifying compositional relations. This is likely due to us giving explicit compositional relation supervision during pre-training.

We also perform ablation studies to evaluate the impact of atomic and composition relations acquired by LEAF on the subsets MATRES-C and TB-Dense-C. As shown in Table 4, we find that BERT$_{BASE}$ trained with only compositional relations performs better on both datasets than the model trained with only atomic relations. It even surpasses BERT$_{BASE}$ + LEAF, which is trained with the whole set of acquired relation supervision. This verifies that the compositional relations extracted are effective at assisting the model in tackling challenging compositional relation extraction. However, as shown in Table 3, training with the mere compositional relations does not bring better overall performance on MATRES and TB-Dense. Overall, training with all the relations obtained by LEAF is a better solution that achieves competitive overall extraction performance and predicts challenging temporal relations with greater accuracy.

4.5 Case Study

In this section, we examine specific instances where the model demonstrates an ability to grasp patterns that were not seen during pre-training as well as instances which display the model's capacity to effectively learn atomic and compositional patterns.

We present cases that confirm the effectiveness of exposing the model to out extracted patterns patterns during pre-training. In Figure 3, we observe examples where the model learns to correctly identify atomic and compositional relations after pre-training. These are examples in which the model fails to identify the relationship correctly without pre-training, and succeeds after pre-training. This shows the effectiveness of our patterns, equipping the model with a robust understanding of complex relations, enhancing its ability to make accurate

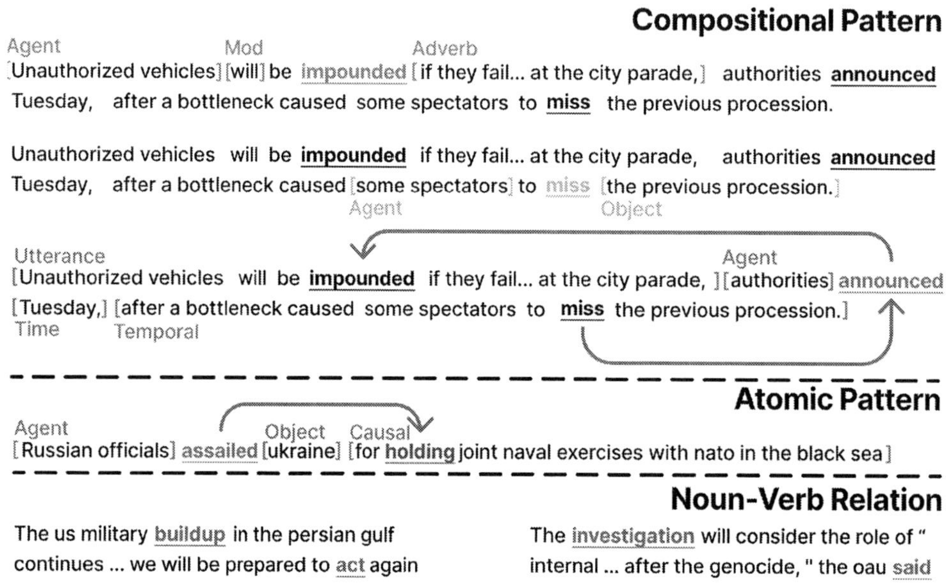

Figure 3: Examples of relations that were learned by pre-training with acquired patterns. These are instances in which the model labels the relation incorrectly without pre-training, and correctly after pre-training. For the compositional pattern, we see the event "announced" revealing a relation between "impounded" and "miss" (sentence 3). These otherwise do not have a trivial relation, because "miss" is not in the arguments of "impounded" (sentence 1) and "impounded" is not in the arguments of "miss" (sentence 2). Our model effectively identifies this relation after pre-training. For the atomic pattern, we see that vanilla RoBERTa fails on atomic relations, while LEAF can help to capture this case. For the noun-verb relation sentences, we see two examples where the model learns relations between a noun event (in red) and a verb event (in blue), despite not having seen any during pre-training.

predictions and adapt to new, unseen data.

Because the SRL parser only annotates verb events during pre-training, our model only sees verb-verb relations during pre-training. Despite this fact, LEAF has shown a remarkable ability to learn noun-verb relations that are not acquired without the pattern supervision. This is evidenced by the two examples illustrated in Figure 3. The model's ability to grasp these relations suggests that the patterns we provided during training have a potential beyond their explicit supervision.

5 Conclusions

In conclusion, our proposed LEAF framework demonstrates the effectiveness of using diverse linguistic structures to extract rich temporal knowledge of events from large-scale corpora. The extracted knowledge is able to enhance language models via a simple pre-training procedure. Our approach outperforms or rivals previous models on MATRES and TB-Dense, and excels at identifying complex compositional event relations.

6 Limitations

Our model's scope for event relations does not include all types of events. Specifically, the captured temporal relationships used for pre-training supervision does not cover noun-verb and noun-noun event pairs. Another limitation is that our model is only as good as the SRL annotations are. If the SRL annotations are noisy, then so will be our data. Also, due to the limits of computation resources, the scale of our base models are only around 110M parameters. We hope to extend to larger-scale experiments once better computational resources are available for use.

Acknowledgement

We would like to thank the anonymous reviewers for the insightful feedback and constructive suggestions. We also greatly appreciate the help of UCLA undergraduate students Eric Lin and Eric Wu in verifying the accuracy of our collected relations. This research is partially supported by an ONR grant #N00014-23-1-2780 and a Cisco Sponsored Research Award.

References

Miguel Ballesteros, Rishita Anubhai, Shuai Wang, Nima Pourdamghani, Yogarshi Vyas, Jie Ma, Parminder Bhatia, Kathleen McKeown, and Yaser Al-Onaizan. 2020. Severing the edge between before and after: Neural architectures for temporal ordering of events. In *Proceedings of the 2020 Conference on Empirical Methods in Natural Language Processing (EMNLP)*, pages 5412–5417, Online. Association for Computational Linguistics.

Taylor Cassidy, Bill McDowell, Nathanael Chambers, and Steven Bethard. 2014. An annotation framework for dense event ordering. In *Proceedings of the 52nd Annual Meeting of the Association for Computational Linguistics (Volume 2: Short Papers)*, pages 501–506, Baltimore, Maryland. Association for Computational Linguistics.

Nathanael Chambers, Taylor Cassidy, Bill McDowell, and Steven Bethard. 2014. Dense event ordering with a multi-pass architecture. *Transactions of the Association for Computational Linguistics*, 2:273–284.

Fei Cheng and Yusuke Miyao. 2017. Classifying temporal relations by bidirectional LSTM over dependency paths. In *Proceedings of the 55th Annual Meeting of the Association for Computational Linguistics (Volume 2: Short Papers)*, pages 1–6, Vancouver, Canada. Association for Computational Linguistics.

Yao Cheng, Peter Anick, Pengyu Hong, and Nianwen Xue. 2013. Temporal relation discovery between events and temporal expressions identified in clinical narrative. *Journal of Biomedical Informatics*, 46:S48–S53. Supplement: 2012 i2b2 NLP Challenge on Temporal Relations in Clinical Data.

Timothy Chklovski and Patrick Pantel. 2004. VerbOcean: Mining the web for fine-grained semantic verb relations. In *Proceedings of the 2004 Conference on Empirical Methods in Natural Language Processing*, pages 33–40, Barcelona, Spain. Association for Computational Linguistics.

Jacob Devlin, Ming-Wei Chang, Kenton Lee, and Kristina Toutanova. 2019. BERT: Pre-training of deep bidirectional transformers for language understanding. In *Proceedings of the 2019 Conference of the North American Chapter of the Association for Computational Linguistics: Human Language Technologies, Volume 1 (Long and Short Papers)*, pages 4171–4186, Minneapolis, Minnesota. Association for Computational Linguistics.

Jennifer D'Souza and Vincent Ng. 2013. Classifying temporal relations with rich linguistic knowledge. In *Proceedings of the 2013 Conference of the North American Chapter of the Association for Computational Linguistics: Human Language Technologies*, pages 918–927, Atlanta, Georgia. Association for Computational Linguistics.

Matt Gardner, Joel Grus, Mark Neumann, Oyvind Tafjord, Pradeep Dasigi, Nelson F. Liu, Matthew Peters, Michael Schmitz, and Luke Zettlemoyer. 2018. AllenNLP: A deep semantic natural language processing platform. In *Proceedings of Workshop for NLP Open Source Software (NLP-OSS)*, pages 1–6, Melbourne, Australia. Association for Computational Linguistics.

Tanya Goyal and Greg Durrett. 2019. Embedding time expressions for deep temporal ordering models. In *Proceedings of the 57th Annual Meeting of the Association for Computational Linguistics*, pages 4400–4406, Florence, Italy. Association for Computational Linguistics.

David Graff, Junbo Kong, Ke Chen, and Kazuaki Maeda. 2003. English gigaword. *Linguistic Data Consortium, Philadelphia*, 4(1):34.

Rujun Han, I-Hung Hsu, Jiao Sun, Julia Baylon, Qiang Ning, Dan Roth, and Nanyun Peng. 2021a. ESTER: A machine reading comprehension dataset for reasoning about event semantic relations. In *Proceedings of the 2021 Conference on Empirical Methods in Natural Language Processing*, pages 7543–7559, Online and Punta Cana, Dominican Republic. Association for Computational Linguistics.

Rujun Han, Xiang Ren, and Nanyun Peng. 2021b. ECONET: Effective continual pretraining of language models for event temporal reasoning. In *Proceedings of the 2021 Conference on Empirical Methods in Natural Language Processing*, pages 5367–5380, Online and Punta Cana, Dominican Republic. Association for Computational Linguistics.

Quzhe Huang, Yutong Hu, Shengqi Zhu, Yansong Feng, Chang Liu, and Dongyan Zhao. 2023. More than classification: A unified framework for event temporal relation extraction. In *Proceedings of the 61st Annual Meeting of the Association for Computational Linguistics (Volume 1: Long Papers)*, pages 9631–9646, Toronto, Canada. Association for Computational Linguistics.

EunJeong Hwang, Jay-Yoon Lee, Tianyi Yang, Dhruvesh Patel, Dongxu Zhang, and Andrew McCallum. 2022. Event-event relation extraction using probabilistic box embedding. In *Proceedings of the 60th Annual Meeting of the Association for Computational Linguistics (Volume 2: Short Papers)*, pages 235–244, Dublin, Ireland. Association for Computational Linguistics.

Carina Kauf, Anna A. Ivanova, Giulia Rambelli, Emmanuele Chersoni, Jingyuan S. She, Zawad Chowdhury, Evelina Fedorenko, and Alessandro Lenci. 2022. Event knowledge in large language models: the gap between the impossible and the unlikely.

Mayuko Kimura, Lis Kanashiro Pereira, and Ichiro Kobayashi. 2022. Effective masked language modeling for temporal commonsense reasoning. In *2022*

Joint 12th International Conference on Soft Computing and Intelligent Systems and 23rd International Symposium on Advanced Intelligent Systems (SCIS&ISIS), pages 1–4.

Hee-Jin Lee, Yaoyun Zhang, Min Jiang, Jun Xu, Cui Tao, and Hua Xu. 2018. Identifying direct temporal relations between time and events from clinical notes. *BMC Medical Informatics and Decision Making*, 18(Suppl 2):49.

Qian Li, Jianxin Li, Jiawei Sheng, Shiyao Cui, Jia Wu, Yiming Hei, Hao Peng, Shu Guo, Lihong Wang, Amin Beheshti, and Philip S. Yu. 2022. A survey on deep learning event extraction: Approaches and applications.

Yinhan Liu, Myle Ott, Naman Goyal, Jingfei Du, Mandar Joshi, Danqi Chen, Omer Levy, Mike Lewis, Luke Zettlemoyer, and Veselin Stoyanov. 2019. Roberta: A robustly optimized bert pretraining approach.

Junru Lu, Xingwei Tan, Gabriele Pergola, Lin Gui, and Yulan He. 2022. Event-centric question answering via contrastive learning and invertible event transformation. In *Findings of the Association for Computational Linguistics: EMNLP 2022*, pages 2377–2389, Abu Dhabi, United Arab Emirates. Association for Computational Linguistics.

Mingyu Derek Ma, Jiao Sun, Mu Yang, Kung-Hsiang Huang, Nuan Wen, Shikhar Singh, Rujun Han, and Nanyun Peng. 2021. EventPlus: A temporal event understanding pipeline. In *Proceedings of the 2021 Conference of the North American Chapter of the Association for Computational Linguistics: Human Language Technologies: Demonstrations*, pages 56–65, Online. Association for Computational Linguistics.

Inderjeet Mani, Marc Verhagen, Ben Wellner, Chong Min Lee, and James Pustejovsky. 2006. Machine learning of temporal relations. In *Proceedings of the 21st International Conference on Computational Linguistics and 44th Annual Meeting of the Association for Computational Linguistics*, pages 753–760, Sydney, Australia. Association for Computational Linguistics.

Paramita Mirza. 2014. Extracting temporal and causal relations between events. In *Proceedings of the ACL 2014 Student Research Workshop*, pages 10–17, Baltimore, Maryland, USA. Association for Computational Linguistics.

Qiang Ning, Zhili Feng, and Dan Roth. 2017. A structured learning approach to temporal relation extraction. In *Proceedings of the 2017 Conference on Empirical Methods in Natural Language Processing*, pages 1027–1037, Copenhagen, Denmark. Association for Computational Linguistics.

Qiang Ning, Hao Wu, Rujun Han, Nanyun Peng, Matt Gardner, and Dan Roth. 2020. TORQUE: A reading comprehension dataset of temporal ordering questions. In *Proceedings of the 2020 Conference on Empirical Methods in Natural Language Processing (EMNLP)*, pages 1158–1172, Online. Association for Computational Linguistics.

Qiang Ning, Hao Wu, and Dan Roth. 2018. A multi-axis annotation scheme for event temporal relations. In *Proceedings of the 56th Annual Meeting of the Association for Computational Linguistics (Volume 1: Long Papers)*, pages 1318–1328, Melbourne, Australia. Association for Computational Linguistics.

OpenAI. 2023. Chatgpt. `https://openai.com/blog/chatgpt/`. Accessed on May 3, 2023.

Emily Pitler and Ani Nenkova. 2009. Using syntax to disambiguate explicit discourse connectives in text. In *Proceedings of the ACL-IJCNLP 2009 Conference Short Papers*, pages 13–16, Suntec, Singapore. Association for Computational Linguistics.

Alexander M. Rush, Sumit Chopra, and Jason Weston. 2015. A neural attention model for abstractive sentence summarization. *Proceedings of the 2015 Conference on Empirical Methods in Natural Language Processing*.

Peng Shi and Jimmy Lin. 2019. Simple BERT models for relation extraction and semantic role labeling. *CoRR*, abs/1904.05255.

Fiona Anting Tan, Ali Hürriyetoğlu, Tommaso Caselli, Nelleke Oostdijk, Tadashi Nomoto, Hansi Hettiarachchi, Iqra Ameer, Onur Uca, Farhana Ferdousi Liza, and Tiancheng Hu. 2022. The causal news corpus: Annotating causal relations in event sentences from news. In *Proceedings of the Thirteenth Language Resources and Evaluation Conference*, pages 2298–2310, Marseille, France. European Language Resources Association.

Xingwei Tan, Gabriele Pergola, and Yulan He. 2021. Extracting event temporal relations via hyperbolic geometry. In *Proceedings of the 2021 Conference on Empirical Methods in Natural Language Processing*, pages 8065–8077, Online and Punta Cana, Dominican Republic. Association for Computational Linguistics.

Haoyu Wang, Muhao Chen, Hongming Zhang, and Dan Roth. 2020. Joint constrained learning for event-event relation extraction. In *Proceedings of the 2020 Conference on Empirical Methods in Natural Language Processing (EMNLP)*, pages 696–706, Online. Association for Computational Linguistics.

Meiguo Wang, Benjamin Yao, Bin Guo, Xiaohu Liu, Yu Zhang, Tuan-Hung Pham, and Chenlei Guo. 2022a. Joint goal segmentation and goal success prediction on multi-domain conversations. In *Proceedings of the 29th International Conference on Computational Linguistics*, pages 505–509, Gyeongju, Republic of Korea. International Committee on Computational Linguistics.

Xiaozhi Wang, Yulin Chen, Ning Ding, Hao Peng, Zimu Wang, Yankai Lin, Xu Han, Lei Hou, Juanzi Li, Zhiyuan Liu, Peng Li, and Jie Zhou. 2022b. MAVEN-ERE: A unified large-scale dataset for event coreference, temporal, causal, and subevent relation extraction. In *Proceedings of the 2022 Conference on Empirical Methods in Natural Language Processing*, pages 926–941, Abu Dhabi, United Arab Emirates. Association for Computational Linguistics.

Haoyang Wen and Heng Ji. 2021. Utilizing relative event time to enhance event-event temporal relation extraction. In *Proceedings of the 2021 Conference on Empirical Methods in Natural Language Processing*, pages 10431–10437, Online and Punta Cana, Dominican Republic. Association for Computational Linguistics.

QunLi Xie, JunLan Pan, Tao Liu, BeiBei Qian, XianChuan Wang, and Xianchao Wang. 2022. A survey of event relation extraction. In *Frontier Computing*, pages 1818–1827, Singapore. Springer Nature Singapore.

Chenhan Yuan, Qianqian Xie, and Sophia Ananiadou. 2023. Zero-shot temporal relation extraction with chatgpt.

Chong Zhang, Jiagao Lyu, and Ke Xu. 2023. A storytree-based model for inter-document causal relation extraction from news articles. *Knowledge and Information Systems*, 65:827–853.

Shuaicheng Zhang, Qiang Ning, and Lifu Huang. 2022. Extracting temporal event relation with syntax-guided graph transformer. In *Findings of the Association for Computational Linguistics: NAACL 2022*, pages 379–390, Seattle, United States. Association for Computational Linguistics.

Xinyu Zhao, Shih-Ting Lin, and Greg Durrett. 2021. Effective distant supervision for temporal relation extraction. In *Proceedings of the Second Workshop on Domain Adaptation for NLP*, pages 195–203, Kyiv, Ukraine. Association for Computational Linguistics.

Ben Zhou, Qiang Ning, Daniel Khashabi, and Dan Roth. 2020a. Temporal common sense acquisition with minimal supervision. In *Proceedings of the 58th Annual Meeting of the Association for Computational Linguistics*, pages 7579–7589, Online. Association for Computational Linguistics.

Guangyu Zhou, Muhao Chen, Chelsea J T Ju, Zheng Wang, Jyun-Yu Jiang, and Wei Wang. 2020b. Mutation effect estimation on protein–protein interactions using deep contextualized representation learning. *NAR Genomics and Bioinformatics*, 2(2). Lqaa015.

Appendix

A List of Atomic Patterns

In Table 5, we provide a comprehensive list of patterns used to extract the data. The top section outlines general semantic tag patterns. If a target event possesses any of these arguments, all argument events will hold the specified temporal relationship with the target event. The bottom section includes tag and beginning word patterns, consisting of a three-letter capitalized tag followed by a word. If an argument begins with such a keyword, all events within the argument will hold the temporal relation with the target event. The `to` pattern specifies that all semantic arguments beginning with `to` indicate that the target event occurs before the events in the tag. `Modal verbs` indicates that any argumentative event modified by a modal verb will hold the designated temporal relationship with the target event.

B Dataset Statistics

In Table 6, we display the statistics for both datasets. Both datasets provide gold event labels, and the task is to predict the temporal relation between two provided events.

C ChatGPT Prompts

Below are the three ChatGPT prompts that we averaged the performance over. For three-shot, we simply repeated the prompt four times, with the first three times also including the answer to the passage. Note that all examples are the ones we used for MATRES. For TB-Dense, because there are more labels, we added more options for ChatGPT to choose from. For each example, the example sentence replaces {sentence}, and the names of the left and right event replace {left_event} and {right_event}.

1. Context: {sentence}
   Based on the above paragraph, what can we conclude about the events "{left_event}" and "{right_event}"?
   Please choose one of the following:
   - "{left_event}" started before "{right_event}"
   - "{left_event}" started after "{right_event}"
   - "{left_event}" and "{right_event}" started simultaneously
   - The temporal relationship between "{left_event}" and "{right_event}" is vague

2. Read the following and determine the temporal relationship between the events "{left_event}" and "{right_event}":
   Context: {sentence}
   Options:
   - "{left_event}" started before "{right_event}"
   - "{left_event}" started after "{right_event}"
   - "{left_event}" and "{right_event}" started simultaneously
   - The temporal relationship between "{left_event}" and "{right_event}" is vague

3. Description: Given a passage, and two events "{left_event}" and "{right_event}", determine the temporal relationship between the events, choosing between one of the following options:
   - "{left_event}" started before "{right_event}"
   - "{left_event}" started after "{right_event}"
   - "{left_event}" and "{right_event}" started simultaneously
   - The temporal relationship between "{left_event}" and "{right_event}" is vague
   Passage: {sentence}

Names	Temporal Relations	Example Sentences	Explanations
CAU	After	John cooked noodles [because he was hungry].	John cooked after he was hungry
PRP	Before	John cooked noodles [for the family gathering].	John cooked before the family gathering
PPT	After	John cooked [freshly made noodles].	The noodles were made before John cooked them
to	Before	John cooked noodles [to cure his boredom]	John cooked before his boredom was cured
TMP when	After	[When he got hungry], John cooked noodles.	John cooked after he got hungry
TMP following...	After	John cooked noodles [following a request from Adam].	John cooked after Adam requested
TMP after...	After	John cooked noodles [after Adam arrived].	John cooked after Adam arrived
TMP before...	Before	John cooked noodles [before Adam arrived].	John cooked before Adam arrived
TMP during...	Simultaneous	John cooked noodles[during the storm].	It stormed while John cooked noodles
TMP while...	Simultaneous	John cooked noodles [while it was snowing].	It snowed while John cooked noodles
TMP as...	Simultaneous	John cooked noodles [as Adam arrived].	Adam arrived while John cooked noodles
ADV while...	Simultaneous	John cooked noodles, [while Adam was unamused by his jokes].	Adam was unamused while John cooked noodles
ADV if...	After	John cooks noodles [if he is bored].	John cooks after he is bored
Modal Verbs	Before	John cooked noodles and [Adam will eat them].	John cooks noodles before Adam eats

Table 5: Full list of atomic patterns. Three letter abbreviations indicate semantic tags. Patterns that only consist of a tag (e.g., PPT) indicate that all events in that tag hold the respective temporal relation to the target verb. The patterns that have a tag (e.g., TMP) and a word (e.g., during) indicate the pattern whose semantic tag starts with the word.

	Train	Validation	Test	Labels
MATRES	5,036	1,296	827	Vague, before, after, simultaneous
TB-Dense	4,032	629	1,427	Vague, before, after, simultaneous, includes, is_included

Table 6: Statistics for both datasets. Note that TB-Dense has all of the labels of MATRES, plus two additional labels: includes and is_included.

A Graph-Guided Reasoning Approach for Open-ended Commonsense Question Answering

Zhen Han[1]*, **Yue Feng**[1], **Mingming Sun**[1]
[1]Cognitive Computing Lab, Baidu Research
hanzhen02111@163.com, sunmingming01@baidu.com

Abstract

Recently, end-to-end trained models for multiple-choice commonsense question answering (QA) have delivered promising results. However, such question-answering systems cannot be directly applied in real-world scenarios where answer candidates are not provided. Hence, a new benchmark challenge set for open-ended commonsense reasoning (OpenCSR) has been recently released, which contains natural science questions without any predefined choices. On the OpenCSR challenge set, many questions require implicit multi-hop reasoning and have a large decision space, reflecting the difficult nature of this task. Existing work on OpenCSR sorely focuses on improving the retrieval process, which extracts relevant factual sentences from a textual knowledge base, leaving the important and non-trivial reasoning task outside the scope. In this work, we extend the scope to include a reasoner that constructs a question-dependent open knowledge graph based on retrieved supporting facts and employs a sequential subgraph reasoning process to predict the answer. The subgraph itself can be seen as a concise and compact graphical explanation of the prediction. Experiments on two OpenCSR datasets show that the proposed model achieves great performance on benchmark OpenCSR datasets.

1 Introduction

Commonsense reasoning has long been considered an essential topic in artificial intelligence. Most approaches work on the setting of *multiple-choice question answering* [8, 3], which selects an answer choice by scoring the question-choice pairs. However, the multiple-choice setting is not applicable in many real-world scenarios since many question-answering tasks do not provide answer candidates. As a step towards making commonsense reasoning research more realistic and useful, open-ended commonsense reasoning (OpenCSR) has been introduced [9], which explores a commonsense knowledge corpus to answer commonsense questions. OpenCSR often requires multi-hop reasoning, i.e., the model should conclude the answer by reasoning over two or more facts from the knowledge corpus, which makes this task much more challenging. Lin et al. [9] proposed a retrieval-based method, called *DrFact*, by combining the maximum inner product search and symbolic links between facts. However, DrFact does not put much effort on the reasoning module to re-rank the retrieved facts. To this end, we proposed an integrated subgraph reasoning approach for OpenCSR with end-to-end learning, which iteratively employs a retriever to extract question-relevant facts from a knowledge corpus and a reasoner over the extracted facts. Given a commonsense question, the proposed approach applies DPR [6] to extract relevant facts from a textual knowledge corpus, converts the retrieved natural language facts into a graph-structured format using Open Information Annotation (OIA) [10] and performs subgraph reasoning on the constructed joint OIA-graph using a multi-relational graph attention network. Specifically, the reasoner first performs entity linking from the giving question to the joint OIA-graph. Then it starts from the linked entities (nodes), and iteratively samples relevant edges with a pruning procedure to form an enclosing subgraph around the question. The reasoning procedure takes into account both structural information, i.e., graph structure of the joint OIA graph, and semantic information, i.e., language representation of questions and facts. After several rounds of retrieval and pruning, the model predicts the answer from the concepts in the subgraph.

Our contributions are as follows: (1) we investigate how to perform a cooperative retrieval-and-reasoning in open-ended commonsense question answering. To the best of our knowledge, our

*work done while internship at Baidu.

Proceedings of the 2nd Workshop in Pattern-based Approaches to NLP in the Age of Deep Learning, pages 20–24
December 6, 2023.

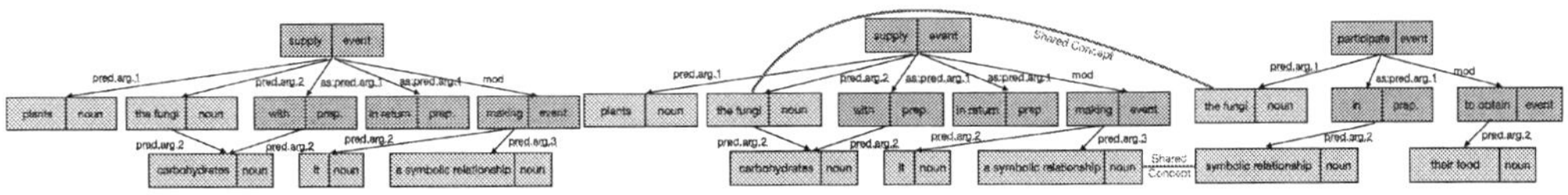

(a) (b)

Figure 1: (**a**) The OIA graph of "Plants supply the fungi with carbohydrates, in return, making it a symbiotic relationship." There are two types of nodes: constant and predicate. Constant nodes are simple nominal phrases while predicate nodes include simple verbal phrases and prepositional phrases. Edges in OIA graphs are labeled. *pred.arg.n* denotes the n-th arguments of a predicate node, *mod* indicates the modification, and *as:pred.arg.n* expresses an reversed relation of *pred.arg.n*. (**b**) The joint OIA graph consists of two factoid sentences that share the concepts "fungi" and "symbiotic relationship".

work is the first retrieve-and-reasoning approach for OpenCSR. (2) We present experimental results that show our model achieves great results on the benchmark OpenCSR dataset with an ablation study demonstrating the performance gain of integration structural information and semantic information. (3) The proposed method can potentially homogenize structured, i.e., knowledge base, and unstructured commonsense knowledge, i.e., textual corpus for answering open-ended commonsense questions since it can unify both knowledge formats into a graph-structured format.

2 Related Work

Commonsense Reasoning Traditional commonsense reasoning (CSR) techniques are mainly designed for multiple-choice QA. For instance, to independently score each decision, KagNet [8] and MHGRN [3] both leverage external commonsense knowledge graphs as structural priors. Although effective in selecting the best response for a multiple-choice question, these techniques are less useful for real-world situations because answer candidates are frequently unavailable. By fine-tuning a text-to-text transformer, UnifiedQA [7] generated answers to questions. However, a drawback of multiple-choice QA models is that they do not provide intermediate explanations for their answers, making them less suitable in many real-world scenarios. Lin et al. [9] introduced the open-ended commonsense reasoning and proposed DrFact to directly retrieve relevant facts, and then use the concepts mentioned in the top-ranked facts as answer predictions.

Subgraph Reasoning Many recent works learn representations of localized subgraphs. Alsentzer et al. [1] introduced a subgraph neural network to learn disentangled subgraph representations using a novel subgraph routing mechanism. Teru et al. [11] proposed a graph neural network that reasons over local subgraph structures and performs inductive relation predictions. Han et al. [4] developed an explainable reasoning framework for forecasting future links on temporal knowledge graphs by employing a sequential reasoning process over local subgraphs.

3 Our Approach

Retrieving Relevant Facts Following the dense passage retrieval work [6], we use a bi-encoder transformer architecture that learns to maximize the inner product of the representation of a question and the relevant factual sentences from the knowledge corpus containing correct answers to the given question.

Constructing Question-dependent Joint OIA-Graph Following the steps in [10], we convert each retrieved factual sentence into an OIA-graph as shown in Figure 1a. For each node in an OIA graph, we link it with nodes in the OIA graphs of other sentences that include the same concept. We label this kind of link as *shared concepts*. As shown in Figure 1b, the factoid sentences "Plants supply the fungi with carbohydrates, in return, making it a symbiotic relationship." and "Fungi participate in symbiotic relationships to obtain their food." shares the same concepts "fungi" and "symbiotic relationship". Then, we construct a joint OIA-graph $\mathcal{G}_{joint}$ by linking nodes that share the same concepts in different OIA graphs.

Subgraph Reasoning on the Joint OIA-Graph Inspired by [5], we conduct reasoning on a dynamically expanded inference graph $\mathcal{G}_{inf}$ extracted from the joint OIA-graph. Given a commonsense question q, we build an initial inference graph via **entity linking** between the question q and the joint OIA-graph. We find all nodes of $\mathcal{G}_{joint}$ that share the same concepts as q includes. We set such OIA-

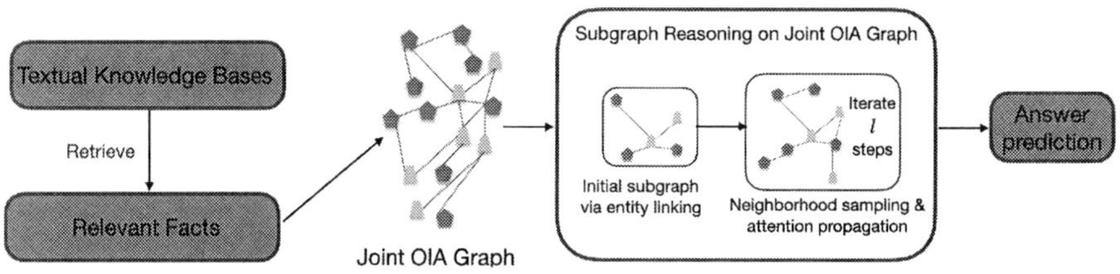

Figure 2: Model Architecture.

nodes to be the initial nodes of the inference graph $\mathcal{G}_{inf}$. The inference graph expands by sampling one-hop neighbors of initial nodes in $\mathcal{G}_{joint}$. Besides, we propose a semantic-following operation to build skip connections between the initial nodes and their multi-hop neighbors. Taking a node v in $\mathcal{G}_{inf}$ as an example, we compute the inner-product similarity between its representation and the representation of other nodes in $\mathcal{G}_{joint}$ obtained by the retrieval and add the top K nodes into $\mathcal{G}_{inf}$ by linking them with v. The contribution of the semantic-following has two folds: 1) It speeds up the reasoning process and broadens the receptive field of the subgraph reasoner by adding skip connections between multi-hop neighbors; 2) It allows the subgraph reasoner to take into account both semantic-relevant and symbolic-linked nodes regarding a given question. Next, we feed $\mathcal{G}_{inf}$ into a relational graph attention layer that takes node embedding as the input, computes an attention score for each edge indicating the relevance to the given question, and produces a question-dependent representation for each node using message passing. Instead of treating all neighbors with equal importance in the massage passing, we take the question information into account and assign varying importance levels to each neighbor by calculating the following question-dependent attention score:

$$e^l_{vu}(q, p_k) = \mathbf{W}^l_s(\mathbf{h}^{l-1}_v||\mathbf{p}^{l-1}_k||\mathbf{h}^{l-1}_q)^T \mathbf{W}^l_t(\mathbf{h}^{l-1}_u||\mathbf{p}^{l-1}_k||\mathbf{h}^{l-1}_q), \tag{1}$$

where $e^l_{vu}(q, p_k)$ is the attention score of the edge (v, p_k, u) regarding the question q, p_k corresponds to the edge type between the source node v and the target node u, $\mathbf{W}^l_s$ and $\mathbf{W}^l_t$ are two weight matrices for capturing the dependencies between question representations and source node features specified for source node and target node, respectively. $\mathbf{p}_k$ is the edge embedding indicating the relationship between u and v. $\mathbf{h}^{l-1}_v$ denotes the hidden representation of the node v at the $(l-1)^{th}$ inference step. When $l = 1$, i.e., for the first layer, $\mathbf{h}^0_v$ is the aggregated token representation from Bert. Then, we compute the normalized attention score $\alpha^l_{vu}(q, p_k)$ using the *softmax function*. Once obtained, we aggregate the representations of the sampled neighbors of node v denoted as $\hat{\mathcal{N}}_v$ and weight them using the normalized attention scores, which are written as

$$\mathbf{h}^l_v(q) = \sum_{u \in \hat{\mathcal{N}}_v} \alpha^l_{vu}(q, p_k)\mathbf{h}^{l-1}_u(q). \tag{2}$$

Answer Prediction We compute the plausibility score $s^l_{v,q}$ of node v to be the answer of question q at the lth inference step as follows:

$$s^l_{v,q} = s_{mips}(\mathbf{q}, \mathbf{f}_v) + \sum_{u \in \hat{\mathcal{N}}_v} \sum_{p_k \in \mathcal{P}_{uv}} \alpha^l_{uv}(q, p_k) a^{l-1}_{u,q}, \tag{3}$$

where $s_{mips}(\mathbf{q}, \mathbf{f}_v)$ denotes the relevance score of the retrieved fact f_v, which mentions the node v, regarding the question q by the maximum inner product search. Since the same concept may appear in different nodes in the inference graph, we aggregate the plausibility score of nodes that share the same concept to assign each concept a unique attention score:

$$s^l_{c_i,q} = g(s^l_{v,q}|v(c) = c_i), \quad \text{for } v \in \mathcal{V}_{\mathcal{G}_{inf}}, \tag{4}$$

where $s^l_{c_i,q}$ denotes the plausibility score of concept c_i, $\mathcal{V}_{\mathcal{G}_{inf}}$ is the set of nodes in inference graph $\mathcal{G}_{inf}$. $v(c)$ represents the concept included in node v, and $g(\cdot)$ represents a score aggregation function. Here we use the maximum function.

Inference Graph Expansion and Pruning After several iterations of expansion, the inference graph $\mathcal{G}_{inf}$ would grow rapidly and cover almost all nodes. To prevent the inference graph from exploding, we reduce the graph size by pruning the edges with a small plausibility score and keeping the edges with K largest contribution scores. After running

Datasets	ARC-Open				OBQA-Open			
Model	H@50	H@100	R@50	R@100	H@50	H@100	R@50	R@100
DPR	68.67	78.62	28.93	38.63	54.47	67.73	15.17	22.34
DrKIT	67.63	77.89	27.57	37.29	61.74	75.92	18.18	27.10
DrFact	71.60	80.38	31.48	40.93	69.01	80.03	21.27	30.32
Our model	72.76	80.38	31.09	40.24	62.30	73.80	18.11	26.83

Table 1: Results of the Hit@K and Rec@K (K=50/100) in % on OpenCSR.

L inference steps, the model selects the concept with the highest plausibility score in $\mathcal{G}_{inf}$ as the answer to the given question, where the inference graph itself serves as a graphical explanation.

Loss Function We use the binary cross-entropy as the loss function, which is

$$\mathcal{L} = -\frac{1}{|\mathcal{Q}|}\sum_{q\in\mathcal{Q}}\frac{1}{|\mathcal{C}_q^{inf}|}\sum_{c_i\in\mathcal{C}_q^{inf}}(y_{c_i,q}\log(\frac{s_{c_i,q}^L}{\sum_{c_j\in\mathcal{C}_q^{inf}} s_{c_j,q}^L}) + (1-y_{c_i,q})\log((1-\frac{s_{c_i,q}^L}{\sum_{c_j\in\mathcal{C}_q^{inf}} s_{c_j,q}^L}))),$$

where $\mathcal{C}_q^{inf}$ represents the set of concepts in the inference graph of the question q, $y_{c_i,q}$ represents the binary label that indicates whether c_i is an answer for q, and Q denotes the question set. $s_{c_i,q}^L$ denotes the plausibility score of concept c_i at the final inference step.

4 Experiments

Fact corpus and concept vocabulary Following settings in [9], GenericsKB-Best corpus serves as the main commonsense knowledge source that contains 1,025,413 unique facts. All sentences in the corpus are provided with concepts, which are frequent noun chunks, using the spaCy toolkit. There are 80,524 concepts in total.

Datasets and evaluation metrics We evaluate our model on two benchmark open-ended commonsense reasoning datasets, i.e., ARC-Open and OBQA-Open [9], that contain 6600 and 5288 questions, separately. Every question could be answered using various concepts, where the average answer is 6.8 and 7.7 in ARC-Open and OBQA-Open. Each dataset provides the set of true answer concepts for each question. We use two metrics, Hits@K and Recall@K, where Hits@K denotes the percentage of times that at least one true concept appears in the top k of ranked concepts.

Experimental Results We compare our model with DPR [6], DrKIT [2], and DrFact [9]. Recall that our model applies DPR as the retriever so it is a straightforward baseline. And DrFact is the strongest baseline in OpenCSR. As shown in Table 1, our model outperforms DPR and DrKIT on ARC-Open and achieves on-par performance as DrFact. All results are averaged over three trials. We provide implementation details in Appendix B and attach the source code in the supplementary material.

Datasets	ARC-Open			
Model	H@50	H@100	R@50	R@100
Model w/ SC	72.76	80.38	31.09	40.24
Model w/o SC	71.74	79.65	30.56	39.75

Table 2: Ablation Study on ARC-Open: we investigate the gain of adding skip connections (SC) to semantically relevant multi-hop neighbors.

Ablation Study Recall that the proposed subgraph reasoner takes into account both the structurally linked one-hop neighbors and semantically relevant multi-hop neighbors by expanding the inference graph $\mathcal{G}_{inf}$. Table 2 shows an ablation study in that we disable the reasoner to add semantically relevant multi-hop neighbors while inference graph expansion called *Model w/o SC*, demonstrating the performance gain of integrating both structural and semantic information.

5 Conclusion

We present a novel graph-guided neural symbolic commonsense reasoning approach for the open-ended commonsense reasoning task. Specifically, The proposed method integrates both structural dependency information between facts and semantic information by constructing an open information annotation graph and employing a semantic-following operation. The model achieved state-of-the-art performance on two benchmark datasets while being more interpretable.

Limitations

The proposed model performs a sequential reasoning process, and thus, may cause long inference time when answering requires a quite long multi-hop reasoning chain. Besides, the "share-link", which connects nodes that share the same concept, would have a significant amount in some datasets and make the underlying graph much denser. It would make it difficult for the model to decide the expansion direction of the subgraph.

References

[1] Emily Alsentzer, Samuel Finlayson, Michelle Li, and Marinka Zitnik. Subgraph neural networks. *Advances in Neural Information Processing Systems*, 33:8017–8029, 2020.

[2] Bhuwan Dhingra, Manzil Zaheer, Vidhisha Balachandran, Graham Neubig, Ruslan Salakhutdinov, and William W Cohen. Differentiable reasoning over a virtual knowledge base. *arXiv preprint arXiv:2002.10640*, 2020.

[3] Yanlin Feng, Xinyue Chen, Bill Yuchen Lin, Peifeng Wang, Jun Yan, and Xiang Ren. Scalable multi-hop relational reasoning for knowledge-aware question answering. In *Proceedings of the 2020 Conference on Empirical Methods in Natural Language Processing (EMNLP)*, pages 1295–1309, Online, November 2020. Association for Computational Linguistics.

[4] Zhen Han, Peng Chen, Yunpu Ma, and Volker Tresp. Explainable subgraph reasoning for forecasting on temporal knowledge graphs. In *International Conference on Learning Representations*, 2020.

[5] Zhen Han, Peng Chen, Yunpu Ma, and Volker Tresp. xerte: Explainable reasoning on temporal knowledge graphs for forecasting future links. *arXiv preprint arXiv:2012.15537*, 2020.

[6] Vladimir Karpukhin, Barlas Oguz, Sewon Min, Patrick Lewis, Ledell Wu, Sergey Edunov, Danqi Chen, and Wen-tau Yih. Dense passage retrieval for open-domain question answering. In *Proceedings of the 2020 Conference on Empirical Methods in Natural Language Processing (EMNLP)*, pages 6769–6781, Online, November 2020. Association for Computational Linguistics.

[7] Daniel Khashabi, Sewon Min, Tushar Khot, Ashish Sabharwal, Oyvind Tafjord, Peter Clark, and Hannaneh Hajishirzi. UNIFIEDQA: Crossing format boundaries with a single QA system. In *Findings of the Association for Computational Linguistics: EMNLP 2020*, pages 1896–1907, Online, November 2020. Association for Computational Linguistics.

[8] Bill Yuchen Lin, Xinyue Chen, Jamin Chen, and Xiang Ren. KagNet: Knowledge-aware graph networks for commonsense reasoning. In *Proceedings of the 2019 Conference on Empirical Methods in Natural Language Processing and the 9th International Joint Conference on Natural Language Processing (EMNLP-IJCNLP)*, pages 2829–2839, Hong Kong, China, November 2019. Association for Computational Linguistics.

[9] Bill Yuchen Lin, Haitian Sun, Bhuwan Dhingra, Manzil Zaheer, Xiang Ren, and William W Cohen. Differentiable open-ended commonsense reasoning. *arXiv preprint arXiv:2010.14439*, 2020.

[10] Mingming Sun, Wenyue Hua, Zoey Liu, Xin Wang, Kangjie Zheng, and Ping Li. A predicate-function-argument annotation of natural language for open-domain information expression. In *Proceedings of the 2020 Conference on Empirical Methods in Natural Language Processing (EMNLP)*, pages 2140–2150, 2020.

[11] Komal Teru, Etienne Denis, and Will Hamilton. Inductive relation prediction by subgraph reasoning. In *International Conference on Machine Learning*, pages 9448–9457. PMLR, 2020.

Appendices

A The license of the Artifacts

The datasets we used in this work are proposed by Lin et al. [9] which is licensed under the MIT License.

About the model we proposed in this work, we will release it and give the license, copyright information, and terms of use once the paper gets accepted.

B Implementation

We tune the hyperparameters of our models using the random search and report the best configuration in the source code in the supplementary material. The training costs 73 GPU hours on the ARC-Open dataset and 50 GPU hours on the OBQA-Open dataset with NVIDIA A40 instance.

Generating Irish Text with a Flexible Plug-and-Play Architecture

Simon Mille
ADAPT, Dublin City University
simon.mille@adaptcentre.ie

Elaine Uí Dhonnchadha
Trinity College, Dublin
uidhonne@tcd.ie

Lauren Cassidy
ADAPT, Dublin City University
lauren.cassidy@adaptcentre.ie

Brian Davis
ADAPT, Dublin City University
brian.davis@adaptcentre.ie

Stamatia Dasiopoulou
Independent Researcher
stamatia.dasiopoulou@gmail.com

Anya Belz
ADAPT, Dublin City University
anya.belz@adaptcentre.ie

Abstract

In this paper, we describe M-FleNS, a multilingual flexible plug-and-play architecture designed to accommodate neural and symbolic modules, and initially instantiated with rule-based modules. We focus on using M-FleNS for the specific purpose of building new resources for Irish, a language currently under-represented in the NLP landscape. We present the general M-FleNS framework and how we use it to build an Irish Natural Language Generation system for verbalising part of the DBpedia ontology and building a multilayered dataset with rich linguistic annotations. Via automatic and human assessments of the output texts we show that with very limited resources we can create a system that reaches high levels of fluency and semantic accuracy, while having very low energy and memory requirements.

1 Introduction

Natural Language Generation (NLG) for tasks including dialogue-turn generation and fact verbalisation is increasingly widely used in commercial systems. Despite recent spectacular advances achieved by LLMs, in application contexts where accuracy and reliability are crucial, many commercial systems continue to use the same old template filler systems that have been around at least since the 1980s.[1] The other two main categories of NLG systems are neural language-model based (NLMB) systems, currently extremely popular in research systems, and rule and grammar based (RGB) systems, currently very unpopular. In contrast to template-based (TB) systems, NLMB systems have very high Coverage, while also sharing TB systems' high Fluency and Robustness. However, the disadvantage of an NLMB system is that it cannot be guaranteed that the output will be free of grammatical errors or even that it will be semantically accurate. The latter is of particular concern as NLMB systems cannot be trusted not to omit essential content, make things up, or even insult users. Moreover, such systems also tend not to be built for low-resource languages (LRLs) languages because of the large amounts of data needed to build them. Finally, NLMB systems often suffer from low Variation, and very low Energy Efficiency, with the best current models having shockingly high carbon footprints. RGB systems on the other hand have become increasingly unpopular since the NLP field switched first to statistical systems, then to neural systems. While RGB systems tend to have low Coverage, suprasentential Fluency, and Robustness as well as having to be built manually, they can be guaranteed to have high Accuracy and Grammaticality, as well as being efficient in terms of data and energy requirements, and suitable for LRLs.

According to the European Language Equality report for Irish (Lynn, 2022), Irish is a low-resource language. In a survey of available resources for European languages, on a scale of 1-4, Irish was classified as 4 having "weak or no support", and ranked 31st out of the 33 European languages surveyed. The report identifies a range of language technology gaps, mainly due to the lack of underlying data resources, dedicated funding and skill-sets, and finds that to date there has been little or no system development for Automatic Subtitling, Information Retrieval, Information Extraction, Natu-

[1] E.g. Arria NLG: https://www.arria.com/.

Proceedings of the 2nd Workshop in Pattern-based Approaches to NLP in the Age of Deep Learning, pages 25–42
December 6, 2023. ©2023 Association for Computational Linguistics

Reiter&Dale Tasks	M-FleNS Tasks	M-FleNS Input	M-FleNS Output	Output type
Content determination	—	—	—	—
Discourse planning	Linguistic structuring	Structured data	PredArg	DAG
Sentence aggregation	Text planning*	PredArg	PredArg-Agg	DAG
Lexicalisation	Lexicalisation Comm. structuring Deep sent. structuring Surf. sent. structuring Synt. aggregation*	PredArg(-Agg) PredArg-Lex PredArg-Th DSynt SSynt	PredArg-Lex PredArg-Th DSynt SSynt SSynt-Agg	DAG DAG DT DT DT
REG	REG*	SSynt(-Agg)	SSynt-Pro	DT
Linguistic realisation	Word ord. and agree. resolution Surface form retrieval	SSynt(-Agg/-Pro) DMorph	DMorph SMorph	Chain Chain

Table 1: The M-FleNS architecture (see Appendix D for illustration): the tasks, their respective input, output (used as module name), structure type (DAG = Directed Acyclic Graph; DT = Dependency Tree) and correspondence with Reiter and Dale (1997)'s tasks. * Denotes optional modules, i.e., grammatical texts can be produced without them.

ral Language Generation, Semantic Role Labelling, and other areas. The report recommends a long term strategy of support for dedicated LT education and training, investment in data collection and annotation, and the development of LT tools.

The *Digital Plan for the Irish Language* (Department of Tourism, Culture, Arts, Gaeltacht, Sport Media, 2022) notes that urgent action is needed if Irish is to benefit from the digital revolution and to survive the threat of digital extinction. It notes two complementary approaches, knowledge-based and data-driven machine-learning methods, and states that both are needed and each brings specific advantages. A linguistic knowledge base provides a digital, explicit account of the structure of contemporary Irish which is an important goal in itself, while machine-learning approaches can offer a quick and less labour-intensive route to developing certain technologies. Both approaches are needed and, especially in the context or LRLs, can be combined in specific systems.

In this paper, we present a flexible plug-and-play architecture that addresses both knowledge-based and machine-learning-based gaps in Irish Natural Language Processing, by releasing a generation system and a rich dataset. While the current (single) Multilingual Flexible Neuro-Symbolic (M-FleNS) system is multilingual –generating text also e.g. in English, French, Spanish, and Catalan-, we focus here on its instantiation with rule-based modules for the generation of Irish texts from DBpedia triple sets. Below, we start by describing and motivating our architecture (Section 2). Next we describe the WebNLG dataset, the FORGe generator and the Irish morphology tools (Section 3) we use. We present the extension to WebNLG data-to-text for Irish, and evaluate it via metrics and human assessment; we also present a new Irish dataset with rich linguistic annotations produced with our instantiated architecture (Section 4). We finish with a discussion of related work (Section 5). The generation pipeline,[2] dataset[3] and an interactive demo for the generation of short Wikipedia pages in Irish or English[4] are all publicly available.

2 A plug-and-play architecture for system and resource building

2.1 Modular structure

While end-to-end approaches are popular in current NLG systems (Dušek et al., 2018; Castro Ferreira et al., 2020), they are more data-hungry and computationally far more expensive (therefore more energy intensive) than corresponding modular architectures (Dušek et al., 2020). Furthermore, recent evidence shows that splitting the generation process into sub-steps can lead to better output texts (Castro Ferreira et al., 2019; Moryossef et al., 2019; Puduppully and Lapata, 2021; Kasner and Dusek, 2022). We seek to leverage this advantage by giving our M-FleNS framework a sequential architecture where each module corresponds to specific (sub)tasks of the natural language generation process roughly corresponding to the pipeline architecture originally established by Reiter and Dale (1997). Table 1 lists the M-FleNS modules in terms

[2] https://github.com/mille-s/DCU_TCD-FORGe_WebNLG23

[3] https://github.com/mille-s/Mod-D2T/

[4] https://github.com/mille-s/WikipediaPage_Generator

of the tasks they perform, alongside the tasks/-modules identified in Reiter and Dale's pipeline to which they roughly correspond.[5]

2.2 Rich linguistic representations

Each of the 10 different modules shown in Table 1 provides as output one or more well defined, rich, and linguistically motivated representations. The intermediate representations in M-FleNS are all graphs that can be grouped into three main types: (i) predicate-argument *directed acyclic graphs (DAGs)* for semantic information; (ii) *unordered dependency trees (DTs)* for syntactic information; and (iii) *chains* for morphological information. These intermediate representations loosely follow the different levels of Meaning-Text Theory (Mel'čuk, 1973). In the instantiated version of the pipeline presented in this paper, the input structured data is the WebNLG data (Aquilina et al., 2023), made of DBpedia triple sets, and we use the FORGe grammar-based generator to produce the intermediate representations (Mille et al., 2019) and the Irish NLP toolkit (Dhonnchadha et al., 2003) to produce the final representation: details about the dataset and tools are provided in Section 3.

2.3 Addressing technology gaps

With our modular approach we aim not only at developing a first system for Irish NLG, but also at producing new data that will allow for addressing more of the technology gaps identified in the European Language Equality report. For instance, with the generator we can produce a large amount of semantic and syntactic structures; syntactic structures paired with texts can be used to train syntactic parsers, while semantic structures paired with text can be used to train semantic role labelers. Using in parallel syntactic and semantic structures, tools can be trained that convert one into the other to build smaller modules to be combined with other tools (e.g. an existing syntactic parser). All ten intermediate representations can be also be used for explainability, language teaching, etc. In Section 4.6 we provide details on how we used our architecture to produce linguistically annotated data.

3 Data and tools

In the following subsections, we describe the dataset (WebNLG) and tools (FORGe and Irish NLP) we use in our experiments.

[5]This table is adapted from (Mille et al., 2023).

3.1 The WebNLG dataset

The WebNLG dataset (Aquilina et al., 2023) is a data-to-text benchmark consisting of {input, output} pairs, where the input is a set of n triples ($1 \leq n \leq 7$), the output a set of m texts that verbalise the triple set. In Figure 1, $n = 3$ and $m = 1$.

DBpedia triples are the building blocks of the inputs, and consist of three related elements called a *Property*, a *Subject* and an *Object* in Semantic Web terminology. A Subject (denoted by *DB-Subj* in this paper) is usually an entity that has a Property and a value for this Property, which is the Object (*DB-Obj*). E.g. in Figure 1, the entity *Agra_Airport* is associated with 3 properties: *location*, *operatingOrganisation* and *icaoLocationIdentifier*. The semantics of each property is defined by DBpedia editors,[6] but in most cases, *the Property of the DB-Subj is DB-Obj* makes it clear (e.g., *The location of Agra Airport is India*, *The operating organisation of Agra Airport the Indian Air Force*, and *the ICAO location identifier of Agra Airport is VIAG.*).

WebNLG 2017 (Gardent et al., 2017) consisted of (only) an English task. For WebNLG 2020, the English dataset was extended with more properties, and it also included Russian texts (Castro Ferreira et al., 2020); in both cases, the texts were collected via manual effort (crowdsourcing) . The third edition of the task in 2023 focused on four low-resource languages: Irish, Welsh, Breton and Maltese, for which the texts for the training data are the machine-translated 2020 English texts, while the texts in the test and development data were translated by professional translators. All inputs are the same as the 2020 inputs.

3.2 The FORGe multilingual generator

FORGe (Mille et al., 2019) is a multilingual rule-based generator that takes as input minimal predicate-argument (PredArg) structures. It realises the last four consecutive steps of the traditional NLG pipeline (Reiter and Dale, 1997) (sentence aggregation, lexicalisation,[7] referring expression generation and linguistic realisation, see Table 1). Each of the four steps is implemented as one or more graph transducer(s) that successively map the input PredArg onto different dependency-based intermediate linguistic representations.

[6]See http://mappings.dbpedia.org/index.php/How_to_edit_the_DBpedia_Ontology.

[7]We refer to a more surface-oriented lexicalisation here, with, e.g., function words, as opposed to the "deep" lexicalisation of the main concepts described in Section 4.1.

```
<entry category="Airport" eid="719" shape="(X (X) (X) (X))" shape_type="sibling" size="3">
  <modifiedtripleset>
    <mtriple>Agra_Airport | location | India</mtriple>
    <mtriple>Agra_Airport | operatingOrganisation | Indian_Air_Force</mtriple>
    <mtriple>Agra_Airport | icaoLocationIdentifier | &quot;VIAG&quot;</mtriple>
  </modifiedtripleset>
  <lex comment="" lang="ga" lid="Id3">Tá Aerfort Agra, atá VIAG mar an cód aitheantais
      áite ICAO aige, á reáchtáil ag Aerfhórsa na hIndia.</lex>
</entry>
```

Figure 1: A WebNLG data point (EN: 'Agra airport, whose ICAO identifier is VIAG, is operated by the IAF.')

A mix of language-independent and language-specific rules build these intermediate representations using additional knowledge contained in language-specific dictionaries. From the perspective of multilingualism, there are 3 types (T1-T3) of rules in FORGe: fully language-independent rules (T1, ~82% of all rules); rules that apply to a subset of languages (T2, ~6.5 languages on average, ~3% of rules); and language-specific rules, which apply to one single language (T3, ~15% of rules). In the description of the extensions of FORGe for Irish below, we refer to these three types.

FORGe uses three different dictionaries to store:

- Mappings between concepts and lexical units, e.g. *located {GA={lex=lonnaithe_JJ_01}}*.
- Lexical unit descriptions, e.g. *lonnaithe_JJ_01 {lemma = lonnaithe; pos = JJ; preposition_arg2 = i }*, where *i* 'in' is required on the second argument of *lonnaithe*: *lonnaithe i X* 'located in X'.
- Generic language-specific knowledge, such as the type of word order or morphological agreement triggered by surface-oriented dependencies (e.g. in English a direct object is by default after its governing verb in the sentence, and a determiner receives case, number and gender from its governing noun).

The input PredArg structures are very similar to the *Facts* in ILEX's Content potential structures (O'Donnell et al., 2001), or the *Message triples* in NaturalOWL (Androutsopoulos et al., 2013), with the difference that all predicates in the PredArg structures are generally intended to represent atomic meanings (e.g. *main* + *runway* as opposed to *mainRunway*), allowing for more flexible processing. The first part of the generation pipeline, which produces aggregated predicate-argument graphs, is also comparable to ILEX (O'Donnell et al., 2001), while the surface realisation is largely inspired by MARQUIS (Wanner et al., 2010). FORGe shares not only its general architecture with these two systems, but also the use of lexical resources with subcategorisation information and of a multilingual core of rules.

FORGe was adapted to the WebNLG'20 dataset for the generation of English texts and has a multilingual core of rules, but is not able to generate text in a new language off-the-shelf. However, adapting it to a new language is relatively easy, so it is a good candidate for building the first Irish generator. In Section 4, we report on the extensions we carried out to FORGe so as to be able to generate WebNLG Irish texts. We use the whole FORGe pipeline except for the surface form generation, for which we use the existing Irish NLP tools (see Section 3.3).

3.3 Irish NLP tools

The Irish NLP tools suite[8] includes finite-state transducers for Irish morphology generation (Dhonnchadha et al., 2003). These tools handle tokenisation and morphological analysis/generation of the inflected forms of Irish headwords coded in the finite-state lexicons. The tools were initially developed using xfst (Xerox finite state tools) (Beesley and Karttunen, 2003) and later converted to use foma tools (Hulden, 2009).[9] Finite-state transducers model a two-level morphology where a lexical description is mapped to a surface form, e.g. déan+Verb+VT+FutInd maps to the future tense form *déanfaidh* of the transitive verb *déan* 'make'. The transducers can be used to generate inflected forms of words for NLG and CALL applications, and the same transducers work in the opposite direction for morphological analysis as part of NLP applications including PoS tagging and parsing.

4 M-FleNS for Irish Natural Language Generation

In this section, we describe our pipeline for the generation of Irish texts from DBpedia triples,

[8] https://www.scss.tcd.ie/~uidhonne/irish.utf8.htm

[9] https://fomafst.github.io/

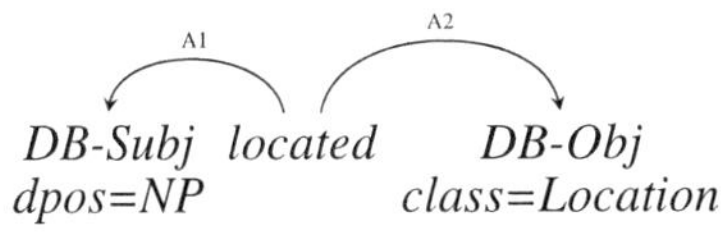

Figure 2: Sample PredArg template corresponding to the *location* property.

including Subject and Object label retrieval and predicate-argument template crafting (4.1), extensions to FORGe and lexical resource building for Irish (4.2), the connection between FORGe and Irish NLP tools (4.3) and post-processing of outputs (4.4). We then provide an evaluation of the generator (4.5) and describe a new dataset (4.6). All resources are available; see Footnotes 2, 3, 4.

4.1 PredArg templates and their instantiation

The linguistic structuring step consists of mapping the WebNLG input triple sets onto abstract linguistic (predicate-argument) structures. For this, we follow the approach of the FORGe submission at WebNLG'17 (Mille et al., 2019), i.e. we use PredArg templates in the PropBank style (Kingsbury and Palmer, 2002) that correspond to each individual property and instantiate them by replacing the DB-Subj and DB-Obj placeholders with their respective lexicalisations. The instantiated templates are then grouped based on their DB-Subj and ordered in descending frequency of appearance of the DB-Subj in the input triple set (e.g. triples with a DB-Subj that has 3 mentions come before those with 2 mentions). Figure 2 shows a PredArg template, instantiated in Figure 4 in Appendix A.

Lexicalisation of properties. We handcrafted templates for all properties of the training, development and test splits of the WebNLG'23 dataset. There are 411 different properties, and since several properties can be verbalised the same way,[10] the total number of unique templates is lower (381).

In an effort to possibly reduce the human effort in the crafting of the templates in future developments of our (or others') system, we tried to reduce to a maximum the number of different templates to cover all properties. After examining the 411 properties and defining corresponding templates, we assigned each property a specific type according to the kind of information that it is transmitting. We defined 23 type labels such as *PART OF/MEMBER OF*, *ORIGIN LOCATION*, *SET MEMBERSHIP*, *[X] HAS [QTY] ENTITY*, etc. Each type is associated with a sentence template and a basic PredArg that can be used to verbalise the properties associated to it. We plan to use these basic labels to speed up the future extension of the generator.

Lexicalisation of DB-Subj and DB-Obj values. For each triple, the property and its pertinent domain and range classes determine whether the DB-Subj/Obj values will be lexicalised using their English or Irish label (human readable name). To obtain the latter, we take advantage of the *owl:sameAs* relation that links the DB-Subj/Obj entity of the English DBpedia to its equivalent entity in the Irish DBpedia version; if no equivalent entity is contained in the localised DBpedia version, we fall back to Google translate,[11] giving as input the English label without any further context.

4.2 Extensions to FORGe

We extended the available version of FORGe in two aspects: (i) manual crafting of the three types of dictionaries, and (ii) implementation of language-specific rules to cover the idiosyncracies of Irish. With respect to dictionaries, we added 457 mappings between concepts and lexical units and as many lexical unit descriptions, and we manually crafted the generic language-specific dictionary. For rules, we implemented 76 rules that apply exclusively to Irish (T3), which represents 2.78% of rules; Table 2 shows the breakdown of language-agnostic and language-specific rules per module. We also activated 65 existing T2 rules for Irish.

As Table 2 shows, 4 modules require Irish-specific rules: deep sentence structuring, surface sentence structuring, word order and agreement resolution and morphology processing; next we list the phenomena that required T3 and most T2 rules.

Deep sentence structuring

Relative particles (T3): the particle *a* is introduced to link the modified noun and the main verb in relative clauses; in case of prepositional relatives, the particle has a different form depending on the tense of the verb (present *a*, past *ar*).

Passive (T3): in Irish there are two alternative constructions where a passive form would be used in English. If the data refers to an action/event, an autonomous main verb form is used, e.g. for the triple `Acharya_Institute_of_Technology | established | 2000`, *bunaíodh*, the autonomous

[10] Properties such as *municipality*, *district*, or *country* are mapped to the same template as *location*, shown in Figure 2.

[11] We used the publicly available *Translator* module of the *googletrans* (version 3.1.0a0) library.

ID	FORGe module	# rl	% lang. ind. rl	# T3 GA rl	% T3 GA rl
1	Text planning	553	99.82	0	0
2	Lexicalisation	183	97.81	0	0
3	Communicative structuring	258	97.29	0	0
4	Deep sentence structuring	345	78.84	3	0.87
5	Surface sentence structuring	477	68.97	17	3.56
6	Syntactic aggregation	215	93.02	0	0
7	Referring Expression Generation	237	96.2	0	0
8	Word order and agreement resolution	265	50.57	17	6.42
9	Morphology processing	201	45.77	39	19.4
	All modules	2,734	81.82	76	2.78

Table 2: Number of rules, proportion of language-independent rules, and number and % of Irish-specific (T3) rules (rl) per FORGe module.

form of the verb *bunaigh* 'to establish' is used, as in *Bunaíodh Institiúid Teicneolaíochta Acharya sa bhliain 2000*, 'Acharya Institute of Technology was established in the year 2000'. Alternatively, where a state/location is referred to, e.g. for the triple `MotorSport_Vision|city|Longfield`, we have *tá*, the present tense of the auxiliary verb *bí* 'to be', and the past participle *lonnaithe* 'located', as in *Tá MotorSport Vision lonnaithe i gcathair Longfield*, 'MotorSport Vision is located in Longfield'.

Non-verbal copula (T3): Irish has two copular constructions. The verbal copula *bí* is used for changeable properties whereas the non-verbal copula *is* is used for more permanent properties such as area code, e.g. for `Darlington | areaCode | 01325` we have *Is é cód ceantair Darlington ná 01325*, where *is* connects *cód ceantair Darlington* 'Darlington area code' with its value, and the pronoun *é* agrees with the gender and number of the noun *cód* 'code'.

Surface sentence structuring

Determiners (T3): a definite determiner is only introduced on a noun *N* if *N*'s dependent is not a definite noun or a proper noun.

Dependencies (T2, 22 rules in common with Catalan, Greek, Spanish, French, Italian and Portuguese): surface-oriented dependencies are introduced as, e.g., *subject, direct object, modifier*, etc.

Word order and agreement resolution

Genitive chains (T3): in a chain of genitive elements, only the last element maintains the genitive case, e.g. in the case of 'the length of the runway of the aerodrome', only the last element 'aerodrome' has genitive case as in *Is é fad rúidbhealach an aeradróim 1,095m*.

Word order class (T3): when an element is established as a member of a class, the class name goes right after the copula, as in *Is milseog é Bionico* 'Bionico is a dessert'.

Possessive pronoun agreement (T3): the semantic number and gender of a possessor triggers agreement on the possessed. In the case of the triple `India | leader | T._S._Thakur`, the copular construction generates the text *Tá T.S. Shakur ina cheannaire ar an India*, 'T. S. Thakur is a leader of India', where we have the present tense of the verbal copula *bí*, followed by the subject *'T. S. Thakur'* and the subject complement *'ina cheannaire ar an India'*. The complement has a possessive pronoun *ina* that agrees in gender and number with the subject, i.e. *ina* is masculine singular reflecting the subject 'T. S. Thakur' and it triggers masculine singular agreement on the noun *cheannaire* 'leader'.

Ellipsis (T3): some rules look for pronouns to elide, in particular in relative and non-verbal copular constructions. Irish is a VSO language so a specific rule checks for repeated subjects on the right of the verb and replaces them with pronouns.[12]

Order between siblings (T2, 29 rules in common with Catalan, Greek, Spanish, French, Portuguese and sometimes Italian): for instance, in many languages, the determiner usually goes before all other dependents of the noun.

Morphology processing

Concatenations (T3): *don* is a contraction of *do an* 'for the' as in *Scríobh Nicholas Brodszky an ceol don scannán* meaning 'Nicholas Brodszky wrote the music **for the** film'.

Prefixes (T3): vowel-initial masculine nouns following the determiner *an* receive a *t-* prefix as in *Rugadh an **t-aisteoir** Bill Oddie in Rochdale* meaning 'The actor Bill Oddie was born in Rochdale'.

[12]Strictly speaking, this rule belongs to the REG module but since it has the same conditions of application as ellipsis in other languages, it was left in this module for the time being.

The preposition *le* triggers a prefix *h-* on following nouns starting with a vowel, and some past verbs get the prefix *d'*.

Mutations (T3): word-initial mutations are common in Irish and fulfil many grammatical functions, for example the noun *cathair* 'city' has various mutations depending on the number and gender of the possessive pronoun, e.g. there is lenition in *mo* ***ch****athair* 'my city', eclipsis in *ár* ***g****cathair* 'our city' and no mutation in *a cathair* 'her city'.

Verbal Adj/N, Prep. declension, V flags (T3): other rules cover the conversion of some adjectives and nouns into their verbal counterparts, the inflection of some prepositions and the insertion of a tag that flags vowel-initial verbs, as required by the morphology generator.

4.3 Interfacing FORGe with Irish NLP tools

In order to match the inputs expected by Irish NLP tools, we process FORGe outputs with regular expressions to replace reserved characters, introduce a '+' separator between morphological tags, and insert single line breaks between consecutive words and double line breaks between consecutive texts.

4.4 Post-processing

The post-processing consists of regular expressions to revert reserved characters to their original form, true-case and clean the texts, and take care of prefixing, hyphenation, contraction, lenition and eclipsis phenomena triggered by the inflected forms of words; see Appendix A for an example.

4.5 Evaluation

We report on both automatic and human evaluations of the quality of the texts generated with our pipeline (DCU/TCD in Tables 3 and 4). Both evaluations were carried out as part of the WebNLG'23 shared task by the task organisers; see details in the task overview paper (Aquilina et al., 2023).

	BLEU	BERT_F1
DCU-NLG	20.40	0.81
DCU/TCD	**16.66**	**0.77**
IREL	15.66	0.78
Cuni-Wue	15.87	0.77
Baseline	11.63	0.76

Table 3: WebNLG'23 automatic evaluation results.

For the automatic evaluations, outputs from all systems were compared to the reference human-translated Irish texts (1,779 test texts), and BLEU (Papineni et al., 2002), TER (Snover et al., 2006), chrF++ (Popović, 2017) and BERTScore (Zhang et al., 2019) were computed; see results in Table 3. For the human assessment, the organisers selected randomly the same 100 outputs for each system (and the corresponding 100 reference texts) and asked professional translators to rate the texts on a scale of 1 to 5 according to 4 criteria: **Fluency** and **Absence of Repetition** to capture the intrinsic quality of the texts, and **Absence of Omission** and **Absence of Additions** to capture the semantic faithfulness of the text with respect to the input triple sets; see Table 4 for results.

System	Flu.	Add.	Omi.	Rep.
Human	4.07	0.81	0.82	0.96
DCU-NLG	3.83	0.83	0.85	0.97
DCU/TCD	**3.35**	**0.84**	**0.81**	**0.89**
IREL	3.39	0.65	0.58	0.94
Cuni-Wue	2.98	0.55	0.51	0.92

Table 4: Results of the WebNLG'23 human evaluation; Human = human-translated texts, Flu. = Fluency, Add. = Absence of addition, Omi. = Absence of omission, Rep. = Absence of repetition.

Considering that all other systems including the baseline are combinations of (very) large language models (to generate English texts) and machine translation (to translate to Irish), we were surprised to see that our rule-based pipeline performed well in the automatic evaluations: we obtained a BLEU score only 4 points below the highest scoring system (a combination of GPT3.5 and Google Translate (Lorandi and Belz, 2023)), and higher that all non-GPT-based submissions. As comparison, for English text generation at WebNLG'20 (Castro Ferreira et al., 2020), the FORGe-based submission was 13 BLEU points lower than the highest scoring system and one of the lowest BLEU overall.[13] Our absolute BLEU score is much lower than FORGe's scores on English at WebNLG'20 (over 40); this is at least partly because BLEU was calculated with only one reference (compared to 2,5 on average in English, which produces higher scores), but it could also be due to the fact that we created our lexicalisations without reference to the gold Irish texts, i.e. surface similarity is likely to be low.

[13]There was significantly more gold data available in English compared to Irish.

The results of the human evaluation show that DCU/TCD-FORGe is on a par with the human references and the best system for Absence of Additions, Absence of Omissions and Repetition (no statistical difference in the scores according to the organisers), but is significantly less good in terms of Fluency. Part of the reason for this can be found in our own preliminary quality assessment of the output texts, during which Irish speakers mentioned that the way the information is packaged into sentences (Text planning task) is often unnatural, which directly affects the Fluency of texts. We plan to address this issue by replacing the text planning module by a statistical component.

Our system does not reach the level that can be achieved with very large language models, but unlike the latter, it is inherently energy- and resource-efficient: our complete pipeline has a disk space of about 8MB and runs with less than 1GB of RAM; it generates the whole WebNLG test set (1,779 texts) in about 15 min (0.5 sec/text). The generation pipeline is also reusable; it currently covers datasets such as E2E (Novikova et al., 2017) or Rotowire (Wiseman et al., 2017) in English, and adapting it to new domains is straightforward.

4.6 A new Irish dataset with rich annotations

Along with our architecture and our generation pipeline, we also release an Irish multilayer dataset with rich linguistically motivated intermediate representations. In order to create the dataset, we apply our whole generation pipeline described in Section 4 and save the intermediate representations in the process. The resulting dataset has ten layers, which correspond to the ten layers shown in Table 1.

Representations at all layers are multi-sentence graphs that can be grouped into the three main types from Section 2: directed acyclic graphs for semantic information, unordered dependency trees for syntactic information, and chains for morphological information. Nodes are connected across layers through individual IDs, and coreference is explicitly marked. Intermediate representations are represented as CoNLL-U tables.[14] Because CoNLL-U is a linear format that we use to represent unordered graphs and trees, we delimit sentences by `<SENT>` at the end of a group of nodes. All lines before `<SENT>` belong to the same sentence, but their relative order in the ConNLL-U file is not relevant. However, the order in which the sentences appear does correspond to their order in the text. For levels that are chains, the order of the lines is the order of the elements in the sentence. Detailed descriptions of format and levels can be found in (Mille et al., 2023); tagsets used, dataset statistics and sample structures are provided in Appendix B, C and D.

Due to the modular system architecture, dataset construction is flexible enough to allow the generation of a myriad of dataset variants in terms of verbalisation, sentence grouping/structuring, output simplicity/complexity, etc., simply by (de)activating optional modules (Table 1) or by introducing variation during the linguistic structuring task –thus providing multiple ways of verbalising each input triple. In contrast to neural generation, our approach ensures that output texts are faithful to the input, and will not contain inaccuracies, biases or offensive language. The dataset is publicly available, see Footnote 3.

5 Related work

Rule-based NLG. There is a long tradition of rule-based natural language generation systems such as REALPRO (Lavoie and Rainbow, 1997), ILEX (O'Donnell et al., 2001), IGEN (Varges and Mellish, 2001), SimpleNLG (Gatt and Reiter, 2009), MARQUIS (Wanner et al., 2010; Bouayad-Agha et al., 2012), OpenCCG (White and Rajkumar, 2012), NaturalOwl (Androutsopoulos et al., 2013), GenDR (Lareau et al., 2018) and others. More recently, RDFJSREALB (Lapalme, 2020) and FORGe (Mille et al., 2019) were adapted to WebNLG, but none were able to generate Irish text. Note that the idea of decomposing the generation process into steps has been the standard before the emergence of end-to-end systems, and that previous work on NLG already based their modules on the Meaning-Text theory, going back to REALPRO (Lavoie and Rainbow, 1997) and MARQUIS (Wanner et al., 2010). It is however the first time that a plug-and-play architecture is proposed with these modules, and the first time that an Irish rule-based NLG system is developed.

Irish datasets and language resources. There are few freely available monolingual Irish corpora, and moreover, domain-specific Irish datasets are scarce. Resources are mostly targeted towards machine translation and/or language analysis tasks. With the exception of the WebNLG 2023 data (and now the data presented in this paper), no datasets exist for text generation tasks (Lynn, 2023).

[14] `https://universaldependencies.org/format.html`

Monolingual corpora. Monolingual data include the New Corpus for Ireland (with fiction, news reports, official documents, etc.) (Kilgarriff et al., 2006), the unshuffled Irish portion of the 2019 OSCAR corpus (Suárez et al., 2019), the Gaois Corpus of Contemporary Irish (Ní Loingsigh et al., 2017), with news media and e-zines, or the Irish Wikipedia Vicipéid,[15] which draws directly from Fréamh an Eolais, an Irish-language encyclopedia of science and technology.[16] Moreover, a corpus of idioms (Ní Loingsigh, 2016) and Universal Dependency treebanks such as Irish UD (Lynn and Foster, 2016), pre-standard Irish UD (Scannell, 2022) and TwittIrish (Cassidy et al., 2022) are available.

Bilingual/Parallel corpora. Significant advances have been made in the collection and availability of bilingual corpora, including: (i) ParaCrawl v7 (Bañón et al., 2020), a collection of parallel corpora crawled from multi-lingual websites; (ii) the Gaois Parallel Corpus[17] of 26M Irish words and 24.5M English words; and in particular, (iii) the Irish-EU English-Irish Parallel Corpus which was a direct outcome of the European Language Resource Coordination project (ELRC[18]). This resource contains 195K+ parallel sentences, collected from various public bodies and government departments released via ELRC-SHARE[19]. In Ireland all national translation data is collected by *eSTÓR*.[20]

Irish tools and Models. The European Language Grid[21] catalogue lists a number of multilingual tools and services that support Irish (e.g. Bitextor, Opus MT, Systran). Irish NLP tools (Uí Dhonnchadha, 2009) offers the only suite of text analysis in Irish. Transformer Language Models (LM) such as multilingual BERT (M-BERT) (Devlin et al., 2019), and the language-agnostic BERT Sentence Embedding (Feng et al., 2022)) support Irish. The monolingual Irish gaBERT LM was trained on over 7.9M sentences, and outperforms baselines for tasks such as dependency parsing and multiword expression identification. (Barry et al., 2022).

6 Conclusions

We have presented a high-accuracy, energy and resource-efficient system for generating Irish text which achieves a satisfactory quality of output. Its modular architecture means that shortcomings can potentially be remedied by training statistical modules, such as a text structuring module for improved fluency, or by including enhanced rule-based modules which can be added to the pipeline.

This type of modular rule-based NLG system is particularly suitable for low-resource languages, where large amounts of training data is not available, and can play an important role in generating accurate fact-based online language content, such as Wikipedia pages. Such systems can be developed incrementally and language documentation is an inherent and valuable by-product of the system. In addition, rule-based systems tend to suffer less from the negative and harmful biases which have been identified in the application of some LLMs.

Limitations

Generation pipeline. Coverage and robustness of rule-based NLG: Although our experiments show that we are able to overcome some of the drawbacks of LLMs, the main bottleneck of any rule-based system remains coverage and robustness. In addition, it can be difficult for someone who is not familiar with the rule systems to edit it, and it usually requires knowledge of the language.

Dataset. Our dataset differs from previous work in that we do not use human-written texts; since texts are synthetic and produced by a deterministic generator, their variety and quality is limited by the knowledge encoded in the generator (in particular, they generally lack the naturalness of human-written texts), and they represent only a fraction of what is possible for a language to express.

The current intermediate representations are well-formed at all layers, but we are conscious that some phenomena would require some additional analysis; as e.g. the syntactic representations of copulas and their *é* pronoun (see Section 4.2).

Acknowledgements

Mille's contribution was funded by the European Union under the Marie Skłodowska-Curie grant agreement No 101062572 (M-FleNS).

Ethics Statement

Given that we do not resort to using language models nor to human evaluation with people who are not authors of this paper, the present work has no ethics implication that we are aware of.

[15] https://dumps.wikimedia.org/gawiki/

[16] https://ga.wikipedia.org/wiki

[17] https://www.gaois.ie/crp/ga/

[18] https://lr-coordination.eu/node/2

[19] https://elrc-share.eu/

[20] https://estor.ie/

[21] https://live.european-language-grid.eu/

References

Ion Androutsopoulos, Gerasimos Lampouras, and Dimitrios Galanis. 2013. Generating natural language descriptions from owl ontologies: the naturalowl system. *Journal of Artificial Intelligence Research*, 48:671–715.

Enrico Aquilina, Anya Belz, Claudia Borg, Liam Cripwell, Claire Gardent, Albert Gatt, John Judge, Michela Lorandi, Anna Nikiforoskaya, William Soto-Martinez, and Craig Thomson. 2023. The 2023 WebNLG shared task on low resource languages: Overview and evaluation results. In *Proceedings of the Workshop on Multimodal, Multilingual Natural Language Generation and Multilingual WebNLG Challenge*, page tbd, Prague, Czech Republic.

Marta Bañón, Pinzhen Chen, Barry Haddow, Kenneth Heafield, Hieu Hoang, Miquel Esplà-Gomis, Mikel L. Forcada, Amir Kamran, Faheem Kirefu, Philipp Koehn, Sergio Ortiz Rojas, Leopoldo Pla Sempere, Gema Ramírez-Sánchez, Elsa Sarrías, Marek Strelec, Brian Thompson, William Waites, Dion Wiggins, and Jaume Zaragoza. 2020. ParaCrawl: Web-scale acquisition of parallel corpora. In *Proceedings of the 58th Annual Meeting of the Association for Computational Linguistics*, pages 4555–4567, Online. Association for Computational Linguistics.

James Barry, Joachim Wagner, Lauren Cassidy, Alan Cowap, Teresa Lynn, Abigail Walsh, Mícheál J Ó Meachair, and Jennifer Foster. 2022. gaBERT–an Irish Language Model. In *Proceedings of the Thirteenth Language Resources and Evaluation Conference*, pages 4774–4788, Marseille,France.

Kenneth R Beesley and Lauri Karttunen. 2003. Finite-state morphology: Xerox tools and techniques. *CSLI, Stanford.*

Nadjet Bouayad-Agha, Gerard Casamayor, Simon Mille, Marco Rospocher, Horacio Saggion, Luciano Serafini, and Leo Wanner. 2012. From ontology to nl: Generation of multilingual user-oriented environmental reports. In *International Conference on Application of Natural Language to Information Systems*, pages 216–221. Springer.

Lauren Cassidy, Teresa Lynn, James Barry, and Jennifer Foster. 2022. TwittIrish: A Universal Dependencies treebank of tweets in modern Irish. In *Proceedings of the 60th Annual Meeting of the Association for Computational Linguistics (Volume 1: Long Papers)*, pages 6869–6884, Dublin, Ireland.

Thiago Castro Ferreira, Claire Gardent, Nikolai Ilinykh, Chris van der Lee, Simon Mille, Diego Moussallem, and Anastasia Shimorina. 2020. The 2020 bilingual, bi-directional WebNLG+ shared task: Overview and evaluation results (WebNLG+ 2020). In *Proceedings of the 3rd International Workshop on Natural Language Generation from the Semantic Web (WebNLG+)*, pages 55–76, Dublin, Ireland (Virtual). Association for Computational Linguistics.

Thiago Castro Ferreira, Chris van der Lee, Emiel van Miltenburg, and Emiel Krahmer. 2019. Neural data-to-text generation: A comparison between pipeline and end-to-end architectures. In *Proceedings of the 2019 Conference on Empirical Methods in Natural Language Processing and the 9th International Joint Conference on Natural Language Processing (EMNLP-IJCNLP)*, pages 552–562, Hong Kong, China. Association for Computational Linguistics.

Department of Tourism, Culture, Arts, Gaeltacht, Sport Media. 2022. Digital plan for the irish language: Speech and language technologies 2023-2027. Technical report, Government of Ireland: Available at `https://assets.gov.ie/250129/1425436f-e1da-4661-8483-92d9ddb4a716.pdf`.

Jacob Devlin, Ming-Wei Chang, Kenton Lee, and Kristina Toutanova. 2019. BERT: Pre-training of deep bidirectional transformers for language understanding. In *Proceedings of the 2019 Conference of the North American Chapter of the Association for Computational Linguistics: Human Language Technologies, Volume 1 (Long and Short Papers)*, pages 4171–4186, Minneapolis, Minnesota. Association for Computational Linguistics.

Uí Dhonnchadha, Caoilfhionn Nic Pháidín, and Josef Van Genabith. 2003. Design, implementation and evaluation of an inflectional morphology finite state transducer for Irish. *Machine Translation*, 18:173–193.

Ondřej Dušek, Jekaterina Novikova, and Verena Rieser. 2018. Findings of the E2E NLG challenge. In *Proceedings of the 11th International Conference on Natural Language Generation*, pages 322–328, Tilburg University, The Netherlands. Association for Computational Linguistics.

Ondřej Dušek, Jekaterina Novikova, and Verena Rieser. 2020. Evaluating the state-of-the-art of end-to-end natural language generation: The e2e nlg challenge. *Computer Speech & Language*, 59:123–156.

Fangxiaoyu Feng, Yinfei Yang, Daniel Cer, Naveen Arivazhagan, and Wei Wang. 2022. Language-agnostic BERT sentence embedding. In *Proceedings of the 60th Annual Meeting of the Association for Computational Linguistics (Volume 1: Long Papers)*, pages 878–891, Dublin, Ireland. Association for Computational Linguistics.

Claire Gardent, Anastasia Shimorina, Shashi Narayan, and Laura Perez-Beltrachini. 2017. Creating training corpora for micro-planners. In *Proceedings of the 55th Annual Meeting of the Association for Computational Linguistics (Volume 1: Long Papers)*, Vancouver, Canada. Association for Computational Linguistics.

Albert Gatt and Ehud Reiter. 2009. SimpleNLG: A realisation engine for practical applications. In *Proceedings of the 12th European Workshop on Natural*

Language Generation (ENLG 2009), pages 90–93, Athens, Greece. Association for Computational Linguistics.

Mans Hulden. 2009. Foma: a finite-state compiler and library. In *Proceedings of the Demonstrations Session at EACL 2009*, pages 29–32, Athens, Greece. Association for Computational Linguistics.

Zdeněk Kasner and Ondrej Dusek. 2022. Neural pipeline for zero-shot data-to-text generation. In *Proceedings of the 60th Annual Meeting of the Association for Computational Linguistics (Volume 1: Long Papers)*, pages 3914–3932, Dublin, Ireland. Association for Computational Linguistics.

Adam Kilgarriff, Michael Rundell, and Elaine Uí Dhonnchadha. 2006. Efficient corpus development for lexicography: building the new corpus for ireland. *Language resources and evaluation*, 40:127–152.

Paul Kingsbury and Martha Palmer. 2002. From TreeBank to PropBank. In *Proceedings of the Third International Conference on Language Resources and Evaluation (LREC'02)*, Las Palmas, Canary Islands - Spain. European Language Resources Association (ELRA).

Guy Lapalme. 2020. RDFjsRealB: a symbolic approach for generating text from RDF triples. In *Proceedings of the 3rd International Workshop on Natural Language Generation from the Semantic Web (WebNLG+)*, pages 144–153, Dublin, Ireland (Virtual). Association for Computational Linguistics.

François Lareau, Florie Lambrey, Ieva Dubinskaite, Daniel Galarreta-Piquette, and Maryam Nejat. 2018. GenDR: A generic deep realizer with complex lexicalization. In *Proceedings of the Eleventh International Conference on Language Resources and Evaluation (LREC 2018)*, Miyazaki, Japan. European Language Resources Association (ELRA).

Benoit Lavoie and Owen Rainbow. 1997. A fast and portable realizer for text generation systems. In *Fifth Conference on Applied Natural Language Processing*, pages 265–268.

Michela Lorandi and Anya Belz. 2023. Data-to-text generation for severely under-resourced languages with GPT-3.5: A bit of help needed from Google Translate. In *Proceedings of the Workshop on Multimodal, Multilingual Natural Language Generation and Multilingual WebNLG Challenge*, page tbd, Prague, Czech Republic.

Teresa Lynn. 2022. Language report Irish. In *European Language Equality: D120 Report on the Irish Language*, pages 1–24. https://european-language-equality.eu/.

Teresa Lynn. 2023. Language report Irish. In *European Language Equality: A Strategic Agenda for Digital Language Equality*, pages 163–166. Springer.

Teresa Lynn and Jennifer Foster. 2016. Universal Dependencies for Irish. In *Proceedings of the 2nd Celtic Language Technology Workshop*, pages 79–92, Paris, France.

Igor A. Mel'čuk. 1973. Towards a linguistic 'Meaning ↔ Text' model. *Trends in Soviet theoretical linguistics*, pages 33–57.

Igor A. Mel'čuk. 1988. *Dependency Syntax: Theory and Practice*. State University of New York Press, Albany, NY.

Simon Mille, Stamatia Dasiopoulou, and Leo Wanner. 2019. A portable grammar-based nlg system for verbalization of structured data. In *Proceedings of the 34th ACM/SIGAPP Symposium on Applied Computing*, pages 1054–1056.

Simon Mille, François Lareau, Anya Belz, and Stamatia Dasiopoulou. 2023. Mod-D2T: A Multi-layer Dataset for Modular Data-to-Text Generation. In *Proceedings of the 16th International Conference on Natural Language Generation*, page tbd, Prague, Czech Republic.

Amit Moryossef, Yoav Goldberg, and Ido Dagan. 2019. Step-by-step: Separating planning from realization in neural data-to-text generation. In *Proceedings of the 2019 Conference of the North American Chapter of the Association for Computational Linguistics: Human Language Technologies, Volume 1 (Long and Short Papers)*, pages 2267–2277, Minneapolis, Minnesota. Association for Computational Linguistics.

Katie Ní Loingsigh. 2016. Towards a lexicon of irish-language idioms. In *Proceedings of the 2nd Celtic Language Technology Workshop*, pages 69–78, Paris, France.

Jekaterina Novikova, Ondřej Dušek, and Verena Rieser. 2017. The E2E dataset: New challenges for end-to-end generation. In *Proceedings of the 18th Annual SIGdial Meeting on Discourse and Dialogue*, pages 201–206, Saarbrücken, Germany. Association for Computational Linguistics.

Katie Ní Loingsigh, Brian Ó Raghallaigh, and Gearóid Ó Cléircín. 2017. The design and development of Corpas na Gaeilge comhaimseartha (corpus of contemporary Irish). In *Proceedings of the 9th International Corpus Linguistics Conference*.

Mick O'Donnell, Chris Mellish, Jon Oberlander, and Alistair Knott. 2001. Ilex: an architecture for a dynamic hypertext generation system. *Natural Language Engineering*, 7(3):225.

Kishore Papineni, Salim Roukos, Todd Ward, and Wei-Jing Zhu. 2002. Bleu: a method for automatic evaluation of machine translation. In *Proceedings of the 40th Annual Meeting of the Association for Computational Linguistics*, pages 311–318, Philadelphia, Pennsylvania, USA. Association for Computational Linguistics.

Maja Popović. 2017. chrF++: words helping character n-grams. In *Proceedings of the Second Conference on Machine Translation*, pages 612–618, Copenhagen, Denmark. Association for Computational Linguistics.

Ratish Puduppully and Mirella Lapata. 2021. Data-to-text generation with macro planning. *Transactions of the Association for Computational Linguistics*, 9:510–527.

Ehud Reiter and Robert Dale. 1997. Building applied natural language generation systems. *Natural Language Engineering*, 3(1):57–87.

Kevin Scannell. 2022. Diachronic parsing of pre-standard Irish. In *Proceedings of the 4th Celtic Language Technology Workshop within LREC2022*, pages 7–13, Marseille, France.

Matthew Snover, Bonnie Dorr, Rich Schwartz, Linnea Micciulla, and John Makhoul. 2006. A study of translation edit rate with targeted human annotation. In *Proceedings of the 7th Conference of the Association for Machine Translation in the Americas: Technical Papers*, pages 223–231, Cambridge, Massachusetts, USA. Association for Machine Translation in the Americas.

Pedro Javier Ortiz Suárez, Benoît Sagot, and Laurent Romary. 2019. Asynchronous pipeline for processing huge corpora on medium to low resource infrastructures. In *7th Workshop on the Challenges in the Management of Large Corpora (CMLC-7)*, Marseille, France. Leibniz-Institut für Deutsche Sprache.

Elaine Uí Dhonnchadha. 2009. *Part-of-speech tagging and partial parsing for Irish using finite-state transducers and constraint grammar*. Ph.D. thesis, Dublin City University.

Sebastian Varges and Chris Mellish. 2001. Instance-based natural language generation. In *Second Meeting of the North American Chapter of the Association for Computational Linguistics*.

Leo Wanner, Bernd Bohnet, Nadjet Bouayad-Agha, Francois Lareau, and Daniel Nicklaß. 2010. MARQUIS: Generation of user-tailored multilingual air quality bulletins. *Applied Artificial Intelligence*, 24(10):914–952.

Michael White and Rajakrishnan Rajkumar. 2012. Minimal dependency length in realization ranking. In *Proceedings of the 2012 Joint Conference on Empirical Methods in Natural Language Processing and Computational Natural Language Learning*, pages 244–255, Jeju Island, Korea. Association for Computational Linguistics.

Sam Wiseman, Stuart Shieber, and Alexander Rush. 2017. Challenges in data-to-document generation. In *Proceedings of the 2017 Conference on Empirical Methods in Natural Language Processing*, pages 2253–2263, Copenhagen, Denmark. Association for Computational Linguistics.

Tianyi Zhang, Varsha Kishore, Felix Wu, Kilian Q Weinberger, and Yoav Artzi. 2019. Bertscore: Evaluating text generation with bert. *arXiv preprint arXiv:1904.09675*.

A Sample input and output structures

The figures in the next page illustrate the generation process starting from an input triple set that corresponds to the following English text:

> *Agra Airport, operated by Indian Air Force, is located in India. Its ICAO location identifier is VIAG.*

Figure 3 shows a WebNLG'23 input, and Figure 4 shows the output of the lexicalisation module. The FORGe, morphology and post-processing outputs are shown in a one-word-per-line format in Table 5. The output Irish text is the following:

> *Tá Agra Airport, reáchtáilte ag Indian Air Force, lonnaithe ins An India. Tá VIAG in a aitheantóir suímh ICAO.*

B Irish dataset: Tagsets used

The edge labels for semantic graphs come mainly from PropBank (Kingsbury and Palmer, 2002), plus some generic labels such as `Location` and `Time`; see Table 6. The ones for deep syntactic trees come from Meaning-Text Theory (Mel'čuk, 1988); see Table 7. As for surface syntactic edge labels, they are our own; see Table 8.

C Irish dataset: Statistics

There are 13,211, 1,667 and 1,779 texts in the training, development and test splits respectively. Tables 9-10 provide an overview of the number of nodes and sentences per text for all splits. Our 10 intermediate layers contain over 2 million nodes.

D Irish dataset: Sample structures

The annotations are released in CoNLL-U format, but because of space constraints, we have truncated the data in Tables 11–20 below: (i) we dropped unused columns and renamed the remaining ones for readability; (ii) we removed feature names to retain only their values; (iii) we omit the metadata, which specifies the text ID, the level of representation (see the captions) and the corresponding text string. The showcased structures all correspond to the same text as in Appendix A.

```
<entry category="Airport" eid="719" shape="(X (X) (X) (X))" shape_type="sibling" size="3">
  <modifiedtripleset>
    <mtriple>Agra_Airport | location | India</mtriple>
    <mtriple>Agra_Airport | operatingOrganisation | Indian_Air_Force</mtriple>
    <mtriple>Agra_Airport | icaoLocationIdentifier | &quot;VIAG&quot;</mtriple>
  </modifiedtripleset>
</entry>
```

Figure 3: A sample WebNLG input with 3 triples (same as Figure 1)

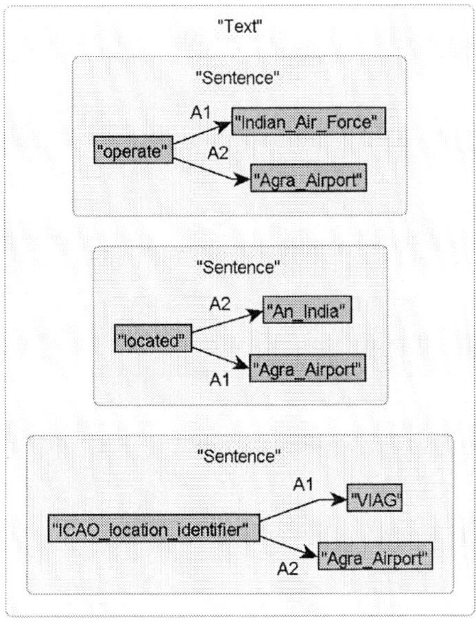

Figure 4: Lexicalisation output: instantiated PredArg templates

FORGe	Morphology	Post-processing
bí+Verb+PresInd	tá	Tá
Agra_Airport+Noun+Masc+Com+Sg	Agra_Airport	Agra Airport
,	,	,
reáchtáilte	reáchtáilte	reáchtáilte
ag	ag	ag
Indian_Air_Force+Noun+Masc+Com+Sg	Indian_Air_Force	Indian Air Force
,	,	,
lonnaithe+Adj+Masc+Com+Sg	lonnaithe	lonnaithe
i	i	ins
An_India+Noun+Masc+Com+Sg	An_India	An India
.	.	.
bí+Verb+PresInd	tá	Tá
VIAG+Noun+Masc+Com+Sg	VIAG	VIAG
i	i	in
a	a	a
aitheantóir+Noun+Masc+Com+Sg	aitheantóir	aitheantóir
suímh	suímh	suímh
ICAO+Noun+Masc+Com+Sg	ICAO	ICAO
.		

Table 5: FORGe, morphology and post-processing outputs (one word per line for convenience)

Label	Description	Example
A0–A6	n-th argument of a predicate or quasi-predicate	speak→ English
Location	location	born→ Paris
Time	time	build→ 1932
NonCore	inverted first argument of a predicate	runway→ second
Set	list of elements	and→ speak
Elaboration	(i) none of governor or dependent are argument of the other (ii) unknown argument slot	above me→ 610m

Table 6: Edge labels of semantic graphs

Label	Description	Example
I–VI	n-th complement of a syntactic predicate	speak→ English
ATTR	modifier	runway→ second
COORD	coordination	staff members→ and
APPEND	parenthetical modifier	Hypermarcas Brazil→ (s.a.)

Table 7: Edge labels of deep syntactic trees

Label	Description
adjunct	backgrounded adverbial
adv	general adverbial (not restrictive nor backgrounded)
agent	between non-finite verb and its 1st argument
analyt_pass	between passive auxiliary and main verb
appos	nominal noun modifier (apposition)
attr	prepositional noun modifier (attributive)
aux_phras	between elements of multi-word proper nouns
compar	between adjective and comparative
compar_conj	complement of a comparative conjunction
coord	between 1st conjunct and conjunction
coord_conj	between conjunction and 2nd conjunct
copul	complement of a copula
det	determiner of a noun
dobj	direct object
iobj	indirect object
modal	between modal verb and main verb
modif	adjectival or participial noun modifier
obl_compl	complement (argument) of a noun
obl_obj	prepositional object (not direct or indirect)
prepos	complement of a preposition
quant	numeral noun modifier (quantificative)
quasi_subj	grammatical (usually empty) subject
restr	restrictive adverbial or modifier (adjacent to governor)
relat	clausal noun modifier (relative)
sub_conj	complement of a subordinating conjunction
subj	subject of verb

Table 8: Edge labels of Irish surface syntactic trees

Layer	N	S
PredArg	152,750	48,776
PredArg-Agg	134,008	31,065
PredArg-Lex	134,008	31,065
PredArg-Comm	143,343	31,065
DSynt	175,019	31,065
SSynt	254,128	31,065
SSynt-Agg	255,499	29,215
REG	254,355	29,215
DMorph	283,593	29,228
Text	285,727	29,228

Table 9: Total number of nodes (N) and sentences (S) per layer.

Layer	N	S	N/S
PredArg	9.2	2.9	3.1
PredArg-Agg	8.0	1.9	4.4
PredArg-Lex	8.0	1.9	4.4
PredArg-Comm	8.6	1.9	4.7
DSynt	10.5	1.9	5.7
SSynt	15.3	1.9	8.3
SSynt-Agg	15.3	1.8	8.9
REG	15.3	1.8	8.8
DMorph	17.0	1.8	9.8
Text	17.2	1.8	9.9

Table 10: Average number of nodes (N), sentences (S) and nodes per sentence (N/S) for each text, per layer.

ID	Semanteme	Features	Head	Rel	Misc
1	located	_	0	root	src=1
2	Agra_Airport	ne	1	A1	coref=0|src=2
3	An_India	location|ne	1	A2	coref=1|src=3
4	<SENT>	_	_	_	_
5	operate	pres	0	root	src=4
6	Indian_Air_Force	ne	5	A1	coref=2|src=6
7	Agra_Airport	def|ne	5	A2	coref=0|src=5
8	<SENT>	_	_	_	_
9	ICAO_location_identifier	def	0	root	src=7
10	Agra_Airport	_	9	A2	coref=0|src=8
11	VIAG	ne	9	A1	coref=3|src=9
12	<SENT>	_	_	_	_

Table 11: Predicate-argument structure (PredArg).

ID	Semanteme	Features	Head	Rel	Misc
1	located	rheme	0	root	src=1
2	An_India	location|ne	1	A2	coref=1|src=3
3	operate	pres	0	root	src=4
4	Indian_Air_Force	ne	3	A1	coref=2|src=6
5	Agra_Airport	ne	1,3	A1,A2	coref=0|src=2
6	<SENT>	_	_	_	_
7	ICAO_location_identifier	def	0	root	src=7
8	Agra_Airport	_	7	A2	coref=0|src=8
9	VIAG	ne	7	A1	coref=3|src=9
10	<SENT>	_	_	_	_

Table 12: Aggregated predicate-argument structure (PredArg-Agg; corresponds to Figure 4).

<table>
<tr><th>ID</th><th>Semanteme</th><th>POS</th><th>Features</th><th>Head</th><th>Rel</th><th>Misc</th></tr>
<tr><td>1</td><td>located</td><td>JJ</td><td>jj|rheme</td><td>0</td><td>root</td><td>src=1</td></tr>
<tr><td>2</td><td>An_India</td><td>NP</td><td>location|ne</td><td>1</td><td>A2</td><td>src=3</td></tr>
<tr><td>3</td><td>operate</td><td>VB</td><td>pres|vb</td><td>0</td><td>root</td><td>src=4</td></tr>
<tr><td>4</td><td>Indian_Air_Force</td><td>NP</td><td>ne</td><td>3</td><td>A1</td><td>src=6</td></tr>
<tr><td>5</td><td>Agra_Airport</td><td>NP</td><td>ne</td><td>1,3</td><td>A1,A2</td><td>coref=0|src=2</td></tr>
<tr><td>6</td><td><SENT></td><td>_</td><td>_</td><td>_</td><td>_</td><td>_</td></tr>
<tr><td>7</td><td>ICAO_location_identifier</td><td>NN</td><td>def|nn</td><td>0</td><td>root</td><td>src=7</td></tr>
<tr><td>8</td><td>Agra_Airport</td><td>NN</td><td>_</td><td>7</td><td>A2</td><td>coref=0|src=8</td></tr>
<tr><td>9</td><td>VIAG</td><td>NP</td><td>ne</td><td>7</td><td>A1</td><td>src=9</td></tr>
<tr><td>10</td><td><SENT></td><td>_</td><td>_</td><td>_</td><td>_</td><td>_</td></tr>
</table>

Table 13: Lexicalised predicate-argument structure (PredArg-Lex).

<table>
<tr><th>ID</th><th>Semanteme</th><th>POS</th><th>Features</th><th>Head</th><th>Rel</th><th>Misc</th></tr>
<tr><td>1</td><td>reáchtáil</td><td>VB</td><td>pres</td><td>0</td><td>root</td><td>src=4</td></tr>
<tr><td>2</td><td>lonnaithe</td><td>JJ</td><td>rheme</td><td>0</td><td>root</td><td>src=1</td></tr>
<tr><td>3</td><td>Agra_Airport</td><td>NP</td><td>ne</td><td>1,2</td><td>A2,A1</td><td>coref=0|src=2</td></tr>
<tr><td>4</td><td>An_India</td><td>NP</td><td>location|ne</td><td>2</td><td>A2</td><td>src=3</td></tr>
<tr><td>5</td><td>Indian_Air_Force</td><td>NP</td><td>ne</td><td>1</td><td>A1</td><td>src=6</td></tr>
<tr><td>6</td><td><SENT></td><td>_</td><td>_</td><td>_</td><td>_</td><td>_</td></tr>
<tr><td>7</td><td>aitheantóir</td><td>NN</td><td>def|rheme</td><td>0</td><td>root</td><td>src=7</td></tr>
<tr><td>8</td><td>Agra_Airport</td><td>NN</td><td>_</td><td>7</td><td>A2</td><td>coref=0|src=8</td></tr>
<tr><td>9</td><td>VIAG</td><td>NP</td><td>ne</td><td>7</td><td>A1</td><td>src=9</td></tr>
<tr><td>10</td><td><SENT></td><td>_</td><td>_</td><td>_</td><td>_</td><td>_</td></tr>
</table>

Table 14: Predicate-argument structure with thematicity (PredArg-Th).

<table>
<tr><th>ID</th><th>Lexeme</th><th>POS</th><th>Features</th><th>Head</th><th>Rel</th><th>Misc</th></tr>
<tr><td>1</td><td>bí</td><td>VB</td><td>fin|decl|act</td><td>0</td><td>root</td><td>src=1</td></tr>
<tr><td>2</td><td>Agra_Airport</td><td>NP</td><td>_</td><td>1</td><td>I</td><td>coref=0|src=2</td></tr>
<tr><td>3</td><td>reáchtáil</td><td>VB</td><td>part|pres</td><td>2</td><td>ATTR</td><td>src=4</td></tr>
<tr><td>4</td><td>Indian_Air_Force</td><td>NP</td><td>_</td><td>3</td><td>I</td><td>src=6</td></tr>
<tr><td>5</td><td>lonnaithe</td><td>JJ</td><td>_</td><td>1</td><td>II</td><td>src=1</td></tr>
<tr><td>6</td><td>An_India</td><td>NP</td><td>location</td><td>5</td><td>II</td><td>src=3</td></tr>
<tr><td>7</td><td><SENT></td><td>_</td><td>_</td><td>_</td><td>_</td><td>_</td></tr>
<tr><td>8</td><td>bí</td><td>VB</td><td>masc|act|fin|decl</td><td>0</td><td>root</td><td>src=7</td></tr>
<tr><td>9</td><td>VIAG</td><td>NP</td><td>_</td><td>8</td><td>I</td><td>src=9</td></tr>
<tr><td>10</td><td>aitheantóir</td><td>NN</td><td>masc|gen|sg</td><td>8</td><td>II</td><td>src=7</td></tr>
<tr><td>11</td><td>Agra_Airport</td><td>NN</td><td>sg</td><td>10</td><td>II</td><td>coref=0|src=8</td></tr>
<tr><td>12</td><td><SENT></td><td>_</td><td>_</td><td>_</td><td>_</td><td>_</td></tr>
</table>

Table 15: Deep syntactic representation (DSynt).

<table>
<tr><th>ID</th><th>Lexeme</th><th>POS</th><th>Features</th><th>Head</th><th>Rel</th><th>Misc</th></tr>
<tr><td>1</td><td>bí</td><td>VB</td><td>decl|fin|ind|pres</td><td>0</td><td>root</td><td>src=1</td></tr>
<tr><td>2</td><td>lonnaithe</td><td>JJ</td><td>acc</td><td>1</td><td>dobj</td><td>src=1</td></tr>
<tr><td>3</td><td>Agra_Airport</td><td>NP</td><td>nom|masc|sg|ne</td><td>1</td><td>subj</td><td>coref=0|src=2</td></tr>
<tr><td>4</td><td>reáchtáil</td><td>VB</td><td>part</td><td>3</td><td>modif</td><td>src=4</td></tr>
<tr><td>5</td><td>ag</td><td>IN</td><td>_</td><td>4</td><td>agent</td><td>src=6</td></tr>
<tr><td>6</td><td>i</td><td>IN</td><td>_</td><td>2</td><td>obl_compl</td><td>src=3</td></tr>
<tr><td>7</td><td>An_India</td><td>NP</td><td>sg|dat|location|masc|ne</td><td>6</td><td>prepos</td><td>src=3</td></tr>
<tr><td>8</td><td>Indian_Air_Force</td><td>NP</td><td>nom|masc|sg|ne</td><td>5</td><td>prepos</td><td>src=6</td></tr>
<tr><td>9</td><td><SENT></td><td>_</td><td>_</td><td>_</td><td>_</td><td>_</td></tr>
<tr><td>10</td><td>bí</td><td>VB</td><td>pres|decl|fin|masc|ind</td><td>0</td><td>root</td><td>src=7</td></tr>
<tr><td>11</td><td>i</td><td>IN</td><td>gen</td><td>10</td><td>obl_obj</td><td>src=7</td></tr>
<tr><td>12</td><td>aitheantóir</td><td>NN</td><td>dat|masc|sg|gen</td><td>11</td><td>prepos</td><td>src=7</td></tr>
<tr><td>13</td><td>ar</td><td>IN</td><td>_</td><td>12</td><td>obl_compl</td><td>src=8</td></tr>
<tr><td>14</td><td>Agra_Airport</td><td>NN</td><td>dat|masc|sg</td><td>13</td><td>prepos</td><td>coref=0|src=8</td></tr>
<tr><td>15</td><td>VIAG</td><td>NP</td><td>nom|masc|sg|ne</td><td>10</td><td>subj</td><td>src=9</td></tr>
<tr><td>16</td><td>suímh ICAO</td><td>NN</td><td>sg|masc|nom</td><td>12</td><td>restr</td><td>src=7</td></tr>
<tr><td>17</td><td>a</td><td>DT</td><td>-</td><td>12</td><td>det</td><td>src=7</td></tr>
<tr><td>18</td><td><SENT></td><td>_</td><td>_</td><td>_</td><td>_</td><td>_</td></tr>
</table>

Table 16: Surface syntactic representation (SSynt).

ID	Lexeme	POS	Features	Head	Rel	Misc
1	bí	VB	ind|sg|sg|decl|fin|pres	0	root	src=1
2	lonnaithe	JJ	sg|sg|acc	1	dobj	src=1
3	i	IN	sg|sg	2	obl_compl	src=3
4	Agra_Airport	NP	sg|nom|sg|masc|masc|ne	1	subj	coref=0|src=2
5	reáchtáil	VB	sg|sg|part	4	modif	src=4
6	ag	IN	sg|sg	5	agent	src=6
7	Indian_Air_Force	NP	nom|masc|sg|masc|sg|ne	6	prepos	src=6
8	An_India	NP	masc|sg|dat|location|masc|sg|ne	3	prepos	src=3
9	<SENT>	_	_	_	_	_
10	bí	VB	pres|sg|sg|decl|fin|masc|masc|ind	0	root	src=7
11	i	IN	sg|sg|gen	10	obl_obj	src=7
12	aitheantóir	NN	dat|sg|masc|gen|masc|sg	11	prepos	src=7
13	ar	IN	sg|sg	12	obl_compl	src=8
14	Agra_Airport	NN	masc|dat|masc|sg|sg	13	prepos	coref=0|src=8
15	VIAG	NP	nom|sg|masc|masc|sg|ne	10	subj	src=9
16	suímh ICAO	NN	sg|sg|masc|nom|masc	12	restr	src=7
17	a	DT	-|sg|sg	12	det	src=7
18	<SENT>	_	_	_	_	_

Table 17: Aggregated surface syntactic representation (SSynt-Agg).

ID	Lexeme	POS	Features	Head	Rel	Misc
1	bí	VB	sg|sg|decl|fin|pres|ind	0	root	src=1
2	lonnaithe	JJ	sg|acc|sg	1	dobj	src=1
3	i	IN	sg|sg	2	obl_compl	src=3
4	Agra_Airport	NP	masc|sg|sg|nom|masc|ne	1	subj	coref=0|src=2
5	reáchtáil	VB	part|sg|sg	4	modif	src=4
6	An_India	NP	location|masc|masc|sg|dat|sg|ne	3	prepos	src=3
7	ag	IN	sg|sg	5	agent	src=6
8	Indian_Air_Force	NP	masc|masc|sg|sg|nom|ne	7	prepos	src=6
9	<SENT>	_	_	_	_	_
10	bí	VB	pres|ind|masc|sg|decl|sg|fin|masc	0	root	src=7
11	i	IN	sg|sg|gen	10	obl_obj	src=7
12	aitheantóir	NN	masc|gen|masc|sg|sg|dat	11	prepos	src=7
13	_PRO_	PP	masc|sg|dat|masc|sg	12	obl_compl	coref=0|src=8
14	suímh ICAO	NN	masc|sg|nom|masc|sg	12	restr	src=7
15	VIAG	NP	masc|sg|sg|nom|masc|ne	10	subj	src=9
16	<SENT>	_	_	_	_	_

Table 18: Pronominalised surface syntactic representation (SSynt-Pro).

ID	Word	POS	Features	Misc
1	bí	VB	pres|vi|decl|fin|sg|ind	src=1
2	Agra_Airport	NP	nom|masc|sg|invar	coref=0|src=2
3	reáchtáil	VB	nom|part|masc|sg|vti	src=4
4	ag	IN	sg	src=6
5	Indian_Air_Force	NP	sg|nom|masc|invar	src=6
6	lonnaithe	JJ	sg|acc|masc	src=1
7	i	IN	sg	src=3
8	An_India	NP	dat|masc|sg|invar	src=3
9	.	_	_	src=-
10	bí	VB	ind|pres|vi|sg|decl|fin|masc	src=7
11	VIAG	NP	nom|masc|sg|invar	src=9
12	i	IN	sg	src=7
13	_PRO_	PP	dat|masc|sg	coref=0|src=8
14	aitheantóir	NN	masc|sg|dat	src=7
15	suímh ICAO	NN	nom|masc|sg	src=7
16	.	_	_	src=-

Table 19: Deep morphological representation (DMorph).

ID	Word	POS	Misc
1	bí%Verb%PresInd	VB	src=1
2	Agra_Airport%Noun%Masc%Com%Sg	NP	coref=0|src=2
3	,	_	src=-
4	reáchtáilte	VB	src=4
5	ag	IN	src=6
6	Indian_Air_Force%Noun%Masc%Com%Sg	NP	src=6
7	,	_	src=-
8	lonnaithe%Adj%Masc%Com%Sg	JJ	src=1
9	i	IN	src=3
10	An_India%Noun%Masc%Com%Sg	NP	src=3
11	.	_	src=-
12	bí%Verb%PresInd	VB	src=7
13	VIAG%Noun%Masc%Com%Sg	NP	src=9
14	i	IN	src=7
15	a	PP	coref=0|src=8
16	aitheantóir%Noun%Masc%Com%Sg	NN	src=7
17	suímh ICAO%Noun%Masc%Com%Sg	NN	src=7
18	.	_	src=-

Table 20: Surface morphological representation (SMorph; corresponds to Table 5).

Symbolic Planning and Code Generation for Grounded Dialogue

Justin T. Chiu
Cornell Tech
jtc257@cornell.edu

Wenting Zhao
Cornell University
wz346@cornell.edu

Derek Chen
Columbia University
dc3761@columbia.edu

Saujas Vaduguru
Carnegie Mellon University
svadugur@andrew.cmu.edu

Alexander M. Rush
Cornell Tech
arush@cornell.edu

Daniel Fried
Carnegie Mellon University
dfried@cs.cmu.edu

Abstract

Large language models (LLMs) excel at processing and generating both text and code. However, LLMs have had limited applicability in grounded task-oriented dialogue as they are difficult to steer toward task objectives and fail to handle novel grounding. We present a modular and interpretable grounded dialogue system that addresses these shortcomings by composing LLMs with a symbolic planner and grounded code execution. Our system consists of a reader and planner: the reader leverages an LLM to convert partner utterances into executable code, calling functions that perform grounding. The translated code's output is stored to track dialogue state, while a symbolic planner determines the next appropriate response. We evaluate our system's performance on the demanding ONECOMMON dialogue task, involving collaborative reference resolution on abstract images of scattered dots. Our system substantially outperforms the previous state-of-the-art, including improving task success in human evaluations from 56% to 69% in the most challenging setting.

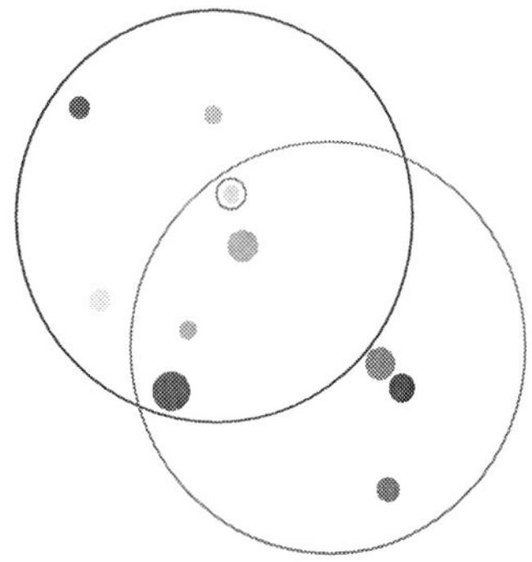

SPC:	Do you see a pair of dots, where the top left dot is medium-sized and grey and the bottom right dot is medium-sized and dark
Human:	No
SPC:	Do you see a pair of dots, where the top dot is small-sized and light and the bottom dot is medium-sized and grey
Human:	Yes I see them. Is there a small grey dot above the small light dot?
SPC:	No. Is there a large size and dark color dot to the left and below those?
Human:	Yes and there is a small grey dot below them as well for me.
SPC:	Yes. Let's select the small size and light color one.
SPC:	<select>
Human:	<select>

Figure 1: An example grounded dialogue from ONECOMMON. Our dialogue agent, SPC, and a human partner have different but overlapping circular views of a shared board. The agent and partner must collaborate through dialogue in order to find and select a shared dot. ONECOMMON demands careful, grounded reasoning.

1 Introduction

Success in grounded task-oriented dialogue requires intentional communication guided by strategic planning (Cohen and Perrault, 1979; Traum, 1994; Walker et al., 2004; Rieser and Lemon, 2009; Bakhtin et al., 2022, *inter alia*). Dialogue agents must read partner utterances, update their beliefs, then make a plan that furthers their goal. These plans must take into account both dialogue history and grounding, such as in an image. In end-to-end systems based solely on large language models (LLMs), this process is implicit and therefore difficult to control, requiring extra supervision (Christiano et al., 2023) or expensive search (Lu et al., 2022) to improve. While recent work has taken steps to rectify implicit reasoning via planning in language space, where intermediate steps are generated by an LLM (Wei et al., 2022), there is no guarantee that these approaches result in plans that further task progress. Additionally, planning in language space is expensive, requiring inference in an LLM (Yarats and Lewis, 2017; Guez et al., 2012).

Rather than implicit or heuristic reasoning, we are interested in explicit reasoning and planning over symbolic actions. Symbolic actions are controllable by construction, allowing system designers to easily build in task-specific knowledge (He et al., 2018; Bakhtin et al., 2022). This controlla-

Proceedings of the 2nd Workshop in Pattern-based Approaches to NLP in the Age of Deep Learning , pages 43–53
December 6, 2023.

bility is crucial for obtaining task-specific success using general tools, even with LLMs.

We provide an example from ONECOMMON, a particularly challenging grounded dialogue game (Udagawa and Aizawa, 2019). The goal of ONECOMMON is to, through dialogue, identify one dot in common with your partner, who has an overlapping but different view of an underlying set of dots, illustrated in Figure 1. The challenge in ONECOMMON is grounding the contextual spatial relationships described in language to dots.

Recent work has utilized code-generation for grounded language understanding (Dídac et al., 2023). In particular, they translate natural language questions to code as an intermediate representation, then execute that code to obtain an answer. Code has a couple appealing properties as an intermediate representation: First, modern language models are trained on a mixture of code and natural language, affording them the capability of, with some accuracy, translating between the two (Chen et al., 2021). Second, code acts as a compositional knowledge representation. This allows code-generation systems to perform grounded compositional reasoning, provided a library of Python functions that perform grounding (Liang et al., 2022).

We present a system, Symbolic Planning and Code-generation (SPC), that *reads* by translating partner utterances into code and *plans* based on symbolic reasoning over what to say next. Code as a compositional knowledge representation closely mirrors the compositional nature of utterances, which are composed of grounded parts. SPC plans by optimizing expected information gain, which has been shown to be effective at building a key aspect of collaborative dialogue: common ground (Yu et al., 2019; White et al., 2021; Chiu et al., 2022). Symbolic planning allows SPC to explicitly and efficiently optimize for task success while taking advantage of task-specific properties.

We evaluate our SPC system on the most challenging subset of the ONECOMMON task, comparing our system to the previous state-of-the-art supervised system for the task (Fried et al., 2021). In both evaluations with human partners and automated self-play evaluations, we find that our approach substantially outperforms the previous state-of-the-art in task accuracy, improving from 56% to 69% accuracy, and obtains comparable task accuracy to human-human pairs on average.

2 Related Work

Prior work on collaborative reference games focuses on building common ground (He et al., 2017; Haber et al., 2019; Khani et al., 2018). Prior work by Fried et al. (2021) implements an approximation of pragmatic reasoning on ONECOMMON, but plans in language space and utilizes supervised models for mapping language to symbols. Khani et al. (2018) plan in symbolic space, but without natural language. We plan in symbolic space and map from language to symbols via code generation.

Dialogue systems have a long history of reasoning with symbolic actions. When available, symbolic actions have been found to improve the performance of dialogue systems, especially in the setting of grounded dialogue (Winograd, 1971; Young, 2006; He et al., 2018; Andreas et al., 2020; Bakhtin et al., 2022). The closest work to ours is CICERO, which utilizes symbolic planning in a system for DIPLOMACY, a dialogue and strategy game that requires negotiation and coordination between players (Bakhtin et al., 2022). CICERO requires a supervised dataset to train their system. We use code LLMs which require minimal supervision beyond constructing a small perceptual grounding API.

Planning in dialogue systems has recently eschewed symbolic actions in favor of planning directly in text, where systems either perform rollouts, tree-search, or other forms of intermediate reasoning in language. This allows system designers to avoid manually defining symbolic actions (Yarats and Lewis, 2017; Jang et al., 2020; Gandhi et al., 2023). However, the accuracy of language-space planners is still low in many settings (Fried et al., 2021; Valmeekam et al., 2023). We focus on symbolic planning, where planning is defined in a space that ensures accuracy and controllability.

With the recent progress in large language modeling, code generation for modular grounded systems has quickly gained interest. Grounded code generation systems do not require task-specific training data, making them cheap to apply. A body of work utilizes a large language model for instruction following by generating Python code that makes calls to lower-level perception libraries (Liang et al., 2022; Dídac et al., 2023; Gupta and Kembhavi, 2022; Gao et al., 2023). This extends prior work on executable semantic parsing (Liang, 2016; Johnson et al., 2017; Cheng et al., 2018) with large language models. Concurrent work has also utilized code-generation to interpret language, integrated with symbolic reasoning (Wong et al., 2023). We apply these advances to the setting of grounded task-oriented dialogue, where code generation grounds language to symbolic actions for use in explicit planning.

3 Overview: Reference Games

Collaborative reference games pair an agent and a partner in order to build common ground through natural language dialogue (Haber et al., 2019; Khani et al., 2018; He et al., 2017; Udagawa and Aizawa, 2019). Mirroring realistic scenarios, many reference games are also partially observable, where the agent and partner have different perspectives, and so they must resolve ambiguity.

ONECOMMON (Udagawa and Aizawa, 2019), as shown in Figure 1, is a reference game that exemplifies two challenges: grounding and planning. In ONECOMMON, the agent and partner see different but overlapping views of a set of dots, and the goal is to find and select one dot common to both players' views. Grounding in ONECOMMON is particularly difficult due to the dot-based visual context, which requires abstract spatial reasoning. Planning is complicated by the partial observability caused by differing perspectives, which require agents to use complex referring expressions in order to avoid ambiguity.[1] We focus on ONECOMMON due to its simplicity and difficulty.

Our approach to grounded reference games separates symbolic reasoning from language, allowing explicit steering. Our system, Symbolic Planning and Code-generation (SPC), breaks down a turn into three procedures: reading, planning, and writing. Reading and writing convert from language to symbols and vice versa, while planning reasons in purely symbolic space.

The agent maintains a belief distribution over possible worlds, z, representing task-specific unknowns. The goal of dialogue is to gain information about z until the agent is confident enough to end the game. At each turn, the agent **reads** the partner's utterance u, converting it into a symbolic action, $p(x|u)$. This symbolic action potentially builds upon the action x' of a previous utterance, u'. The agent then **plans** in symbolic space. The system uses reasoning to update its belief state, $p(z|u) = \sum_x p(z|x)p(x|u)$, then produces a response y^* of what to say next, which it describes in language to the partner. There is additionally a templated write module for generating a response from y^* described in Appendix C.

In ONECOMMON, given a set of dots $\mathcal{D}$, the state $z \in \{0,1\}^{|\mathcal{D}|}$ represents which dots the agent believes are contained (1) and not contained (0) in the partner's view, illustrated in Figure 3. We call a set of dots a *configuration*. The action representation of partner, x and x', and agent utterances, y^*, alike is also a configuration in $\{0,1\}^{|\mathcal{D}|}$, as well as any answers or confirmations to previous questions.

4 Reading: From Language to Symbols

Reading in SPC requires interpreting utterances to a grounded symbolic action, which in turn facilitates the planning stage. Consider the following exchange:

> Agent: *Do you see a triangle of dark dots?*
> Partner: *Yes, is there a small grey one below it?*

Reading has several challenges. First, reading requires grounding utterances in context, e.g. the shapes and relations. Second, utterances are compositional. For example, the partner utterance builds on top of the previous utterance through coreference. Finally, a reading system must act quickly, as real-time dialogue systems require reasonable response times.

4.1 Code Generation

In SPC, reading is implemented as code generation. Given a dialogue, we generate Python code[2] which is then used as a meaning function to produce a distribution over all valid interpretations of the utterance's symbolic action (Figure 2). The code calls perceptual library functions with grounded semantics, drawn from a task-specific API. This perceptual library allows the system to both ground elements of the utterance and compositionally build upon previous utterances. Consider the following abbreviated example, based on ONECOMMON:

[1]The contexts in ONECOMMON were constructed to make referring expressions challenging and context-dependent. For example, if the agent sees only light dots, a relatively 'dark' dot for the agent may not be considered dark at all by the partner.ONECOMMON is an ideal testbed for pragmatic methods that reason about contextual meaning. While our approach does not address pragmatics, we hope future work will.

[2]We target Python as our code representation since it is well-understood by large language models. However, in principle, our system could target other languages such as Prolog or SQL.

```
from perceptual_library import is_small, ...
dot1, dot2, dot3, ... = get_dots()
```

Agent: *Do you see a triangle of dark dots?*

```
agent_configs = set([
  Config(dot1, dot2, dot3),
  Config(dot3, dot4, dot1)
])
```

Partner: *Yes, is there a small grey one below it?*

```
def turn(prev_configs):
  configs = set()
  for prev_config in prev_configs:
    for dot in single_dots(exclude=prev_config):
      if (
        is_small(dot)
        and is_grey(dot)
        and is_below(dot, prev_config)
      ):
        configs.add(Config(dot, prev_config))
  return configs
partner_configs_x = turn(agent_configs)
```

The code in the meaning function is imperative, but represents a set of declarative constraints representing $p(x|u)$.[3] The meaning function for the partner turn, `turn(prev_configs)`, takes as input the distribution over symbolic actions of a previous turn, $p(x')$, and yields a set of possible interpretations of the current turn, $p(x|u) = \sum_{x'} p(x|u, x')p(x')$.[4] Because utterances can have multiple valid interpretations due to ambiguity, `prev_configs` represents a distribution.[5]

Within `turn`, we consider all valid configurations while marginalizing over x', i.e. interpretations in `prev_configs`. For each interpretation, each `dot` is considered. If the new `dot` satisfies the semantics of the utterance, checked step-by-step via grounded perceptual library functions such as `is_small(d)`, then it is a valid interpretation of the current utterance and is used to create a new `Config`.

The perceptual library functions are drawn from a manually-defined library. For ONECOMMON, we define these functions using domain-specific knowledge:

```
def is_small(d): return d.size < -0.3
```

The perceptual library for ONECOMMON can be

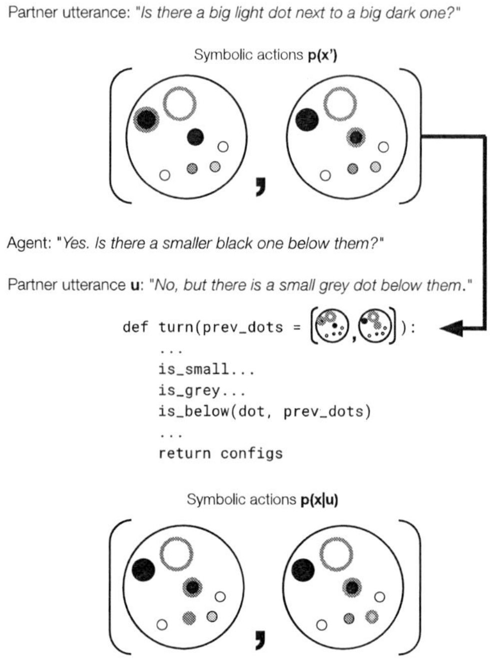

Figure 2: Overview of Reading. The generated meaning function for utterance u takes the previous symbolic action distribution $p(x')$ from a prior turn and yields the interpretations $p(x|u)$, using code as a compositional representation (Section 4).

found here.

4.2 Prompting

Reading is implemented with large language model (LLM) code generation. While LLMs can generate accurate code, full code specifications (Section 4.1) are lengthy and therefore too slow to generate for real-time use. We break down code generation into four steps, where some steps do not require any calls to an LLM. Decreasing the number of output tokens guarantees a speedup, assuming consistent latency. See the code for details on the code LLM and prompts we use.[6]

Dialogue Act: Classify partner utterances as one of three dialogue acts: Start a NEW line of questioning, ask a FOLLOW-UP question, END the dialogue.

Reference: Predict which previous turn x' the utterance is following up on, if any:

Agent: *Do you see a triangle?*

Partner: *Yes, is there a small grey dot below it?*

```
dialogue act: follow-up
refer: turn 1
```

[3]In ONECOMMON, the distribution over symbolic actions $p(x|u)$ is represented as represented as a categorical distribution over configurations with probabilities based on the size of the circumcircle.

[4]The symbolic action of a previous turn x' may also depend on other previous utterances u'. For simplicity, we omit that in the notation.

[5]SPC is able to intentionally produce ambiguous descriptions if that improves task success, as illustrated in this example.

[6]We release the code here.

The system grounds the dots mentioned in the previous turn: `agent_configs`, which is stored by the system. This allows referring to other turns besides the previous.

Constraint Generation: Predict the new dots mentioned in the partner utterance alongside code fragments that express the semantics, without the boilerplate code, in the example above:

Partner: *Yes, is there a small grey one below it?*

```
1 new dot
is_small(dot)
is_grey(dot)
is_below(dot, prev_dots)
```

Compose: Finally, we utilize a template to compose all of this information back into the full code representation for execution.

5 Planning: From Symbols to Responses

To perform well in collaborative reference games, it is essential to build common ground quickly and accurately by carefully reasoning about what information has been gathered so far, as well as what to say next. SPC addresses these desiderata by planning in symbolic space, over the symbolic actions produced by reading.

We have two challenges: First, to incorporate the new information from the partner's utterance while accounting for task-specific grounding as well as dialogue history. Second, given this new information, the system must decide either to end the game or how to improve the probability of success.

Planning requires us to model the actions of the partner given the shared state. To do this we need task specific models of our partner, $p(x \mid z)$, and our partner's reponse to us, $p(x|z, y)$. In ONECOMMON, we model both of these by a heuristic function considering set overlap and dot proximity, described in Appendix D.

5.1 Belief update

Starting from a prior over the previous belief $p(z)$, we incorporate probabilistic evidence from the utterance $p(x|u)$. This requires marginalizing over all valid symbolic actions x from the reading step. In practice, $p(x|u)$ is sparse, and symbols x with non-zero support are very similar. We therefore approximate this marginalization with a point estimate:

$$\begin{aligned} p(z|u) &= \sum_x p(z|x)p(x|u) \\ &= \sum_x \frac{p(x|z)p(z)}{p(x)} p(x|u) \\ &\approx \sum_x \frac{p(x|z)p(z)}{p(x)} 1(x = x^*) \\ &\propto p(x^* \mid z)p(z), \end{aligned} \quad (1)$$

where $x^* = \text{argmax}_x\, p(x|u)$.

We give an example of this process in Figure 3. In this case, a 'big light dot next to a big dark one' could have two valid interpretations, the big light dot and the black dot to the left, or the other black dot to the right. We approximate this distribution with the most likely interpretation x^*. In ONECOMMON, we use the most compact[7] as x^*, yielding the black dot on the left. The belief state is then updated to $p(z|u)$, shown in Figure 3 (center).

5.2 Planning

Given the updated belief, SPC then plans its next action. The challenge here is to ensure task success, e.g. finding one dot in common. This requires both exploring by building common ground, then exploiting that knowledge to win the game.

We formalize exploration as the expected information gain, a quantity that codifies how much the agent can expect to learn about possible worlds z after taking an action (Lindley, 1956). That action then elicits a response from the partner, providing information about the uncertain world state. For example, if the agent has asked about a set of dots and already received a 'no', then asking further questions about those dots would not reduce uncertainty.

Formally, we optimize

$$y^* = \underset{y}{\text{argmax}}\, H[z|u] - \mathbb{E}_{x_y|y}\left[H[z \mid u, y, x_y]\right], \quad (2)$$

where $H[z|u]$ is the entropy of the current belief[8] and $H[z \mid u, y, x_y]$ the entropy of the posterior distribution. This second term is the key part of the objective. Assuming that we take action y, the expectation considers all hypothetical future

[7]We define the compactness of a configuration as the radius of the circumcircle. An ideal approximation would take into account more context, such as the relative sizes.

[8]The belief entropy $H[z|u]$ in the definition of information gain is constant with respect to the plan x, and can be dropped from the objective.

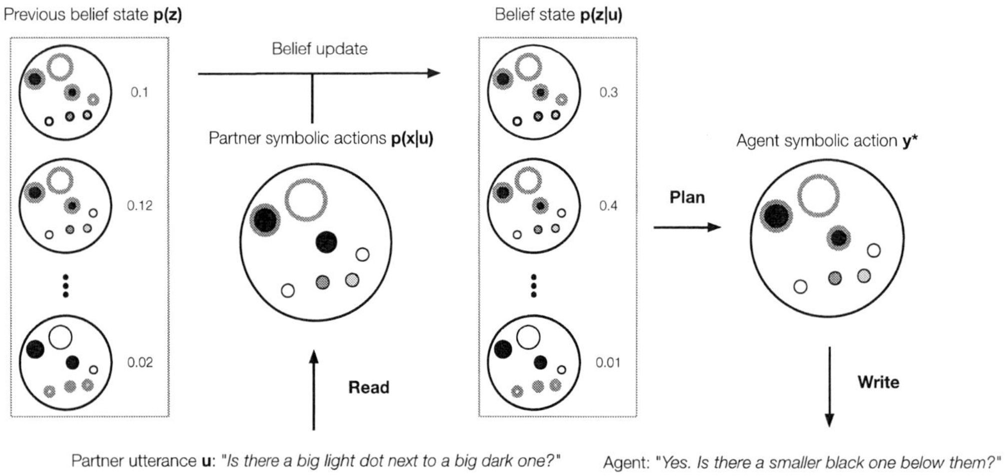

Figure 3: Overview of Planning. Partner utterances are interpreted by a meaning function generated by a code LLM (read), producing a distribution over valid symbolic interpretations, $p(x|u)$. This is used to symbolically update the belief state, $p(z|u)$, increasing the probability of worlds (shared dots) that are consistent with x. This belief state is used to symbolically plan the agent's next utterance, y^*, by optimizing the expected information gain, which is described to the partner (write).

partner responses x_y. We are penalized if after seeing these responses, we are still uncertain about the common ground z. This objective therefore encourages actions that reduce uncertainty. [9]

SPC chooses to exploit and end the game with the following heuristic: If the system is confident in success, i.e. the probability of task success is greater than hyperparameter θ (set to 0.8), SPC ends the game.

6 Experimental Setup

We conduct two evaluations of SPC on the ONECOMMON task. We compare to the state-of-the-art baseline system of Fried et al. (2021), which we refer to as Imitate. Imitate is a pipelined system, where each part is fully supervised. Imitate uses a neural representation of dialogue history in combination with a neural-CRF reference resolution module to understand grounded language. In order to generate, Imitate relies on a pragmatic planning procedure, which plans in a mixture of symbolic and language space, prioritizing descriptions of dots that are easily understood.

We first perform human evaluation, evaluating the task success of systems when paired with human partners. This setting is challenging, requiring the system to handle both the linguistically diverse utterances and a range of strategies of human partners. We recruit 19 workers from Amazon's Mechanical Turk to play with one of three partners: SPC, the most successful past system for the task (Fried et al., 2021), or another human. We pay \$15 per hour, with \$1.00 per game at an average of 4 minutes per game. We additionally give a bonus of \$0.15 for every game. We use 100 visual contexts from the most difficult[10] partition of ONECOMMON. We pay workers $\$1.00$ per game, with a $\$0.15$ bonus if they win. We collect 287 completed dialogues in total, where both players selected a dot.

We secondarily evaluate systems in self-play, where systems are paired with a copy of themselves. This isolates strategic efficiency by ensuring the agent's partner has the same skill as the agent. The 200 games share the same contexts across systems.

We include an additional system in self-play, GPT4 2-shot[11], which gets two full human dialogues as examples. Each human dialogue example starts with a description of the context the agent sees. The full prompts can be viewed here.

Parameterization For code generation, during the reading phase we use GPT-4[12] (OpenAI, 2023).

[9] The distribution $p(x_y|y) = \sum_z p(x_y|y, z)p(z)$ also uses the partner response model $p(x_y|y, z)$.

[10] The number of shared dots is four.

[11] We do not include GPT4 2-shot in human evaluation, as its self-play evaluation is very poor.

[12] Specifically `gpt-4-0613`.

Agent	Success	Turns	Games
SPC	68.8%	7.77	96
Imitate	55.6%	6.61	117
Human	67.6%	5.03	74
Human†	65.8%	4.97	2,189

Table 1: The average success rate, average number of turns, and total number of games between agents and human partners on the hardest setting of ONECOMMON, with 4 shared dots. † indicates statistics from the ONECOMMON dataset (Udagawa and Aizawa, 2019).

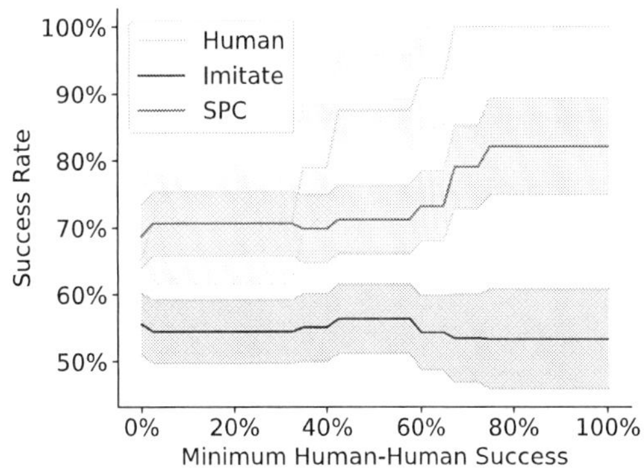

Figure 4: Success rate of the different agent types with human partners, with progressive filtering of human partners by their success rate along the x-axis. Shaded regions give standard errors.

Agent	Avg $|u|$	Median $|u|$
SPC	6.95	4
Imitate	9.62	8
Human	15.06	14

Table 2: The average and median number of words per utterance by human partners for different agent types in human evaluation.

The symbolic actions in ONECOMMON consist of sets of dots and confirmations, while the belief over symbolic states, $p(z)$, captures which dot configurations are shared and is designed to account for dot proximity. Further details on the prior are given in Appendix D. The symbolic partner models, $p(x \mid z)$ and $p(x \mid y, z)$, are drawn from Chiu et al. (2022), and incorporate a similar bias based on dot proximity.

7 Results

Human evaluation In human evaluation, SPC obtains substantially higher task accuracy than the baseline model of Fried et al. (2021), and is comparable to human performance on average. This demonstrates that the combination of symbolic information-gain planning and code-generation in SPC is more effective than the baseline's language-space planning objective and supervised reference resolution.

We see a more nuanced story when conducting a skill-based analysis of the human evaluation results, presented in Figure 4. A worker's skill is given by their average success rate with other human partners. The x-axis of the graph, the minimum success rate, increasingly filters workers from left to right: the left side of the graph shows all workers, while the far right shows only those workers who won nearly all of their human-human games. Skilled human partners have a higher success rate with other humans, as opposed to when partnered with SPC. Additionally, the success rate of SPC improves with human skill, while the success rate of human partners with the baseline system, Imitate, remains relatively constant across skill levels, implying that SPC is more responsive than the baseline to strategies used by humans.

SPC also takes more turns on average than both the baseline and human-human games. We hypothesize that this difference is caused by shorter human partner responses to the system, and therefore less information shared by the human partner. In Table 2, we confirm that the average and median number of words per human utterance are significantly lower for humans partnered with SPC than any other agent type.

Self-play Similarly to human evaluation, SPC outperforms the baseline Imitate system in self-play as shown in Table 3. Compared to the baseline, SPC takes more turns on average, but has a higher success rate. We attribute both the longer games and higher success to symbolic planning, which ensures conservative playing. Interestingly, SPC self-play takes fewer turns on average than SPC-human pairings. We hypothesize that this is due to both copies of SPC communicating a consistent amount of information every turn. This also highlights the importance of human evaluation, which evaluates with a large population of partners.

We also find that GPT4 2-shot performs poorly in self-play. We attribute this to overly-agreeable responses, where the agents choose a dot without

Agent	Success	Avg # turns
SPC	84.0%	4.83
Imitate	63.5%	3.31
GPT4 2-shot	19.0%	9.26
Human†	65.8%	4.97

Table 3: The success rate of different agents in 200 self-play games on the hardest setting of ONECOMMON, with 4 shared dots. A higher success rate is better. The human performance is from the ONECOMMON dataset (Udagawa and Aizawa, 2019).

Prompt style	Acc	Time (s)	Len
SPC	86.7%	5	36
Full	84.0%	18	176

Table 4: The average accuracy, speed, and output length (number of tokens) for the sequential and full code generation methods in our benchmark reading task.

thorough verification or reasoning. This occurs despite the much longer dialogues, in comparison to all other agent types.

8 Analysis

Qualitative analysis We present a qualitative example of a dialogue between SPC and a human partner in Figure 5. This long dialogue illustrates the benefits of explicit belief updates and planning: The conversation starts off with many rejections, which the agent uses to deduce the shared configurations. Eventually, a common set of dots is found and the game ends in a success. Without explicit planning, it would have been unlikely for SPC to have succeeded at the end of the conversation.

Reading speed analysis We perform a speed ablation of the code-generation prompt in SPC. SPC uses a sequence of steps for reading, involving dialogue act classification, code fragment generation, and composing the full code representation based on the output of these steps. We compare this to a prompt that generates the full meaning function.

We evaluate both of these prompts in a reading task, where the goal is to read utterances generated by SPC and recover the underlying plans, measured by accuracy. In Table 4, we see that both styles of prompts have similar similar accuracy, but the sequential, decomposed approach is much faster due to shorter outputs.

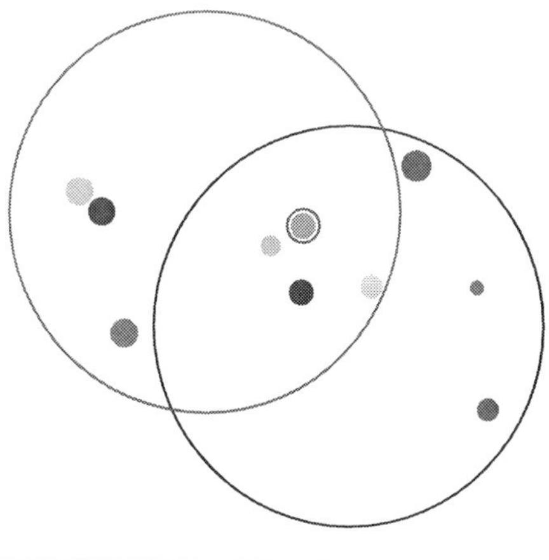

SPC: Do you see a pair of dots, where the bottom dot is medium-sized and dark and the top dot is small-sized and light
Human: No. Do you see a pair of medium sized dots, close together, one is dark grey the other light grey. The light grey one is slightly above and the left of the dark one.
SPC: No. Do you see a pair of dots, where the left dot is medium-sized and dark and the right dot is medium-sized and light
Human: No, do you see a lone medium sized grey dot?
SPC: No. Do you see a pair of dots, where the left dot is medium-sized and light and the right dot is small-sized and grey
Human: No. do you see a pair where the right one is medium and grey and the left one is smaller and lighter. The smaller one is slightly below the medium sized one.
SPC: Yes. Is there a medium size and light color dot to the right and below those?
Human: Yes
SPC: Let's select the medium size and grey color one.
Human: <select>
SPC: <select>

Figure 5: An example dialogue between SPC and a human partner.

9 Conclusion

We present Symbolic Planning and Code-generation (SPC), a method that approaches grounded task-oriented dialogue by separating symbolic reasoning from language. Our approach uses an LLM to generate executable code functions which represent the meaning of utterances, mapping from language to symbolic actions. We then symbolically track task progress using Bayesian reasoning, and explicitly plan the best actions to take next using an information gain objective. Despite using minimal supervision, beyond a task-specific API and few-shot examples, our approach substantially outperforms the state-of-the-art system for the ONECOMMON task in both human evaluations and automatic self-play evaluations.

Our work contrasts with recent work on planning in language space, which reasons implicitly (Wei et al., 2022; Yarats and Lewis, 2017; Guez et al., 2012). While less flexible than language reasoning, symbolic reasoning is both interpretable and modular. Future work should seek to improve the flexibility of symbolic reasoning (Wong et al., 2023).

Our work also represents a first step toward using general-purpose code as a representation for downstream dialogue and interaction tasks. Future work might explore code-based representations that afford more flexible interaction with people, e.g., representing a broader range of user actions, both linguistic and grounded, to construct broadly useful interactive systems. An ideal system would be able to synthesize these representations with minimal manual intervention.

Acknowledgements

We thank Vivian Chen, Sanjiban Choudhury, Ge Gao, Omer Gul, Sedrick Keh, Woojeong Kim, Celine Lee, Jack Morris, Chenran Ning, Jacob Sharf, Alane Suhr, Nicholas Tomlin, Anne Wu, and Jiawei Zhou for discussions, game-playing, and feedback at various points in the process.

We also thank the Mechanical Turkers of Turker Nation for their efforts in game-playing.

JC is supported by NSF #2242302. AMR is supported by a Sloan Fellowship and NSF CAREER #2037519. SV and DF were supported by gifts from Google and from Autodesk Research.

Limitations

Our system performs code execution given human input, opening our system to several risks, such as code injection and unauthorized access. Future work must strive to integrate code execution capabilities in a secure manner.

Our approach also requires the manual engineering of a domain-specific API, as well as a symbolic representation. Future work should seek to alleviate the amount of manual engineering in order to improve flexibility. We hope that methods in program synthesis can provide a solution.

References

Jacob Andreas, John Bufe, David Burkett, Charles Chen, Josh Clausman, Jean Crawford, Kate Crim, Jordan DeLoach, Leah Dorner, Jason Eisner, Hao Fang, Alan Guo, David Hall, Kristin Hayes, Kellie Hill, Diana Ho, Wendy Iwaszuk, Smriti Jha, Dan Klein, Jayant Krishnamurthy, Theo Lanman, Percy Liang, Christopher H. Lin, Ilya Lintsbakh, Andy McGovern, Aleksandr Nisnevich, Adam Pauls, Dmitrij Petters, Brent Read, Dan Roth, Subhro Roy, Jesse Rusak, Beth Short, Div Slomin, Ben Snyder, Stephon Striplin, Yu Su, Zachary Tellman, Sam Thomson, Andrei Vorobev, Izabela Witoszko, Jason Andrew Wolfe, Abby Wray, Yuchen Zhang, and Alexander Zotov. 2020. Task-oriented dialogue as dataflow synthesis. *CoRR*, abs/2009.11423.

Anton Bakhtin, Noam Brown, Emily Dinan, Gabriele Farina, Colin Flaherty, Daniel Fried, Andrew Goff, Jonathan Gray, Hengyuan Hu, Athul Paul Jacob, Mojtaba Komeili, Karthik Konath, Minae Kwon, Adam Lerer, Mike Lewis, Alexander H. Miller, Sasha Mitts, Adithya Renduchintala, Stephen Roller, Dirk Rowe, Weiyan Shi, Joe Spisak, Alexander Wei, David Wu, Hugh Zhang, and Markus Zijlstra. 2022. Human-level play in the game of diplomacy by combining language models with strategic reasoning. *Science*, 378(6624):1067–1074.

Mark Chen, Jerry Tworek, Heewoo Jun, Qiming Yuan, Henrique Ponde de Oliveira Pinto, Jared Kaplan, Harri Edwards, Yuri Burda, Nicholas Joseph, Greg Brockman, Alex Ray, Raul Puri, Gretchen Krueger, Michael Petrov, Heidy Khlaaf, Girish Sastry, Pamela Mishkin, Brooke Chan, Scott Gray, Nick Ryder, Mikhail Pavlov, Alethea Power, Lukasz Kaiser, Mohammad Bavarian, Clemens Winter, Philippe Tillet, Felipe Petroski Such, Dave Cummings, Matthias Plappert, Fotios Chantzis, Elizabeth Barnes, Ariel Herbert-Voss, William Hebgen Guss, Alex Nichol, Alex Paino, Nikolas Tezak, Jie Tang, Igor Babuschkin, Suchir Balaji, Shantanu Jain, William Saunders, Christopher Hesse, Andrew N. Carr, Jan Leike, Josh Achiam, Vedant Misra, Evan Morikawa, Alec Radford, Matthew Knight, Miles Brundage, Mira Murati, Katie Mayer, Peter Welinder, Bob McGrew, Dario Amodei, Sam McCandlish, Ilya Sutskever, and Wojciech Zaremba. 2021. Evaluating large language models trained on code.

Jianpeng Cheng, Siva Reddy, Vijay Saraswat, and Mirella Lapata. 2018. Learning an executable neural semantic parser.

Justin T Chiu, Wenting Zhao, Daniel Fried, and Alexander M Rush. 2022. Modeling perspective-dependent ambiguity in collaborative dialogue. In *The Third Wordplay: When Language Meets Games Workshop*.

Paul Christiano, Jan Leike, Tom B. Brown, Miljan Martic, Shane Legg, and Dario Amodei. 2023. Deep reinforcement learning from human preferences.

Philip R. Cohen and C. Raymond Perrault. 1979. Elements of a plan-based theory of speech acts. *Cognitive Science*.

Surís Dídac, Sachit Menon, and Carl Vondrick. 2023. Vipergpt: Visual inference via python execution for reasoning. *arXiv preprint arXiv:2303.08128*.

Daniel Fried, Justin T. Chiu, and Dan Klein. 2021. Reference-centric models for grounded collaborative dialogue. In *Proceedings of EMNLP*.

Kanishk Gandhi, Dorsa Sadigh, and Noah D. Goodman. 2023. Strategic reasoning with language models.

Luyu Gao, Aman Madaan, Shuyan Zhou, Uri Alon, Pengfei Liu, Yiming Yang, Jamie Callan, and Graham Neubig. 2023. Pal: Program-aided language models.

Arthur Guez, David Silver, and Peter Dayan. 2012. Efficient bayes-adaptive reinforcement learning using sample-based search. *CoRR*, abs/1205.3109.

Tanmay Gupta and Aniruddha Kembhavi. 2022. Visual programming: Compositional visual reasoning without training.

Janosch Haber, Tim Baumgärtner, Ece Takmaz, Lieke Gelderloos, Elia Bruni, and Raquel Fernández. 2019. The photobook dataset: Building common ground through visually-grounded dialogue. *CoRR*, abs/1906.01530.

He He, Anusha Balakrishnan, Mihail Eric, and Percy Liang. 2017. Learning symmetric collaborative dialogue agents with dynamic knowledge graph embeddings. *CoRR*, abs/1704.07130.

He He, Derek Chen, Anusha Balakrishnan, and Percy Liang. 2018. Decoupling strategy and generation in negotiation dialogues. *CoRR*, abs/1808.09637.

Youngsoo Jang, Jongmin Lee, and Kee-Eung Kim. 2020. Bayes-adaptive monte-carlo planning and learning for goal-oriented dialogues. In *The Thirty-Fourth AAAI Conference on Artificial Intelligence, AAAI 2020, The Thirty-Second Innovative Applications of Artificial Intelligence Conference, IAAI 2020, The Tenth AAAI Symposium on Educational Advances in Artificial Intelligence, EAAI 2020, New York, NY, USA, February 7-12, 2020*, pages 7994–8001. AAAI Press.

Justin Johnson, Bharath Hariharan, Laurens van der Maaten, Judy Hoffman, Li Fei-Fei, C. Lawrence Zitnick, and Ross Girshick. 2017. Inferring and executing programs for visual reasoning.

Fereshte Khani, Noah Goodman, and Percy Liang. 2018. Planning, inference and pragmatics in sequential language games. *Transactions of the Association for Computational Linguistics*, 6:543–555.

Jacky Liang, Wenlong Huang, Fei Xia, Peng Xu, Karol Hausman, Brian Ichter, Pete Florence, and Andy Zeng. 2022. Code as policies: Language model programs for embodied control. In *arXiv preprint arXiv:2209.07753*.

Percy Liang. 2016. Learning executable semantic parsers for natural language understanding.

D. V. Lindley. 1956. On a Measure of the Information Provided by an Experiment. *The Annals of Mathematical Statistics*, 27(4):986 – 1005.

Ximing Lu, Sean Welleck, Peter West, Liwei Jiang, Jungo Kasai, Daniel Khashabi, Ronan Le Bras, Lianhui Qin, Youngjae Yu, Rowan Zellers, Noah A. Smith, and Yejin Choi. 2022. Neurologic a*esque decoding: Constrained text generation with lookahead heuristics.

OpenAI. 2023. Gpt-4 technical report.

Verena Rieser and Oliver Lemon. 2009. Natural language generation as planning under uncertainty for spoken dialogue systems. In *Proceedings of the 12th Conference of the European Chapter of the ACL (EACL 2009)*, pages 683–691, Athens, Greece. Association for Computational Linguistics.

David R Traum. 1994. A computational theory of grounding in natural language conversation. Technical report, Rochester University Department of Computer Science.

Takuma Udagawa and Akiko Aizawa. 2019. A natural language corpus of common grounding under continuous and partially-observable context. *Proceedings of the AAAI Conference on Artificial Intelligence*, 33(01):7120–7127.

Karthik Valmeekam, Sarath Sreedharan, Matthew Marquez, Alberto Olmo, and Subbarao Kambhampati. 2023. On the planning abilities of large language models (a critical investigation with a proposed benchmark).

M A Walker, S J Whittaker, A Stent, P Maloor, J Moore, M Johnston, and G Vasireddy. 2004. Generation and evaluation of user tailored responses in multimodal dialogue. *Cognitive Science*, 28(5):811–840.

Jason Wei, Xuezhi Wang, Dale Schuurmans, Maarten Bosma, Ed H. Chi, Quoc Le, and Denny Zhou. 2022. Chain of thought prompting elicits reasoning in large language models. *CoRR*, abs/2201.11903.

Julia White, Gabriel Poesia, Robert Hawkins, Dorsa Sadigh, and Noah Goodman. 2021. Open-domain clarification question generation without question examples. In *Proceedings of the 2021 Conference on Empirical Methods in Natural Language Processing*, pages 563–570, Online and Punta Cana, Dominican Republic. Association for Computational Linguistics.

Terry Winograd. 1971. Procedures as a representation for data in a computer program for understanding natural language.

Lionel Wong, Gabriel Grand, Alexander K. Lew, Noah D. Goodman, Vikash K. Mansinghka, Jacob Andreas, and Joshua B. Tenenbaum. 2023. From word models to world models: Translating from natural language to the probabilistic language of thought.

Denis Yarats and Mike Lewis. 2017. Hierarchical text generation and planning for strategic dialogue. *CoRR*, abs/1712.05846.

Steve Young. 2006. Using pomdps for dialog management. In *2006 IEEE Spoken Language Technology Workshop*, pages 8–13.

Lili Yu, Howard Chen, Sida I. Wang, Yoav Artzi, and Tao Lei. 2019. Interactive classification by asking informative questions. *CoRR*, abs/1911.03598.

A Prompt details

All prompts rely on few-shot prompting. Reformat has 5 few-shot examples, Classify has two dialogues with 15-turns total, Confirm has 9 examples, and Understand has two dialogues with 15 turns total. All examples were based loosely on 10 examples from the human-human games collected in OneCommon by Udagawa and Aizawa (2019). The same prompts were used in every context. The full prompts can be found here.

B Prompt ablation

We present an additional experiment on how the choice of few-shot examples affects the code constraint generation prompt, which is a key component of the reading step. The code constraints express the relationships between the mentioned dots, e.g. whether they form a triangle or their relative positions, shapes, and colors.

We take the first human utterance from 20 games in human evaluation and examine whether the parsed answer changes when the prompt examples are changed. The 15 examples in the constraint generation prompt were labeled by hand. Since we cannot sample another 15 examples, we instead sub-sample 5 random examples out of 15 for a 5-shot prompt. We report the average agreement between 5-shot prompts and the original 15-shot prompt across 5 trials: 99%, with a standard deviation of 2%. This implies the constraint generation prompt is not sensitive to prompt example choice at the 5-shot level and prompts could be further optimized.

We perform the same experiment with 5 trials of 1-shot prompts and see an average agreement rate of 34% with a standard deviation of 42%. This implies that given a single example, the prompt example matters.

We also find that a zero-shot prompt is unable to generate output in the correct format.

C Writing

We utilize three templates for writing, one for each dialogue act.

START: `Do you see a pair of dots, where the {position} dot is {size}-sized and {color} and the {position} dot is {size}-sized and {color}?`

FOLLOW-UP: `Is there a {size} size and {color} color dot {position} those?`

SELECT: `Let's select the {size} size and {color} color one. <selection>`

D Parameterization

We give the parameterization of the belief prior, $p(z)$ for ONECOMMON.

Our goal in designing the prior is to ensure that the closer dots are, the more likely they are to be of the same state: either all shared or not. This reflects the contiguity of ONECOMMON perspectives.

The prior is given by

$$p(z) \propto \exp(f(z)), \tag{3}$$

where $f(z)$ is given the sum of the edges of a minimum spanning tree for the dots in z. The weights of this spanning tree are determined by the rank of how close the dots are to each other. The edge between the nearest neighbor of a dot and the dot itself gets assigned a weight of 0, the 2nd nearest neighbor a weight of 1, and so on.

E Relation to prior work in semantic parsing and dialogue state tracking

Prior work in semantic parsing for dialogue state tracking, such as in SMCalFlow (Andreas et al., 2020), does not ground in a visual context and also requires strategic, collaborative planning due to OneCommon's symmetric roles. Agents must both give and request information strategically. This type of strategic reasoning is not explored in prior works in semantic parsing and dialogue state tracking. Our technical contribution is unifying grounded language understanding and strategic symbolic reasoning with code generation. In particular, the reading phase of SPC was designed for spatial reasoning in OneCommon.

Towards Zero-Shot Frame Semantic Parsing with Task Agnostic Ontologies and Simple Labels

Danilo Ribeiro[1,2,*], **Omid Abdar**[1,*], **Jack Goetz**[1], **Mike Ross**[1], **Annie Dong**[1], **Kenneth Forbus**[2], **Ahmed Mohamed**[1]
[1]Meta AI, {jrgoetz, mikeross, asyd, ahmedkm}@meta.com,
[2]Northwestern University, {dnribeiro, forbus}@u.northwestern.edu,

Abstract

Frame semantic parsing is an important component of task-oriented dialogue systems. Current models rely on a significant amount training data to successfully identify the intent and slots in the user's input utterance. This creates a significant barrier for adding new domains to virtual assistant capabilities, as creation of this data requires highly specialized NLP expertise. In this work we propose OpenFSP, a framework that allows for easy creation of new domains from a handful of simple labels that can be generated without specific NLP knowledge. Our approach relies on creating a small, but expressive, set of domain agnostic slot types that enables easy annotation of new domains. Given such annotation, a matching algorithm relying on sentence encoders predicts the intent and slots for domains defined by end-users. Experiments on the TopV2 dataset shows that our model trained on these *simple labels* have strong performance against supervised baselines.

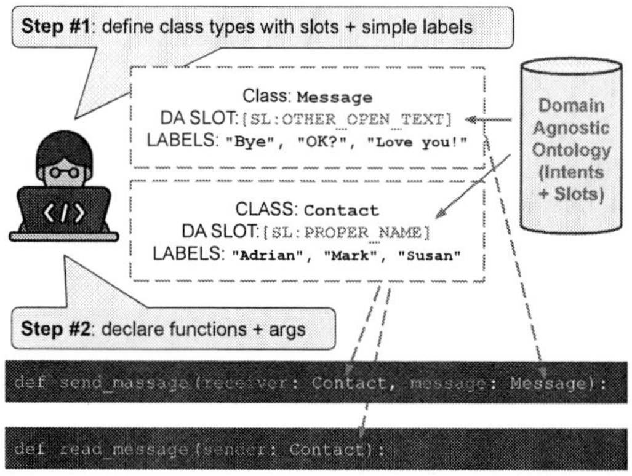

Figure 1: Illustration of proposed OpenFSP framework with a domain agnostic ontology and simple labels provided by the software developer (natural language textual examples). OpenFSP can facilitate the development of new domains and automatic construction of new ontologies by decoding functions or API specifications.

1 Introduction

Frame semantic parsing is an important subproblem with many applications, and in particular is critical for task-oriented dialogue assistants to identify the desired action (intent) and specific details (slots) (Coucke et al., 2018; Gupta et al., 2019). This is typically modeled as a semantic parsing problem (usually solved via a combination of ML and rules) with custom ontology that reflects capabilities of the system. Creation of this custom ontology, and annotation of consistent data is highly non-trivial, and typically requires specialized skills (Ahmad et al., 2021). This limits extension of the ontology and generation of parsing data to a small group of experts.

On the other hand, intent-slot concepts map well to functions and arguments of an API call, a paradigm well understood by software developers. Therefore, making extension to the parser is the primary blocker to enabling support for new capabilities (domains) within a task-oriented assistant system. As shown in Figure 1, our goal is to enable non-NLP experts to define allowed intent-slot combinations, and provide a small amount of non-NLP specialized labels, which we call *simple labels*. These data enable the creation of a parser for those intent-slot combinations. This new problem definition lies somewhere between zero-shot and few-shot learning. It requires zero fully annotated semantic parse examples, but does require some human produced labels.

To this end, we develop a framework called ***Open F**rame **S**emantic **P**arser* (OpenFSP). OpenFSP takes as input the developer's defined functions and their annotations to augment an existing assistant system for new tasks. Underlying OpenFSP is a two module model consisting of a *general semantic parser* and a *matching module*. The gen-

*These authors contributed equally.

Proceedings of the 2nd Workshop in Pattern-based Approaches to NLP in the Age of Deep Learning, pages 54–63
December 6, 2023.

eral semantic parser can identify the intent and slots according to the pre-defined domain agnostic ontology, while the matching module will take this intermediate representation and match them to the specific function and arguments defined in the domain specific ontology.

In summary, our contributions are: (1) we formalize a new framework, namely OpenFSP, that allows for easy development of new domains without much expertise knowledge from software developers (2) we define a general-purpose domain agnostic ontology by analysing the semantic similarity of slots from `TopV2` (Chen et al., 2020b), a well established task-oriented semantic parsing dataset (3) we propose an approach consisting of a parser and a matching module that can outperform strong baselines in the *simple labels* setting.

2 Related Work

Data-Efficient Semantic Parsing In one of the first attempts to use data-efficient methods to perform frame semantic parsing, (Bapna et al., 2017) applied recurrent neural networks to perform semi-supervised intent classification and slot filling (IC/SF) while leveraging natural language descriptions of slot labels. The work of Krone et al. (2020) more clearly formalized few-shot learning for IC/SF, while providing a few-shot split of three public datasets. Wilson et al. (2019) implemented and deployed a kiosk virtual assistant, which could handle multiple modalities by learning from a few examples using analogical learning.

Multiple low resource IC/SF approaches were proposed (Chen et al., 2020b; Desai et al., 2021; Yin et al., 2022; Basu et al., 2022). All of these approaches either rely on a non-trivial amount of training data (hundreds to thousands of examples), or use a fixed set of intents and slots, making it harder to adapt to new domains. Our matching module shares some similarities with retrieval based systems (Yu et al., 2021; Shrivastava et al., 2022), however these methods learn from standard utterance and semantic frames, instead of simple textual labels for each slot and intent. This is an important differentiator, as the annotation of even a small number of semantic frames requires overcoming a significant knowledge barrier.

Sentence Encoders for Language Understanding One key aspect of our matching module is to encode the textual spans using sentence encoders. These models have the advantage of working well in low resource settings, and have been used in many applications including natural language inference (Conneau et al., 2017), semantic textual similarity (Reimers and Gurevych, 2019), dense passage retrieval (Karpukhin et al., 2020; Izacard and Grave, 2021), natural language explanations (Neves Ribeiro et al., 2022), and many others. The idea of using sentence embeddings for text classification has been previously explored (Perone et al., 2018; Piao, 2021). Most notably, the work of Tunstall et al. (2022) proposed SETFIT, a prompt-free model that can learn text classification tasks from a handful of examples. However, none of these works directly applied to semantic parsing which require multiple consistent predictions from the input utterance.

Task-Oriented Ontologies Task-oriented dialogue systems are natural language interfaces for a system that parses user utterances. A common approach in these systems is the use of ontologies to represent domain information (Wessel et al., 2019). In general, such ontologies can be created manually using rule-based techniques, which is a highly accurate but time consuming and expensive approach that usually requires domain experts (Meditskos et al., 2020), or via ontology induction approaches using machine learning (Poon and Domingos, 2010). While these approaches both involve trade-offs, curated ontologies can also be created via simplification of an existing ontology based on custom needs (Kutiyanawala et al., 2018; Laadidi and Bahaj, 2018). On the other hand, our work simplifies the ontological creation by abstracting the existing functions and arguments defined by the application itself.

3 Problem Definition

The standard frame semantic parsing has two main tasks which maps the input utterance x with tokens $x_1, \ldots, x_n$ to some structured output frame $\boldsymbol{y}$. For the *slot-filling* task, the output frame F consists of a set of m non-overlapping spans and their respective labels $F = \{(s_i, e_i, l_i)\}_{i=1}^{m}$ indicating that subsequence $\boldsymbol{x}_{[s_i:e_i]}$ has label $l_i \in \mathcal{L}$, where $\mathcal{L}$ is the set of possible labels (e.g., the text span "noon tomorrow" has the label `SL:DATE_TIME`). The *intent classification* assigns a label to the whole utterance. For simplicity, we assume that the intent can be thought of as another slot filling with $s_i = 0$ and $e_i = n$, with l_i as the intent type.

To simplify annotation efforts, we define an on-

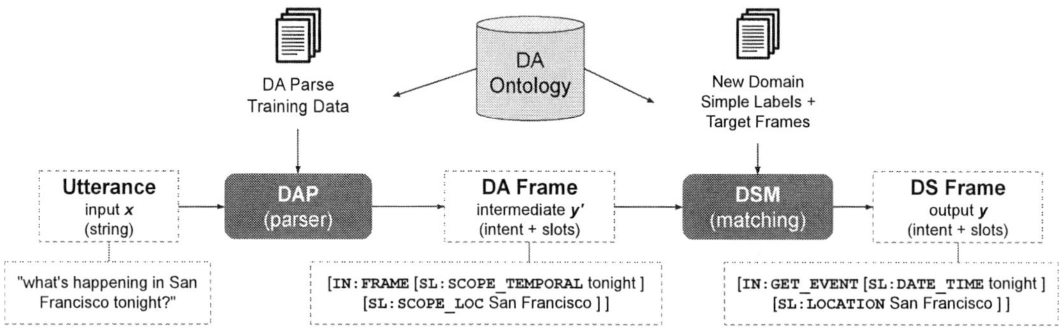

Figure 2: System overview with two components, namely the *domain agnostic parser* (DAP) and the *domain specific matching* (DSM).

tology with a set of domain-agnostic labels $\mathcal{L}_A$, where $|\mathcal{L}_A| << |\mathcal{L}|$. These domain-agnostic labels can be interpreted as generic "label types", with an existing many-to-one mapping $\psi : \mathcal{L} \to \mathcal{L}_A$ between the two sets. This mapping is further described in Appendix A.1. In our proposed simple label setting, training data for new domains will not include $\boldsymbol{x}$, but only a subsequence of the tokens defined by the frame spans. The number of examples for each slot will be relatively small, with 5 to 50 examples per slot type. The set of all possible domain specific target frames F^* (i.e., defined functions and their arguments) is assumed to be known a priory.

4 Approach

Our model is comprised of two main components, the *domain agnostic parser* (DAP) and the *domain specific matching* (DSM). The system overview is shown in Figure 2. The DAP is trained to take the input utterance x and output a domain agnostic frame F_A, where span labels belong to $\mathcal{L}_A$. Afterwards the DSM module will score the potential domain specific frames from F^* according to their similarity to the domain agnostic frame F_A.

The DAP module can be any frame semantic parser. Ours is built on a span-pointer network (Shrivastava et al., 2021), which is a non-autoregressive parser that replaces the decoding from text generation with span predictions. It is trained on domain agnostic data obtained from existing domain specific data using the slot label function ψ.

The DSM module has to learn a similarity function between a text span and its slot label (same applies to intents). Since the slot label scoring function has to be done in a few-shot setting, the DSM module uses a sentence encoder ϕ (Reimers and Gurevych, 2019) with a classification head on top. The module modifies a pre-trained transformer language model fine tuned to output semantically meaningful sentence embeddings.

The sentence encoder ϕ is tailored to work on generic text, minimizing the distance between semantically similar sentences while maximizing the distance of dissimilar sentences. We use a classification head H over the produced sentence embedding of a given text span $\boldsymbol{x}$. Therefore, the probability score of a label l_i can be computed as follows:

$$P(l_i|\boldsymbol{x}) = \frac{exp(H(\phi(\boldsymbol{x}))_i)}{\sum_{j=1}^{|\mathcal{L}|} exp(H(\phi(\boldsymbol{x}))_j)} \tag{1}$$

Note that the input training data does not contain fully annotated domain specific frames (only text and their intent-slot labels). For this reason, the DSM module has to aggregate these individual intent and slot probability scores to predict the full frame scores. The similarity score for a target domain specific frame $F = \{(s_i, e_i, l_i)\}_{i=1}^{|F|}$ given a query domain agnostic parse $F_A = \{(s_i^A, e_i^A, l_i^A)\}_{i=1}^{|F_A|}$ is given by:

$$sim(F, F_A) = \max_{F' \in \mathfrak{S}(F)} \frac{1}{|F'|} \sum_{i=1}^{|F'|} P(l_i|\boldsymbol{x}_{[s_i^A:e_i^A]}) \tag{2}$$

Where $\mathfrak{S}(F)$ is the set of all slot permutations of F. To make the final prediction, we also check that the typing between domain agnostic and domain specific types match. Therefore DSM selects the best frame $F \in F^*$ using the formula:

$$\arg\max_{F \in F^*} \begin{cases} 0 & \text{if } \exists i : \psi(l_i) \neq l_i^A \\ sim(F, F_A) & \text{otherwise} \end{cases} \quad (3)$$

Note that for each new domain, only a very small set of parameters are trained (namely, the classification head H), which makes this approach computationally efficient.

4.1 Data

We conduct experiments using the `TopV2` (Chen et al., 2020b), a multi-domain dataset containing intent and slot annotations for task-oriented dialogue systems. We select a subset of the data points, ignoring the ones containing more than one intent (even though our method would also work for nested frames) or utterances with `IN:UNSUPPORTED` intent label. The final dataset contains a total of eight different domains (namely: `alarm`, `event`, `messaging`, `music`, `navigation`, `reminder`, `timer`, and `weather`). The dataset is then split into train (104278), evaluation (14509) and test (32654) sets.

5 Experiments

5.1 Evaluation Setup

We conduct experiments to evaluate how well a model can adapt to a new unseen domain by leveraging the "simple labels" for this new domain. To simulate this adaptation process we perform multiple test rounds, where each of the eight `TopV2` domains are treated as unseen domains. We use *frame accuracy* as a metric, which refers to the ratio of examples where the system correctly predicts all the frame's spans and labels. The results for each left-out domain are averaged to obtain the final metrics. Each label $l_i \in \mathcal{L}$ of the unseen domain will be assigned a few textual examples that will be used for training. In our experiments we use 5, 10 and 50 examples per unseen domain's label.

5.2 Baselines

The first two methods are used as baselines and can be seen as soft upper bounds. They do not follow the "simple labels" settings, and use the full training data for the new domains instead. Other two methods are used to further evaluate the different implementation choices of the model, as ablation studies.

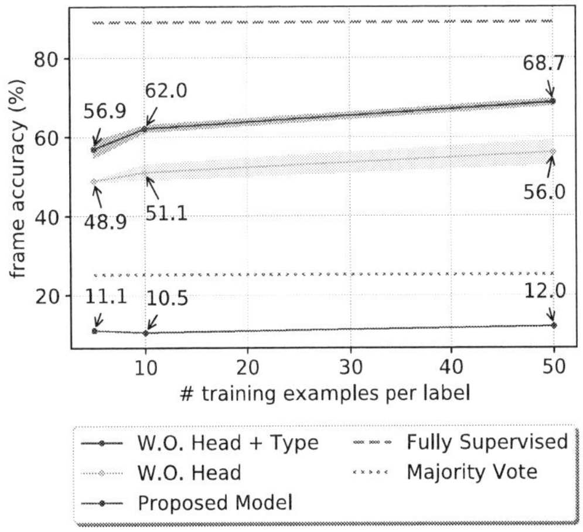

Figure 3: Main experiment results with different number of examples per label.

Majority Vote This simple method always selects the most commonly occurring intent and slots for a given domain. It uses the DAP module to generate F_A, and assigns the domain specific labels according to the number of occurrences of $F \in F^*$ (such that $|F| = |F_A|$) in the training data.

Fully Supervised Uses the same architecture as the DAP (semantic parser) module, but it is trained using the full training data. Despite not being at all a fair comparison with the *simple label* settings, we include these baseline results as a way to visualize the best-case scenario.

W.O. Head This method does not use a classification head H, instead, it predicts the class label by selecting the example with highest semantic similarity with the input text using the cosine similarity score.

W.O. Head + Type This method not only uses the classification head, but also disregards the type constraint in Equation 3 such that the best frame is always $\arg\max_{F \in F^*} (sim(F, F_A))$.

5.3 Implementation Details

The span-pointer architecture used by the DAP module is a encoder-decoder model based on RoBERTa (Liu et al., 2019), with the encoder containing 12 layers and the decoder containing 1 layer. We train the model for 85 epochs using a learning rate of $1.67 \cdot 10^{-5}$. The sentence encoder used in the DSM module is built on top of a 36 layer XLM-R model (Conneau et al., 2019) fine-tuned

Eval. Setting	messa.	alarm	music	event	navig.	remind.	timer	weath.	avg.
Standard	86.7	67.6	55.5	73.9	60.6	58.5	72.7	79.6	69.4
+ Golden Parse	93.9	50.1	60.7	88.7	60.7	78.7	78.7	89.1	75.1
+ Recall@3	92.9	78.8	65.0	82.2	75.0	68.9	78.9	90.2	79.0
+ Intent Acc.	96.9	82.3	76.6	97.9	78.6	61.5	80.4	85.7	82.5

Table 1: Break down of results by domain for different evaluation settings. The results shown correspond to a single run of our proposed model with 50 labels per example.

to capture general sentence similarity. When fine-tuning the models we used a machine containing two NVIDIA Tesla P100 graphics processing units. Note that the underlying models used are relatively small when compared to current large language models (Sanh et al., 2019) and would be suitable for "on-the-edge" device computation.

5.4 Results

We perform three test runs with different random seeds for each evaluation setting, which influences both the model initialization and the set of training examples per label. The main results are shown in Figure 3. The baselines using the full training data (i.e., *Fully Supervised* and *Majority Vote*) are shown as dashed lines, and their results do not change according to the x-axis. The remaining results show the mean (and standard deviation as the shaded region) among the three test runs.

The results show that our proposed model outperforms most of the baselines, with numbers comparable to the *fully supervised* baseline (77.9% of its frame accuracy with 50 examples per label), even though it relies on a much smaller and simplified version of the training data.

There are a few other takeaways. First, we notice that increasing the number of "simple label" training examples significantly improves the frame accuracy. However, only five training examples is enough to produce decent results. More examples also seem to increases the variance of the models without a classification head. Second, the type filtering from Equation 3 is one key aspect of why the system can perform so well with so few example. Because of the generic nature of the domain agnostic ontology, filtering out invalid frames greatly reduces the size of the target space F^*, with a size reduction of 96% for certain domains such as `messaging`.

5.4.1 Results Break Down

To obtain further insights on the model, we show the results broken down by domain in Table 1. We used our proposed model trained on 50 examples per label, and different evaluation settings described as follows. The *Standard* settings are the same as the ones displayed in Figure 3. The *Golden Parse* assumes that the DAP module outputs only correct domain agnostic parses (i.e., the best-case scenario for the parser). The *Recall@3* results uses the same model as the *Standard* setting, but checks if the correct answer is in the top-3 scored matches (instead of top-1) from DSM. Finally, the *Intent Acc.* setting evaluates if the model correctly predicts the intent of the given input utterance. These results help us answer the following questions:

How much error from the parser gets propagated? We can notice from the *Golden Parse* results that there is a reasonable improvement (8.2% increase) in accuracy when using the gold test frames. This means that incorrect parses from the DAP module certainly propagates forward and improving the DAP module could certainly benefit the system as a whole.

Is the matching module nearly missing the right answer? When looking *Recall@3* results, we notice a significantly larger improvement in results (13.8% increase). With an average mean reciprocal ranking among all domains of 74.9. Having a high frame score values in the top-3 is significant considering that on average the size among all domains for the target space F^* is around 279.8 frames.

5.5 Error Analysis and Future Work

To understand the mistakes made by the OpenFSP system we perform some error analysis and suggest some possible improvement avenues for future work. For this analysis we use the development set and randomly sampled 100 output frames from different domains. We manually categorize the errors as follows.

Parsing Errors We notice that 45% of the errors are due to parsing errors. This includes cases when the DAP module predicts an incorrect number of slots (∼93% among parsing errors) or when the number of slots are correct, but some of the slots have the incorrect labels (∼7% among parsing errors). A future direction could be to use the DAP and DSM modules to over-generate valid frames and rank (Varges, 2006; Zhang and Wan, 2022), which could circumvent parsing errors.

Intent Classification Error Another common error was the mislabeling of the utterance's intent, corresponding to 32% of the manually categorized examples. This kind of error would often happen between semantically similar intents (e.g., `IN:PREVIOUS_TRACK_MUSIC` and `IN:REPLAY_MUSIC` in the `music` domain) and with examples from `TopV2` that were labeled as unsupported (e.g., `IN:UNSUPPORTED_WEATHER` and `IN:UNSUPPORTED_MUSIC`) that often have out of scope questions that are harder to classify (e.g., "What is the hottest temperature this month"). One possible future direction would be to use Contrastive Learning (Chen et al., 2020a; Basu et al., 2022) that could improve the classification boundary of similar examples.

Slot Classification Error The last 23% of the errors were due to slot type misclassification. Again, semantically similar slot types are more challenging to classify. For instance, in the `alarm` domain `SL:DATE_TIME_RECURRING`, `SL:DATE_TIME`, `SL:PERIOD` and `SL:DURATION` were particularly hard to classify since they were all part of the same domain agnostic type `SL:SCOPE_TEMPORAL`. Another common issue was identifying proper names (∼21% of the slot classification errors), including artist, event, album, and playlist names. A future direction would be to integrate a named entity recognition module to help classify slots involving proper names.

6 Conclusion

In this work we propose OpenFSP, a framework designed to simplify the process of adapting an existing task-oriented dialogue system to new domains. This framework enables non-experts to automatically build new domain ontologies from well defined software engineering concepts such as functions and arguments. We define a general-purpose domain agnostic ontology, that when combined with textual examples of new slots and intents (which we call *simple labels*), provides sufficient data to adapt the system to a new domain.

Finally, we propose a two-module system that can use these simple labels to reasonably parse input utterances into the domain specific frames. Our experiments show that the proposed model outperforms strong baselines and is able to obtain results comparable with a fully supervised model (achieving 77.9% of its semantic frame accuracy). We hope that our work will facilitate the development of new assistant capabilities, allowing end-users to interact with more software applications through natural language.

Limitations

Domain-agnostic (DA) slots represent the overal semantic space covered by underlying TopV2 slots. Given their coarse-grain nature, DA slots are likely to be distributed more or less evenly across all domains. This assumption is key when training the parser on data that does not contain a particular target domain. In addition, we find that our approach is also sensitive to the types of linguistic structures accounted for by each DA slot and works best when these structures are consistent across domains.

More specifically, we conducted a series of leave-one-out (LOO) experiments where a separate parser was learned for each domain using training data from all other domains and then tested on test data from the domain in question exclusively. Error analysis of 100 randomly selected predictions in our LOO model for the "alarm" domain revealed that 32% of the errors were utterances such as "I want alarms set for next Monday at 6.00am and 7.00am" where the model predicted [`SL:SCOPE_TEMPORAL` for next monday at 6.00am] and [`SL:SCOPE_TEMPORAL` 7.00am]] whereas a compound [`SL:SCOPE_TEMPORAL` for next monday at 6.00am and 7.00am]] slot was expected. Upon closer inspection, we observed that these [`SL:SCOPE_TEMPORAL` X and Y] compound nominal constructions appear predominantly (83.3%) in the alarm domain, hence causing inaccurate predictions in a LOO model for this domain.

For these types of errors to be mitigated in our approach, [`SL:SCOPE_TEMPORAL` X and

Y] constructions would need to either be more evenly distributed across all domains, or re-annotated as [[SL:SCOPE_TEMPORAL X] and [SL:SCOPE_TEMPORAL Y]] in the alarm domain to improve homogeneity in the data.

Ethics Statement

No private data or non-public information was used in this work.

References

Wasi Ahmad, Jianfeng Chi, Tu Le, Thomas Norton, Yuan Tian, and Kai-Wei Chang. 2021. Intent classification and slot filling for privacy policies. In *Proceedings of the 59th Annual Meeting of the Association for Computational Linguistics and the 11th International Joint Conference on Natural Language Processing (Volume 1: Long Papers)*, pages 4402–4417, Online. Association for Computational Linguistics.

Ankur Bapna, Gökhan Tür, Dilek Z. Hakkani-Tür, and Larry Heck. 2017. Towards zero-shot frame semantic parsing for domain scaling. In *Interspeech*.

Samyadeep Basu, Amr Sharaf, Karine Ip Kiun Chong, Alex Fischer, Vishal Rohra, Michael Amoake, Hazem El-Hammamy, Ehi Nosakhare, Vijay Ramani, and Benjamin Han. 2022. Strategies to improve few-shot learning for intent classification and slot-filling. In *Proceedings of the Workshop on Structured and Unstructured Knowledge Integration (SUKI)*, pages 17–25, Seattle, USA. Association for Computational Linguistics.

Ting Chen, Simon Kornblith, Mohammad Norouzi, and Geoffrey Hinton. 2020a. A simple framework for contrastive learning of visual representations. In *International conference on machine learning*, pages 1597–1607. PMLR.

Xilun Chen, Asish Ghoshal, Yashar Mehdad, Luke Zettlemoyer, and Sonal Gupta. 2020b. Low-resource domain adaptation for compositional task-oriented semantic parsing. In *Proceedings of the 2020 Conference on Empirical Methods in Natural Language Processing (EMNLP)*, pages 5090–5100, Online. Association for Computational Linguistics.

Alexis Conneau, Kartikay Khandelwal, Naman Goyal, Vishrav Chaudhary, Guillaume Wenzek, Francisco Guzmán, Edouard Grave, Myle Ott, Luke Zettlemoyer, and Veselin Stoyanov. 2019. Unsupervised cross-lingual representation learning at scale. *arXiv preprint arXiv:1911.02116*.

Alexis Conneau, Douwe Kiela, Holger Schwenk, Loïc Barrault, and Antoine Bordes. 2017. Supervised learning of universal sentence representations from natural language inference data. In *Proceedings of the 2017 Conference on Empirical Methods in Natural Language Processing*, pages 670–680, Copenhagen, Denmark. Association for Computational Linguistics.

Alice Coucke, Alaa Saade, Adrien Ball, Théodore Bluche, Alexandre Caulier, David Leroy, Clément Doumouro, Thibault Gisselbrecht, Francesco Caltagirone, Thibaut Lavril, et al. 2018. Snips voice platform: an embedded spoken language understanding system for private-by-design voice interfaces. *arXiv preprint arXiv:1805.10190*.

Shrey Desai, Akshat Shrivastava, Alexander Zotov, and Ahmed Aly. 2021. Low-resource task-oriented semantic parsing via intrinsic modeling. *arXiv preprint arXiv:2104.07224*.

Arshit Gupta, John Hewitt, and Katrin Kirchhoff. 2019. Simple, fast, accurate intent classification and slot labeling for goal-oriented dialogue systems. In *Proceedings of the 20th Annual SIGdial Meeting on Discourse and Dialogue*, pages 46–55, Stockholm, Sweden. Association for Computational Linguistics.

Gautier Izacard and Edouard Grave. 2021. Leveraging passage retrieval with generative models for open domain question answering. In *Proceedings of the 16th Conference of the European Chapter of the Association for Computational Linguistics: Main Volume*, pages 874–880, Online. Association for Computational Linguistics.

Vladimir Karpukhin, Barlas Oguz, Sewon Min, Patrick Lewis, Ledell Wu, Sergey Edunov, Danqi Chen, and Wen-tau Yih. 2020. Dense passage retrieval for open-domain question answering. In *Proceedings of the 2020 Conference on Empirical Methods in Natural Language Processing (EMNLP)*, pages 6769–6781, Online. Association for Computational Linguistics.

Jason Krone, Yi Zhang, and Mona Diab. 2020. Learning to classify intents and slot labels given a handful of examples. In *Proceedings of the 2nd Workshop on Natural Language Processing for Conversational AI*, pages 96–108, Online. Association for Computational Linguistics.

Aliasgar Kutiyanawala, Prateek Verma, and Zheng Yan. 2018. Towards a simplified ontology for better e-commerce search. *ArXiv*, abs/1807.02039.

Yassine Laadidi and Mohamed Bahaj. 2018. Simplification of owl ontology sources for data warehousing. In *Proceedings of the 2018 International Conference on Software Engineering and Information Management*, ICSIM2018, page 77–81, New York, NY, USA. Association for Computing Machinery.

Yinhan Liu, Myle Ott, Naman Goyal, Jingfei Du, Mandar Joshi, Danqi Chen, Omer Levy, Mike Lewis, Luke Zettlemoyer, and Veselin Stoyanov. 2019. Roberta: A robustly optimized bert pretraining approach. *ArXiv*, abs/1907.11692.

Georgios Meditskos, Efstratios Kontopoulos, Stefanos Vrochidis, and Ioannis Kompatsiaris. 2020. Converness: Ontology-driven conversational awareness and context understanding in multimodal dialogue systems. *Expert Systems*, 37(1):e12378.

Danilo Neves Ribeiro, Shen Wang, Xiaofei Ma, Rui Dong, Xiaokai Wei, Henghui Zhu, Xinchi Chen, Peng Xu, Zhiheng Huang, Andrew Arnold, and Dan Roth. 2022. Entailment tree explanations via iterative retrieval-generation reasoner. In *Findings of the Association for Computational Linguistics: NAACL 2022*, pages 465–475, Seattle, United States. Association for Computational Linguistics.

Christian S Perone, Roberto Silveira, and Thomas S Paula. 2018. Evaluation of sentence embeddings in downstream and linguistic probing tasks. *arXiv preprint arXiv:1806.06259*.

Guangyuan Piao. 2021. Scholarly text classification with sentence bert and entity embeddings. In *Trends and Applications in Knowledge Discovery and Data Mining: PAKDD 2021 Workshops, WSPA, MLMEIN, SDPRA, DARAI, and AI4EPT, Delhi, India, May 11, 2021 Proceedings 25*, pages 79–87. Springer.

Hoifung Poon and Pedro Domingos. 2010. Unsupervised ontology induction from text. In *Proceedings of the 48th annual meeting of the Association for Computational Linguistics*, pages 296–305.

Nils Reimers and Iryna Gurevych. 2019. Sentence-BERT: Sentence embeddings using Siamese BERT-networks. In *Proceedings of the 2019 Conference on Empirical Methods in Natural Language Processing and the 9th International Joint Conference on Natural Language Processing (EMNLP-IJCNLP)*, pages 3982–3992, Hong Kong, China. Association for Computational Linguistics.

Victor Sanh, Lysandre Debut, Julien Chaumond, and Thomas Wolf. 2019. DistilBERT, a distilled version of BERT: smaller, faster, cheaper and lighter. In *5th Workshop on Energy Efficient Machine Learning and Cognitive Computing @ NeurIPS 2019*.

Akshat Shrivastava, Pierce Chuang, Arun Babu, Shrey Desai, Abhinav Arora, Alexander Zotov, and Ahmed Aly. 2021. Span pointer networks for non-autoregressive task-oriented semantic parsing. In *Findings of the Association for Computational Linguistics: EMNLP 2021*, pages 1873–1886, Punta Cana, Dominican Republic. Association for Computational Linguistics.

Akshat Shrivastava, Shrey Desai, Anchit Gupta, Ali Elkahky, Aleksandr Livshits, Alexander Zotov, and Ahmed Aly. 2022. Retrieve-and-fill for scenario-based task-oriented semantic parsing. *arXiv preprint arXiv:2202.00901*.

Lewis Tunstall, Nils Reimers, Unso Eun Seo Jo, Luke Bates, Daniel Korat, Moshe Wasserblat, and Oren Pereg. 2022. Efficient few-shot learning without prompts. *arXiv preprint arXiv:2209.11055*.

Sebastian Varges. 2006. Overgeneration and ranking for spoken dialogue systems. In *Proceedings of the Fourth International Natural Language Generation Conference*, pages 20–22.

Michael Wessel, Girish Acharya, James Carpenter, and Min Yin. 2019. Ontovpa—an ontology-based dialogue management system for virtual personal assistants. In *Advanced Social Interaction with Agents: 8th International Workshop on Spoken Dialog Systems*, pages 219–233. Springer.

Jason R Wilson, Kezhen Chen, Maxwell Crouse, Constantine Nakos, Danilo Neves Ribeiro, Irina Rabkina, and Kenneth D Forbus. 2019. Analogical question answering in a multimodal information kiosk. In *Proceedings of the Seventh Annual Conference on Advances in Cognitive Systems*.

Pengcheng Yin, John Wieting, Avirup Sil, and Graham Neubig. 2022. On the ingredients of an effective zero-shot semantic parser. In *Proceedings of the 60th Annual Meeting of the Association for Computational Linguistics (Volume 1: Long Papers)*, pages 1455–1474, Dublin, Ireland. Association for Computational Linguistics.

Dian Yu, Luheng He, Yuan Zhang, Xinya Du, Panupong Pasupat, and Qi Li. 2021. Few-shot intent classification and slot filling with retrieved examples. In *Proceedings of the 2021 Conference of the North American Chapter of the Association for Computational Linguistics: Human Language Technologies*, pages 734–749, Online. Association for Computational Linguistics.

Yunxiang Zhang and Xiaojun Wan. 2022. MOVER: Mask, over-generate and rank for hyperbole generation. In *Proceedings of the 2022 Conference of the North American Chapter of the Association for Computational Linguistics: Human Language Technologies*, pages 6018–6030, Seattle, United States. Association for Computational Linguistics.

A Appendix

A.1 Domain Agnostic Ontology

To create our domain-agnostic ontology, we manually reviewed all existing slots in the TopV2 ontology and categorized the semantic nature of each slot. We then conflated semantically-similar TopV2 slots under overarching, domain-agnostic terms that cover the overall semantic space of the underlying TopV2 slots. For instance, we categorize slots that indicate the user is requesting a "to-do item", "reminder," and "alarm" as roughly the overall "deliverable" item that is being requested, hence conflating the domain-specific slots SL:TODO, SL:METHOD_TIMER, and SL:ALARM_NAME under the domain-agnostic slot SL:DELIVERABLE. Table 2 contains the mapping between the TopV2 ontology and the domain agnostic ontology used in this work.

Domain-agnostic (DA) slots	Domain-specific (DS) slots
SL:DELIVERABLE	SL:TYPE_REACTION, SL:TODO, SL:TODO_NEW SL:METHOD_TIMER, SL:TIMER_NAME, SL:ALARM_NAME
SL:RECIPIENT	SL:RECIPIENT, SL:PERSON_REMINDED_ADDED, SL:PERSON_REMINDED_REMOVED, SL:PERSON_REMINDED, SL:ATTENDEE_REMOVED, SL:ATTENDEE_ADDED
SL:SCOPE_TEMPORAL	SL:DATE_TIME, SL:DATE_TIME_RECURRING, SL:DURATION, SL:PERIOD, SL:RECURRING_DATE_TIME, SL:TIME_ZONE, SL:DATE_TIME_DEPARTURE, SL:DATE_TIME_ARRIVAL, SL:FREQUENCY, SL:RECURRING_DATE_TIME_NEW, SL:DATE_TIME_NEW, SL:SCOPE_TEMPORAL_RECURRING
SL:SCOPE_LOC	SL:LOCATION, SL:POINT_ON_MAP, SL:LOCATION_HOME, SL:LOCATION_USER, SL:LOCATION_MODIFIER, SL:WAYPOINT_ADDED, SL:LOCATION_WORK
SL:SCOPE_DISAM	SL:ORDINAL, SL:TYPE_CONTENT, SL:GROUP, SL:RESOURCE, SL:CONTENT_EMOJI, SL:TYPE_CONTACT, SL:MUTUAL_EMPLOYER, SL:MUTUAL_SCHOOL, SL:TYPE_INFO, SL:MUTUAL_LOCATION, SL:CONTACT_RELATED, SL:MUSIC_GENRE, SL:UNIT_DISTANCE, SL:WEATHER_TEMPERATURE_UNIT, SL:MEASUREMENT_UNIT, SL:METHOD_RETRIEVAL_REMINDER
SL:OTHER_OPEN_TEXT	SL:CATEGORY_EVENT, SL:SEARCH_RADIUS, SL:ATTRIBUTE_EVENT, SL:CATEGORY_LOCATION, SL:NAME_EVENT, SL:ATTENDEE, SL:ATTENDEE_EVENT, SL:TYPE_RELATION, SL:ORGANIZER_EVENT, SL:TAG_MESSAGE, SL:CONTENT_EXACT, SL:MUSIC_TYPE, SL:MUSIC_TRACK_TITLE, SL:MUSIC_ALBUM_TITLE, SL:MUSIC_PLAYLIST_TITLE, SL:MUSIC_RADIO_ID, SL:METHOD_TRAVEL, SL:JOB, SL:WEATHER_ATTRIBUTE, SL:OBSTRUCTION_AVOID, SL:ROAD_CONDITION_AVOID, SL:ROAD_CONDITION
SL:NUMS	SL:AMOUNT, SL:AGE
SL:PROPER_NAME	SL:NAME_EVENT, SL:CONTACT, SL:ORGANIZER_EVENT, SL:SENDER, SL:MUSIC_TRACK_TITLE, SL:MUSIC_PROVIDER_NAME, SL:MUSIC_ALBUM_TITLE, SL:MUSIC_ARTIST_NAME, SL:SOURCE, SL:DESTINATION, SL:PATH, SL:PATH_AVOID, SL:WAYPOINT_AVOID, SL:LOCATION_CURRENT, SL:PATH_AVOID, SL:WAYPOINT_AVOID, SL:LOCATION_CURRENT, SL:WAYPOINT, SL:ATTENDEE, SL:NAME_APP

Table 2: Mapping between `TopV2` ontology and our proposed domain agnostic ontology.

Co-evolving Data-driven and NLU-driven Synthesizers for Generating Code in Domain Growth and Data Scarcity

Jiasheng Gu[†], **Zifan Nan**[§], **Zhiyuan Peng**[§], **Xipeng Shen**[§], **Dongkuan Xu**[§]
[†]University of Southern California; [§]North Carolina State University;
gujiashe@usc.edu; nanzf1993@gmail.com; jerrypeng1937@gmail.com
xshen5@ncsu.edu; dxu27@ncsu.edu

Abstract

Natural language programming automatically generates code based on a user's text query. Recent solutions are either data-driven or natural language understanding (NLU)-driven. However, the data-driven synthesizer requires a large number of query-code pairs for training, which hinders its application to low-resource programming languages with growing domains whose functionality and grammar can be actively updated. NLU-driven synthesizers solve this problem, but their code generation is slow and their performance rapidly saturates in the presence of ever-increasing data. In this paper, we propose a circular training framework, *Colead*, which co-evolves both the data-driven synthesizer and the NLU-driven synthesizer to achieve high-quality code generation in the presence of data scarcity and domain growth. The NLU-driven synthesizer generates query-code pairs to update the data-driven synthesizer, which shares a part of its updated model to improve the NLU-driven synthesizers, enabling the co-evolution of both. Experiments show that *Colead* gives better results than the baselines in the presence of domain growth and data scarcity, and *Colead* consistently improves the performance of both data-driven and NLU-driven synthesizers over the co-evolvement.

1 Introduction

Natural language (NL) programming aims to automatically generate programming code based on a user's text query (Xu et al., 2022b). It has gained increasing research interest in recent years and has a wide range of applications, not only providing an intuitive programming interface that democratizes artificial intelligence to common users (Chen et al., 2021) but also reducing the time and labor cost of turning ideas into code implementations (Yaghmazadeh et al., 2017; Desai et al., 2016).

Typical NL programming approaches can be categorized as rule-driven or data-driven. A rule-driven synthesizer generates code through predefined domain-specific rules, which requires expert knowledge. It made progress in early NL programming research (Le et al., 2013) but gradually lost its appeal due to technical difficulties in adapting to different programming languages. In parallel, data-driven synthesizers based on deep learning techniques have dominated recent studies (Bavishi et al., 2019; Gu et al., 2016; Li et al., 2022). They generate code through a neural network model. Training of the models requires large amounts of parallel data (Polosukhin and Skidanov, 2018), where each text prompt is paired with a corresponding piece of code. Data-driven synthesizers tend to outperform rule-driven synthesizers in many general-purpose languages (GPLs), like Python, C++, etc., which have massive parallel data available.

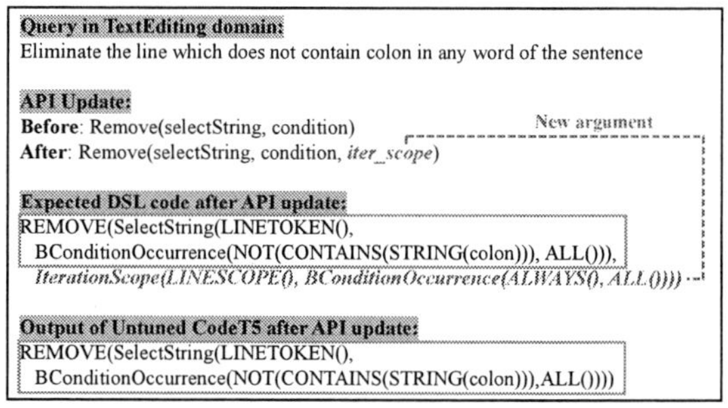

Figure 1: An example of a data-driven model generating code after one API updates in TextEditing (Desai et al., 2016) domain. The API *REMOVE* has a new argument. Without re-training, CodeT5 fails to accommodate this update (shown in blue) and will still generate code for the outdated API (shown in green boxes).

However, there are plenty of domain-specific languages (DSLs) that are low-resource. Some DSLs are dedicated to a specific application domain and has few usages and scarce parallel data. The problem of data scarcity hinders the application of data-driven synthesizers. Another challenging problem is the domain growth of programming languages, which are constantly updated in terms of grammar

Proceedings of the 2nd Workshop in Pattern-based Approaches to NLP in the Age of Deep Learning , pages 64–74
December 6, 2023. ©2023 Association for Computational Linguistics

and functionality. Figure 1 shows an example of a data-driven model (CodeT5) that cannot generate correct code after an API update. To adapt to these updates, data-driven synthesizers require frequent re-training, and it would be labor-intensive and time-consuming to collect new data for the update.

Natural language understanding (NLU)-driven synthesizers have recently been proposed as a compromise between rule-driven and data-driven synthesizers (Nan et al., 2020, 2021; Young et al., 2022; Nan et al., 2022). It circumvents the huge need for parallel data in training by utilizing input user queries and API documentation. Whenever the language is updated with a new API and programming grammar, only the API documentation needs to be modified accordingly to generate the new functional code. However, NLU-driven synthesizers have some limitations. To generate code, grammar and dependency graphs need to be built and traversed, which can be time-consuming and a bottleneck to the speed of code generation. As the training data increases, NLU-driven synthesizers quickly reach performance saturation and become inferior to data-driven synthesizers.

In this paper, we propose a co-evolving framework, *Colead* (for "Co-learning Rule and Data from Documention") that combines NLU-driven and data-driven synthesizers to exploit their complementary strengths and enable code generation in the presence of data scarcity and domain growth (Blum and Mitchell, 1998). *Colead* consists of three key components: a retriever, an NLU-driven synthesizer, and a data-driven synthesizer. The retriever fetches information most relevant to the user's text query from the API documentation. Given the information, the NLU-driven synthesizer constructs a grammar graph and a dependency graph to generate code. The generated code is paired with the user query to train the data-driven synthesizer, which in turn shares its updated encoder with the NLU-driven synthesizer, leading to the co-evolvement of both. We summarize contributions as follows:

- We propose a co-evolving framework, *Colead*, that combines data-driven and NLU-driven synthesizers to achieve their complementary strengths and enable code generation in the presence of data scarcity and domain growth.
- Experimental results on two datasets from distinct domains, Text Editing, and ATIS, demonstrate the effectiveness of *Colead* and show that it can work efficiently in domain growth.
- Our study shows that using both synthesizers together can lead to better performance in solving problems than using only one synthesizer. We show that the NLU-driven synthesizer proves effective in addressing the challenge of limited data availability, while the data-driven synthesizer capitalizes on parallel computing for efficient inference. They complement each other, compensating for their respective drawbacks.

2 Related Work

Large language models pre-trained on vast amounts of code have achieved significant progress in recent years (Li et al., 2022; Chen et al., 2021). These models can be classified as encoder-only, decoder-only, or encoder-decoder. An encoder-only model predicts masked code fragments based on their surroundings. It converts code into effective vector representations and facilitates a myriad of downstream tasks, such as code summarization (Ahmad et al., 2020), code classification (Gilda, 2017), and code clone detection (Ain et al., 2019; Fang et al., 2020). The representative models include CuBERT (Kanade et al., 2020), CodeBERT (Feng et al., 2020), and GraphCodeBERT (Guo et al., 2021). By contrast, a decoder-only model, such as CodeGPT (Lu et al., 2021), CODEGEN (Nijkamp et al., 2022), CERT (Zan et al., 2022), and Codex (Chen et al., 2021), predicts the next token given the previous tokens in an auto-regressive manner. However, these models are not a perfect fit for natural language programming tasks.

An encoder-decoder model first uses an encoder to encode the input sequence and then decodes it with a decoder into an output sequence conditioned on the input sequence. CodeT5 (Wang et al., 2021; Le et al., 2022), PLBART (Ahmad et al., 2021), PolyCoder (Xu et al., 2022a), and AlphaCode (Li et al., 2022) are examples of such models in code. Encoder-decoder models perform well on conditional code generation, such as code annotation, natural language programming, etc. Note that both decoder-only and encoder-decoder models can be employed directly for code generation. These models all share the drawback of requiring an abundance of data.

On the contrary, natural language understanding-driven approaches (Nan et al., 2020, 2021; Young

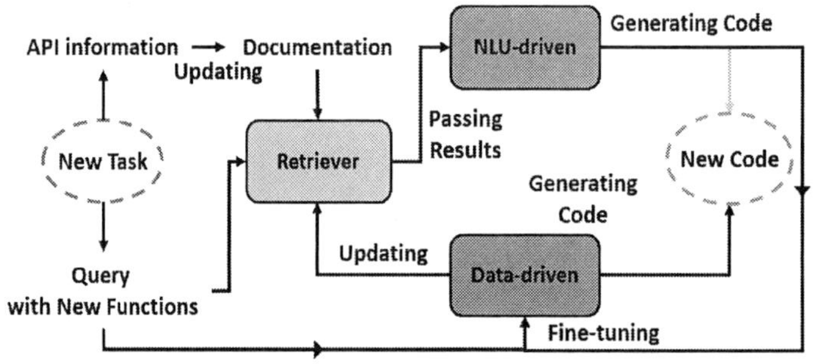

Figure 2: The overview of *Colead*. The main components are the retriever, the NLU-driven synthesizer, and the data-driven synthesizer. Retriever creates a circle by connecting NLU-driven and data-driven components, which serves as a basis for co-evolvement. This circle evolves iteratively to enhance each other's performance.

et al., 2022; Nan et al., 2022) require no training examples. They apply NLP techniques to both natural language (NL) queries and API documentations, extract the key components inside the NL queries and compose the mapped APIs into code expressions following the domain grammar. However, NLU-driven methods are not as powerful as data-driven models when there is a lot of data available for training.

3 Methodology

The major challenge of this work is how to efficiently connect the NLU-driven and data-driven synthesizers so that the joined framework possesses the ability to alleviate data scarcity and domain growth problems while ensuring performance limits and inference speed. The *Colead* framework is proposed to address this challenge, as shown in Fig 2. It has three key components: a retriever, an NLU-driven synthesizer, and a data-driven synthesizer.

3.1 Cycle of Co-evolvement

pThe cycle of co-evolvement is the core of our approach. It starts with the retriever fetching the relevant API documentation based on the user's text query. With the retrieved API documentation and the input query, the NLU-driven synthesizer generates the corresponding code without query-code pairs. Then, the generated code is paired with the query to train the data-driven synthesizer, which in turn shares its well-trained encoder to update the retriever. The updated retriever has a better matching ability and improves the data-driven synthesizer. In this way, the whole process forms a positive circle and co-evolution can be achieved.

The NLU-driven synthesizer, as the teacher of the data-driven synthesizer, reduces the huge demand on human labor to collect query-code pairs, which mitigates the data scarcity issue of DSLs. In addition, the introduced retriever can handle code generation for DSL in domain growth, where the DSL is under active development with frequent updates of new API functions. When new APIs are developed, they only need to be registered in the documentation. New queries from users along with the information retrieved from the updated documentation can be fed into the NLU-driven synthesizer to generate new functional code, which enables the supervised training of the data-driven synthesizer.

3.2 Retriever

The retriever is a shared front end of both the NLU-driven and the data-driven synthesizers. It maps a user's natural language query to the related API description in the documentation.

Specifically, both the natural language query and the API documentation are tokenized by Stanford-CoreNLP (Manning et al., 2014). Initially, exact match is performed based on the description to get the API associated with the query. In other words, the keyword of the query must be present in the API description. Such strict match condition is hard to satisfy, making the retriever fail to retrieve relevant keywords for many queries. To relax the condition and make fuzzy match possible, after the first round of co-evolution, the encoder of the data-driven synthesizer is leveraged to generate dense vector representations of tokens. Two tokens are considered to be matched when the cosine similarity of their vector representations exceeds a pre-defined threshold, which is tuned to have the best result based on experiments.

To realize fuzzy match, the encoder of CodeT5 and SimCSE (Gao et al., 2021) are explored in our

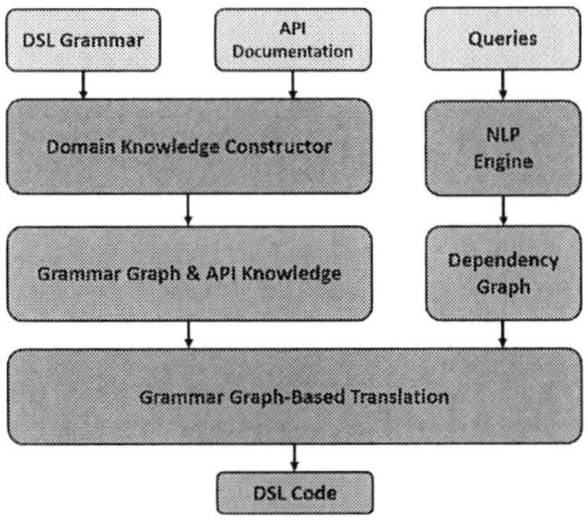

Figure 3: General structure diagram of NLU-driven code generator. It has three main components: a domain knowledge constructor, an NLP engine, and a grammar-graph–based translation module. The grammar graph enables the generated code to follow DSL grammar explicitly. The dependency graph guides the generation of code to follow the logic of the query.

experiment. SimCSE is a simple contrastive learning method that learns embeddings from unlabeled or labeled data. In our experiments, SimCSE is trained only on the queries and API documentation and employed for extracting token embedding.

3.3 NLU-driven Synthesizer

With the retrieved API and user queries, the NLU-driven synthesizer generates the corresponding code by following DSL grammar rules without learning from any specific parallel data.

A typical NLU-driven synthesizer has three components as shown in Fig 3 3: a domain knowledge constructor that processes the domain knowledge to aid code synthesis; an NLP engine that converts an NL-based query to a dependency graph and a grammar-graph–based translation module that generates code based on the dependency graph. The domain knowledge constructor takes two files as input: a document containing all the input and output parameters of the API and their descriptions, and a grammar file containing the context-free grammar written in Backus-Naur form (BNF) (Wikipedia contributors, 2022). The constructor parses the input file and generates two outputs: an API knowledge base for semantic mapping between NL-based queries and APIs, and a grammar graph that defines the search space for code generation. The NLP engine accepts NL-based queries and produces a dependency graph using various NLP techniques, including POS tagging, Lemmatization, NER, and dependency analysis. This dependency graph is

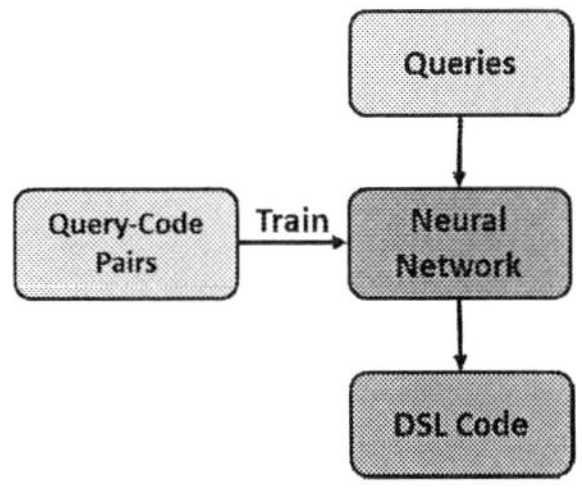

Figure 4: General architecture diagram of a data-driven synthesizer. A data-driven synthesizer can accept natural language queries directly and generate code after training on parallel data. As the training data and model size grow, the performance of the data-driven synthesizer will also progress.

sent to the grammar-graph–based translation module for code generation.

As a "white box" approach, NLU-driven synthesizers are easy to interpret. Synthesis errors can be diagnosed and corrected by humans. However, designing such a synthesizer requires rich expert knowledge. The grammar rules require extensive modifications when adopted to a new program language.

3.4 Data-driven Synthesizer

NLU-driven synthesizers follow grammar rules designed by humans, which cannot cover all situations. The data-driven synthesizer can bridge this gap. It is based on neural networks and outputs the code directly given an input query as Fig 4. The large neural networks have demonstrated impressive success in many NLP tasks, including code generation. We experiment with two pre-trained language models, namely PyCodeGPT (Zan et al., 2022) and CodeT5 (Wang et al., 2021). Our preliminary results show that PyCodeGPT does not perform as well as CodeT5. A possible explanation is that the CodeT5 is an encoder-decoder model, which is more suitable for NL-based code generation. Therefore, we choose CodeT5 as the data-driven synthesizer in our experiments. We also explore CodeT5 in small, base, and large sizes and find that CodeT5-small performed the best. This may be due to the fact that our dataset is small and large models are prone to overfitting.

4 Experiments

Experiments are conducted to answer the following research questions:

- **RQ1:** Can the data-driven synthesizer benefit

DSL	Query	Code
Text Editing	Insert ":" after 1st word.	`INSERT(STRING(:), Position(AFTER(WORDTOKEN()), IntegerSet(INTEGER(1))), IterationScope(LINESCOPE(), BConditionOccurrence(ALWAYS(), ALL())))`
ATIS	I would like to find the cheapest flight from Baltimore to Atlanta	`EXTRACT_ROW_MIN_F(COL_FARE()), AtomicRowPredSet( AtomicRowPred(EQ_DEPARTS(CITY(baltimore), ANY(), ANY(), ANY(), ANY()), EQ_ARRIVES(CITY(atlanta), ANY(), ANY(), ANY(), ANY())))`

Table 1: Examples of Text Editing and ATIS. The text editing language was created to allow consumers to use text editing features without knowing how to program. The Air Travel Information System (ATIS) is a DSL for accessing air travel information.

from the NLU-driven synthesizer of *Colead* in the presence of domain growth?

- **RQ2:** Can NLU-driven synthesizers generate training examples of sufficient quality to address data scarcity?
- **RQ3:** Can the *Colead* enable the NLU-driven synthesizer and the data-driven synthesizer to complete their co-evolvement?

4.1 Experimental Setup

The proposed *Colead* is evaluated on two popular datasets that are collected from different DSLs. Notably, due to the difficulty of collecting DSL data, current DSL datasets typically have only a few hundred entries.

- **Text Editing** [1] is a DSL with 52 APIs in total. It is designed for end-users of Office Suite applications to do text editing without the need of understanding the grammar and semantics of regular expressions, conditionals, loops, etc. The dataset for Text Editing consists of 467 query-code pairs.
- **Air Travel Information System (ATIS)** [2] is a DSL that provides support of predicates and expressions for querying air travel information, such as arrival/departure locations, times, dates, prices, etc. It is based on SQL-style operations, with 51 APIs in total. The dataset of ATIS consists of 535 query-code pairs.

Table 1 presents examples of query-code pairs in two DSL datasets. It can be observed that DSL's grammar format is different from GPL, and DSLs are usually single lines of code to accomplish operations. In addition, because DSLs require functions to be streamlined and compressed, the logic for writing is different from GPL. As a result, data-driven synthesizers trained on the GPLs cannot be deployed for these DSLs without fine-tuning.

We propose to use the Exact Match as the measure, i.e., the generated code is considered correct when it is exactly the same as the original code. Although we do not have test cases to test whether the generated code is correct due to the scarcity of DSL data, it is reasonable to use Exact Match because of the small range of variation in DSLs. We follow the dataset setup commonly used in machine learning, with a ratio of 8:2 for training and validation of the dataset.

Table 3 shows the results of the growing ATIS domain.

4.2 Scenario of Domain Growth

Programming languages are non-static. They are constantly growing and being updated with new functionality. Such domain growth is common in the real world, especially for DSLs.

To answer RQ1, we simulate this situation by incrementally adding and updating the APIs in the DSL documentation and adding new query code pairs associated with these new APIs to the training and validation datasets.

We divide the data into three groups, called Original Task (OT), Incompletely New Task (INT), and Completely New Task (CNT), as described in the caption of Table 2. In the original task, the original DSL implemented only basic API functionality. As the language evolves, new high-level APIs are

[1] shorturl.at/npFIS

[2] shorturl.at/sxyS5

	Stage 1			Stage 2			Stage 3		
	ot	int	cnt	ot	int	cnt	ot	int	cnt
Golden Data	OT			OT+INT			OT+CNT		
	82.54	00.00	00.00	86.13	80.00	00.00	88.88	00.00	80.00
Baseline	OT			OT+INT			OT+CNT		
	-			84.12	43.33	00.00	77.77	00.00	43.33
Ours (*Colead*)	OT			OT+INT			OT+CNT		
	-			85.71	50.00	00.00	85.71	00.00	50.00

Table 2: We train CodeT5 (Wang et al., 2021) on the growing TextEditing domain and use the Exact Match results. i) OT and ot, INT and int, CNT and cnt represent the training and validation set of Original Task(OT), Incompletely New Task(INT) and Complete New Task(CNT). ii) Markers without underlines mean that they belong to the golden dataset. Markers with underlines mean that the code for this dataset is generated from HISyn (Nan et al., 2020). Markers with double underlines mean that the data pairs in this dataset are 5 samples drawn from the correct dataset. iii) In Stage 1, only the Original Task is the subject of experiments. Stage 2 involves both Original Task and Incompletely New Task. In Stage 3, both Original Task and Complete New Task are the subjects of experiments.

	Stage 1			Stage 2			Stage 3		
	ot	int	cnt	ot	int	cnt	ot	int	cnt
Golden Data	OT			OT+INT			OT+CNT		
	79.76	00.00	00.00	96.42	70.83	00.00	95.00	00.00	00.00
Baseline	OT			OT+INT			OT+CNT		
	-			97.61	45.83	00.00	97.38	00.00	56.52
Ours (*Colead*)	OT			OT+INT			OT+CNT		
	-			97.62	25.00	00.00	97.61	00.00	17.39

Table 3: We also train CodeT5 (Wang et al., 2021) on the growing ATIS domain and use the same format as Table 2.

added. They may be incomplete and only partially functional. We refer to the data of these new APIs as Incompletely New Task. Finally, new APIs are developed and completed, bringing data for Completely New Task. For example, in the Original Task in the text editing domain, there is no REMOVE API. As shown in Table 4, the Incompletely New Task introduces the REMOVE API with limited functionality. In the Complete New Task, the IterationScope parameter is added to set the iteration scope to make REMOVE API complete.

Experiments are divided into three stages. In Stage 1, experiments are carried out on Original Task only. In Stage 2, Original Task and Incompletely New Task are included. And in Stage 3, Original Task and Completely New Task are included. We use three different data settings to train CodeT5 (Wang et al., 2021). The results are shown in Table 2. HISyn (Nan et al., 2020) tends to generate multiple code candidates because it is common for HISyn to construct graphs and traverse them to find several paths that satisfy its requirements. We choose to construct the dataset by selecting only

Incompletely New Task (INT)

```
REMOVE(SelectString(NUMBERTOKEN(),
BConditionOccurrence(
BETWEENCOND(STRING(colon),
STRING(colon),IMM()),ALL())))
```

Complete New Task (CNT)

```
REMOVE(SelectString(NUMBERTOKEN(),
BConditionOccurrence(
BETWEENCOND(STRING(colon),
STRING(colon), IMM()), ALL())),
IterationScope(LINESCOPE(),
BConditionOccurrence(ALWAYS(), ALL())))
```

Table 4: Examples of Incompletely New Task (INT) and Complete New Task (CNT). Notably, Original Task (OT) has no new task. Thus, we omit its table illustration for brevity. Compared with INT, the IterationScope is added to the REMOVE API to enable it to set the iteration scope in CNT.

the shortest of all candidates, as the results show that it is better than selecting all candidates. Although selecting all candidates has a larger quantity, a number of incorrect codes introduce noise and reduce data quality. The row "Golden" implies the accuracy that CodeT5 can achieve with exactly the right data. This is the best result we can expect from our strategy. We want the exact matching accuracy of the "Ours" row to be as close as possible to the "Golden" row. Similar results are obtained for ATIS, shown in Table 3.

Stage 1: This stage represents the early development of the DSL, where new tasks have not yet been introduced. At this stage, the training set has only examples of the Original Task. CodeT5 trained on data from the Original Task performs well on the corresponding validation set but has an accuracy of 0 on the validation set of the new task. Although these validation sets belong to the same domain, CodeT5 cannot handle the new API. This indicates that the model trained with the old data cannot handle the new API.

Stage 2: This stage represents a DSL in an intermediate stage, where a new task has been introduced, but it is still incomplete and simple. In order to generate the code for the new task, we need to supplement the corresponding API grammar and description. CodeT5 trained with the data generated by our method accomplishes the same adaptation to the Incompletely New Task as CodeT5 trained with the complete data. By adding the new task-related APIs to the documentation, our method is able to generate data that can be used for training in this stage.

Stage 3: This stage represents a DSL in its final stage, where a new task has been introduced and its development has been completed. Our method requires that both the corresponding grammar and the description in the API documentation be updated to be considered complete. Training data containing complete query-code pairs allows CodeT5 to learn the complete API, completing the migration from Incompletely New Task to Completely New Task. The data generated by our method accomplishes this as well, proving that it not only works on new tasks but can be applied to task updates as well.

From the above three stages, we can observe that our method can consistently provide data to CodeT5 for training in domain growth.

4.3 Scenario of Data Scarcity

Data scarcity occurs frequently in DSLs, as a number of DSLs are designed for specific applications. **To answer RQ2**, we analyze the performance of our method in solving the data scarcity problem. To establish a point of comparison, we set a baseline by including five relevant examples from the new task (specifically, the Incomplete New Task in Stage 2 and the Complete New Task in Stage 3) in the training set. This will be used as a baseline for evaluating the performance of our method.

The results are summarized in Table 2, from which it can be observed that our method outperforms the baseline in all stages. Compared to CodeT5 trained with golden data in Stage 1, the evaluation results of the baseline and $Colead$ on Original Task in Stage 2 increase by 1.58% and 3.17% respectively. This indicates that the commonality of the new task with the old task allows the introduction of new task data to enhance the model's ability to handle the old task. The change in the evaluation results for Incomplete New Task is more pronounced, with the baseline and $Colead$ increasing from 0 to 43.33% and 50.00%, respectively. In Stage 3, the same changes continue to appear for the Completely New Task. To sum up, the above results show that our method can have better help than providing a few positive samples.

4.4 Study of Co-evolvement

To answer RQ3, we experimentally verify the effectiveness of $Colead$ co-evolving on both NLU-driven synthesizers and data-driven synthesizers.

We observe the performance changes of the two synthesizers throughout their co-evolvement. For CodeT5, we use a setup similar to the third stage in Section 4.2, i.e., using the code generated by HISyn for training. For HISyn, since it does not require training, we use the entire dataset for testing. To highlight the role of the retriever, we use documents whose descriptions have not been manually optimized, which places a higher demand on the matching ability of the retriever. We introduce SimCSE (Gao et al., 2021) as the baseline for comparison. The loop starts with an exact match retriever, which is then replaced by a trained CodeT5 encoder. From Table 5, we can observe that $Colead$ leads consistent improvements to CodeT5 during the loop. The "Original" row represents the results of CodeT5 trained on the data generated by HISyn using the exact match retriever.

		CodeT5		HISyn	
		TextEditing	ATIS	TextEditing	ATIS
Baselines	SimCSE	59.59	62.62	22.79	8.95
	Original	56.99	62.62	23.48	10.48
Ours(*Colead*)	Loop 1	58.06	63.55	23.44	10.37
	Loop 2	59.14	**65.42**	24.27	**10.63**
	Loop 3	**60.22**	61.68	**24.42**	10.37

Table 5: Exact Match accuracy of CodeT5 in the loops of *Colead* is on the left. Exact Match accuracy of HISyn with different retrievers in the loops of *Colead* is on the right. The first four lines belong to the Co-evolvement loop of *Colead*. SimCSE is independent of the circle and is not part of it. The bolded numbers are the best results.

Loop 1: From the original to Loop 1, the Exact Match of CodeT5 increases from 56.99% to 58.06% on the TextEditing dataset and from 62.62% to 63.55% on the ATIS dataset, which is contributed by replacing the exact match retriever with the encoder of the CodeT5. Meanwhile, the Exact Match of HISyn slightly decreases but it exceeds the Original later.

Loop 2: CodeT5 continues to improve its performance by 1.08% and 1.87% on the TextEditing and ATIS datasets. We can observe that while SimCSE can outperform Original and Loop 1, *Colead* outperforms SimCSE after Loop 2. HISyn continues to improve by 0.83% and 0.26% on the TextEditing and ATIS datasets, and it outperforms Original and SimCSE.

Loop 3: In Loop 3, CodeT5 and HISyn perform best among these cases on the TextEditing dataset. However, it is observed that the accuracy of ATIS decreased, which is unexpected. By diagnosing the grammar and dependency graphs, we are able to determine the root cause of the errors. Our analysis shows that the fuzzy match retriever increases the number of candidate APIs for mapping. The expansion of the range of candidate APIs exceeds the capability of HISyn, resulting in a degradation of the quality of the generated code.

We analyzed how *Colead* can improve NLU-driven synthesizers with reference to specific examples. Table 6 shows a specific case where the original HISyn generation failed but succeeded in *Colead*. The original HISyn generation fails because the semantic mapping in the retriever is not sufficient to handle the ambiguity of natural language. The updated retriever in *Colead* compensates for this shortcoming. We know from the grammar graph construction log that the original HISyn does not map the word "Remove" to the REMOVE API correctly but the wrong INSERT API. The reason is that the description in the API documentation does not explicitly include "Remove". The fuzzy match retriever is able to correctly match the corresponding API and therefore get the correct code.

Query	Remove colon before every line

Original	`INSERT(STRING(colon),`
	`Position(BEFORE(LINETOKEN()),ALL()),`
	`IterationScope(LINESCOPE(),`
	`BConditionOccurrence(ALWAYS(),ALL())))`

Colead	`REMOVE(SelectString(STRING(colon),`
	`BConditionOccurrence(`
	`BEFORECOND(LINETOKEN(),IMM()),ALL())),`
	`IterationScope(LINESCOPE(),`
	`BConditionOccurrence(ALWAYS(),ALL())))`

Query	Remove colon before every line

Original	`INSERT(STRING(colon),`
	`Position(BEFORE(LINETOKEN()),ALL()),`
	`IterationScope(LINESCOPE(),`
	`BConditionOccurrence(ALWAYS(),ALL())))`

Colead	`REMOVE(`
	`SelectString(STRING(colon),`
	`BConditionOccurrence(`
	`BEFORECOND(LINETOKEN(),IMM()),ALL())),`
	`IterationScope(LINESCOPE(),`
	`BConditionOccurrence(ALWAYS(),ALL())))`

Table 6: Comparison between the original HISyn and *Colead* generated code. In the example of the table, the original is wrong and *Colead* is correct. The original HISyn make a wrong decision for the query because it could not map near-synonyms.

From Table 5, we find that the performance trend of HISyn is similar to that of CodeT5. Although occasionally decreasing at the same time, they consistently improve with the cycle, which proves that they are co-evolving.

5 Discussion

We try ChatGPT (Ouyang et al., 2022a) to accomplish our task and compare it to our approach. To ensure that ChatGPT has the same data situation

Query	Insert colon before every 1st word
Ours	`INSERT(STRING(colon), Position(BEFORE(WORDTOKEN()), IntegerSet(INTEGER(1))), IterationScope(LINESCOPE(), BConditionOccurrence(ALWAYS(), ALL())))`
0-shot ChatGPT	insert ":", start all
5-shot ChatGPT	`INSERT STRING(colon) Position(BEFORE(1st()), ALL()) IterationScope(LINESCOPE(), BConditionOccurrence(ALWAYS(), ALL()))`

Table 7: Comparison between ChatGPT and *Colead* generated code. In the example of the table, 0-shot ChatGPT is completely wrong and *Colead* is correct. But 5-shot ChatGPT performs well.

as our approach, we feed the entire grammar and documentation into ChatGPT. We use the prompt "Based on the above grammar and documentation, write DSL code to accomplish my query" to instruct ChatGPT and prepend 5 query-code pairs in the 5-shot setting.

In Table 7, we observed a difference in performance between ChatGPT and *Colead*. While *Colead* can output exactly the right answer, the performance of 0-shot ChatGPT and 5-shot ChatGPT is very different.

ChatGPT does not require any additional training. It utilizes contextual information to provide inferences, which demonstrates its versatility and adaptability to various tasks. However, if no sample is provided, ChatGPT would not perform well. 0-shot ChatGPT partially understands the request and outputs plausible code. 5-shot ChatGPT generates an almost correct answer, but the grammar is not standardized enough. While correcting it once could easily solve the problem, this step alone incurs significant labor costs, whereas *Colead* is generated strictly according to grammatical rules, and thus has a much smaller probability of grammatical errors.

6 Conclusion and Future Work

Domain growth and data scarcity are two challenges that hinder the application of code generation to DSLs. We have shown that our proposed *Colead* framework can effectively mitigate these problems. Our framework combines NLU-driven and data-driven synthesizers, where the NLU-driven synthesizer alleviates the data-hungry issue of the data-driven one and the data-driven synthesizer provides better semantic mapping for the NLU-driven synthesizer to improve code quality.

Future work should consider code generation by leveraging grammar rules to regularize language models. Components in the NLU-driven synthesizer can be further improved, e.g., semantic mapping, NLP engines, etc. More powerful language models, such as GPT3 (Brown et al., 2020; Ouyang et al., 2022b), can be leveraged to improve the data-driven synthesizer.

Limitations

Number of datasets. Due to the limited number of publicly available DSL datasets, the authors evaluate their method on two DSL datasets. In order to fully validate the capability of the proposed method, it would be desirable to collect more real-world datasets. One potential approach is to manually collect DSL data for a domain, however, this would be costly. Another approach is to apply active learning methods (Ren et al., 2021) to automatically identify relevant datasets as alternative DSL datasets.

Ethics Statement

The authors declare that they adhere to general ethical principles, professional responsibility, principles of professional leadership, and ethical guidelines. In studies involving human participants, all procedures were in accordance with ACL's ethics policy.

References

Wasi Uddin Ahmad, Saikat Chakraborty, Baishakhi Ray, and Kai-Wei Chang. 2020. A transformer-based approach for source code summarization. arXiv preprint arXiv:2005.00653.

Wasi Uddin Ahmad, Saikat Chakraborty, Baishakhi Ray, and Kai-Wei Chang. 2021. Unified pre-training for program understanding and generation. In NAACL-HLT, pages 2655–2668. Association for Computational Linguistics.

Qurat Ul Ain, Wasi Haider Butt, Muhammad Waseem Anwar, Farooque Azam, and Bilal Maqbool. 2019. A systematic review on code clone detection. IEEE Access, 7:86121–86144.

Rohan Bavishi, Caroline Lemieux, Roy Fox, Koushik Sen, and Ion Stoica. 2019. Autopandas: neural-backed generators for program synthesis. Proc. ACM Program. Lang., 3(OOPSLA):168:1–168:27.

Avrim Blum and Tom Mitchell. 1998. Combining labeled and unlabeled data with co-training. In

Proceedings of the eleventh annual conference on Computational learning theory, pages 92–100.

Tom B. Brown, Benjamin Mann, Nick Ryder, Melanie Subbiah, Jared Kaplan, Prafulla Dhariwal, Arvind Neelakantan, Pranav Shyam, Girish Sastry, Amanda Askell, Sandhini Agarwal, Ariel Herbert-Voss, Gretchen Krueger, Tom Henighan, Rewon Child, Aditya Ramesh, Daniel M. Ziegler, Jeffrey Wu, Clemens Winter, Christopher Hesse, Mark Chen, Eric Sigler, Mateusz Litwin, Scott Gray, Benjamin Chess, Jack Clark, Christopher Berner, Sam McCandlish, Alec Radford, Ilya Sutskever, and Dario Amodei. 2020. Language models are few-shot learners. In NeurIPS.

Mark Chen, Jerry Tworek, Heewoo Jun, Qiming Yuan, Henrique Ponde de Oliveira Pinto, Jared Kaplan, Harrison Edwards, Yuri Burda, Nicholas Joseph, Greg Brockman, Alex Ray, Raul Puri, Gretchen Krueger, Michael Petrov, Heidy Khlaaf, Girish Sastry, Pamela Mishkin, Brooke Chan, Scott Gray, Nick Ryder, Mikhail Pavlov, Alethea Power, Lukasz Kaiser, Mohammad Bavarian, Clemens Winter, Philippe Tillet, Felipe Petroski Such, Dave Cummings, Matthias Plappert, Fotios Chantzis, Elizabeth Barnes, Ariel Herbert-Voss, William Hebgen Guss, Alex Nichol, Alex Paino, Nikolas Tezak, Jie Tang, Igor Babuschkin, Suchir Balaji, Shantanu Jain, William Saunders, Christopher Hesse, Andrew N. Carr, Jan Leike, Joshua Achiam, Vedant Misra, Evan Morikawa, Alec Radford, Matthew Knight, Miles Brundage, Mira Murati, Katie Mayer, Peter Welinder, Bob McGrew, Dario Amodei, Sam McCandlish, Ilya Sutskever, and Wojciech Zaremba. 2021. Evaluating large language models trained on code. CoRR, abs/2107.03374.

Aditya Desai, Sumit Gulwani, Vineet Hingorani, Nidhi Jain, Amey Karkare, Mark Marron, Sailesh R, and Subhajit Roy. 2016. Program synthesis using natural language. In ICSE, pages 345–356. ACM.

Chunrong Fang, Zixi Liu, Yangyang Shi, Jeff Huang, and Qingkai Shi. 2020. Functional code clone detection with syntax and semantics fusion learning. In Proceedings of the 29th ACM SIGSOFT International Symposium on Software Testing and Analysis, pages 516–527.

Zhangyin Feng, Daya Guo, Duyu Tang, Nan Duan, Xiaocheng Feng, Ming Gong, Linjun Shou, Bing Qin, Ting Liu, Daxin Jiang, and Ming Zhou. 2020. Codebert: A pre-trained model for programming and natural languages. In EMNLP (Findings), volume EMNLP 2020 of Findings of ACL, pages 1536–1547. Association for Computational Linguistics.

Tianyu Gao, Xingcheng Yao, and Danqi Chen. 2021. SimCSE: Simple contrastive learning of sentence embeddings. In Empirical Methods in Natural Language Processing (EMNLP).

Shlok Gilda. 2017. Source code classification using neural networks. In 2017 14th international joint conference on computer science and software engineering (JCSSE), pages 1–6. IEEE.

Xiaodong Gu, Hongyu Zhang, Dongmei Zhang, and Sunghun Kim. 2016. Deep API learning. CoRR, abs/1605.08535.

Daya Guo, Shuo Ren, Shuai Lu, Zhangyin Feng, Duyu Tang, Shujie Liu, Long Zhou, Nan Duan, Alexey Svyatkovskiy, Shengyu Fu, Michele Tufano, Shao Kun Deng, Colin B. Clement, Dawn Drain, Neel Sundaresan, Jian Yin, Daxin Jiang, and Ming Zhou. 2021. Graphcodebert: Pre-training code representations with data flow. In ICLR. OpenReview.net.

Aditya Kanade, Petros Maniatis, Gogul Balakrishnan, and Kensen Shi. 2020. Learning and evaluating contextual embedding of source code. In ICML, volume 119 of Proceedings of Machine Learning Research, pages 5110–5121. PMLR.

Hung Le, Yue Wang, Akhilesh Deepak Gotmare, Silvio Savarese, and Steven Hoi. 2022. CodeRL: Mastering code generation through pretrained models and deep reinforcement learning. In Advances in Neural Information Processing Systems.

Vu Le, Sumit Gulwani, and Zhendong Su. 2013. Smartsynth: synthesizing smartphone automation scripts from natural language. In MobiSys, pages 193–206. ACM.

Yujia Li, David H. Choi, Junyoung Chung, Nate Kushman, Julian Schrittwieser, Rémi Leblond, Tom Eccles, James Keeling, Felix Gimeno, Agustin Dal Lago, Thomas Hubert, Peter Choy, Cyprien de Masson d'Autume, Igor Babuschkin, Xinyun Chen, Po-Sen Huang, Johannes Welbl, Sven Gowal, Alexey Cherepanov, James Molloy, Daniel J. Mankowitz, Esme Sutherland Robson, Pushmeet Kohli, Nando de Freitas, Koray Kavukcuoglu, and Oriol Vinyals. 2022. Competition-level code generation with alphacode. CoRR, abs/2203.07814.

Shuai Lu, Daya Guo, Shuo Ren, Junjie Huang, Alexey Svyatkovskiy, Ambrosio Blanco, Colin B. Clement, Dawn Drain, Daxin Jiang, Duyu Tang, Ge Li, Lidong Zhou, Linjun Shou, Long Zhou, Michele Tufano, Ming Gong, Ming Zhou, Nan Duan, Neel Sundaresan, Shao Kun Deng, Shengyu Fu, and Shujie Liu. 2021. Codexglue: A machine learning benchmark dataset for code understanding and generation. In NeurIPS Datasets and Benchmarks.

Christopher D. Manning, Mihai Surdeanu, John Bauer, Jenny Rose Finkel, Steven Bethard, and David McClosky. 2014. The stanford corenlp natural language processing toolkit. In ACL (System Demonstrations), pages 55–60. The Association for Computer Linguistics.

Zifan Nan, Hui Guan, and Xipeng Shen. 2020. Hisyn: human learning-inspired natural language programming. In ESEC/SIGSOFT FSE, pages 75–86. ACM.

Zifan Nan, Hui Guan, Xipeng Shen, and Chunhua Liao. 2021. Deep nlp-based co-evolvement for synthesizing code analysis from natural language. In CC '21: 30th ACM SIGPLAN International Conference on Compiler Construction, Virtual Event, Republic of Korea, March 2-3, 2021, pages 141–152. ACM.

Zifan Nan, Xipeng Shen, and Hui Guan. 2022. Enabling near real-time nlu-driven natural language programming through dynamic grammar graph-based translation. In IEEE/ACM International Symposium on Code Generation and Optimization, CGO 2022, Seoul, Korea, Republic of, April 2-6, 2022, pages 278–289. IEEE.

Erik Nijkamp, Bo Pang, Hiroaki Hayashi, Lifu Tu, Huan Wang, Yingbo Zhou, Silvio Savarese, and Caiming Xiong. 2022. A conversational paradigm for program synthesis. CoRR, abs/2203.13474.

Long Ouyang, Jeff Wu, Xu Jiang, Diogo Almeida, Carroll L. Wainwright, Pamela Mishkin, Chong Zhang, Sandhini Agarwal, Katarina Slama, Alex Ray, John Schulman, Jacob Hilton, Fraser Kelton, Luke Miller, Maddie Simens, Amanda Askell, Peter Welinder, Paul Christiano, Jan Leike, and Ryan Lowe. 2022a. Training language models to follow instructions with human feedback.

Long Ouyang, Jeff Wu, Xu Jiang, Diogo Almeida, Carroll L. Wainwright, Pamela Mishkin, Chong Zhang, Sandhini Agarwal, Katarina Slama, Alex Ray, John Schulman, Jacob Hilton, Fraser Kelton, Luke Miller, Maddie Simens, Amanda Askell, Peter Welinder, Paul F. Christiano, Jan Leike, and Ryan Lowe. 2022b. Training language models to follow instructions with human feedback. CoRR, abs/2203.02155.

Illia Polosukhin and Alexander Skidanov. 2018. Neural program search: Solving programming tasks from description and examples. CoRR, abs/1802.04335.

Pengzhen Ren, Yun Xiao, Xiaojun Chang, Po-Yao Huang, Zhihui Li, Brij B Gupta, Xiaojiang Chen, and Xin Wang. 2021. A survey of deep active learning. ACM computing surveys (CSUR), 54(9):1–40.

Yue Wang, Weishi Wang, Shafiq R. Joty, and Steven C. H. Hoi. 2021. Codet5: Identifier-aware unified pre-trained encoder-decoder models for code understanding and generation. In EMNLP (1), pages 8696–8708. Association for Computational Linguistics.

Wikipedia contributors. 2022. Backus–naur form — Wikipedia, the free encyclopedia. [Online; accessed 18-January-2023].

Frank F. Xu, Uri Alon, Graham Neubig, and Vincent Josua Hellendoorn. 2022a. A systematic evaluation of large language models of code. In MAPS@PLDI, pages 1–10. ACM.

Frank F Xu, Bogdan Vasilescu, and Graham Neubig. 2022b. In-ide code generation from natural language: Promise and challenges. ACM Transactions on Software Engineering and Methodology (TOSEM), 31(2):1–47.

Navid Yaghmazadeh, Yuepeng Wang, Isil Dillig, and Thomas Dillig. 2017. Sqlizer: query synthesis from natural language. Proceedings of the ACM on Programming Languages, 1(OOPSLA):1–26.

Mitchell Young, Zifan Nan, and Xipeng Shen. 2022. IDE augmented with human-learning inspired natural language programming. In 44th IEEE/ACM International Conference on Software Engineering: Companion Proceedings, ICSE Companion 2022, Pittsburgh, PA, USA, May 22-24, 2022, pages 110–114. ACM/IEEE.

Daoguang Zan, Bei Chen, Dejian Yang, Zeqi Lin, Minsu Kim, Bei Guan, Yongji Wang, Weizhu Chen, and Jian-Guang Lou. 2022. CERT: continual pre-training on sketches for library-oriented code generation. In IJCAI, pages 2369–2375. ijcai.org.

Complementary Roles of Inference and Language Models in QA

Liang Cheng[†] **Mohammad Javad Hosseini**[‡] **Mark Steedman**[†]
[†]University of Edinburgh [‡]Google Research
L.Cheng-13@sms.ed.ac.uk javadh@google.com steedman@inf.ed.ac.uk

Abstract

Answering open-domain questions through unsupervised methods poses challenges for both machine-reading (MR) and language model (LM) -based approaches. The MR-based approach suffers from sparsity issues in extracted knowledge graphs (KGs), while the performance of the LM-based approach significantly depends on the quality of the retrieved context for questions. In this paper, we compare these approaches and propose a novel methodology that leverages directional predicate entailment (inference) to address these limitations. We use entailment graphs (EGs), with natural language predicates as nodes and entailment as edges, to enhance parsed KGs by inferring unseen assertions, effectively mitigating the sparsity problem in the MR-based approach. We also show EGs improve context retrieval for the LM-based approach. Additionally, we present a Boolean QA task, demonstrating that EGs exhibit comparable directional inference capabilities to large language models (LLMs). Our results highlight the importance of inference in open-domain QA and the improvements brought by leveraging EGs.

1 Introduction

Unsupervised open-domain question answering (QA), the task of learning knowledge from a large collection of documents of diversified topics to answer questions, has been a long-standing challenge in NLP, information retrieval and related fields (Moldovan et al., 2000; Brill et al., 2002; Ferrucci et al., 2010).

The traditional machine-reading (MR) approach first extracts a knowledge graph (KG) from an open-domain corpus and then uses the KG for QA (Harrington and Clark, 2007; Reddy et al., 2014; Khot et al., 2017; Meng et al., 2017). This approach offers *explainability*, since the information in KGs is directly supported by the text. However, the relevant assertions need to be exactly stored in the extracted KG, which is often not the case because assertions can be stated in many different ways, while usually only a small subset of them are available in the KG.

On the other hand, language models have been claimed to be capable of performing a wide range of NLP tasks when used in zero-shot or few-shot prompting mode, including open-domain QA, where they have been argued to act as a latent KG over the pretraining data for querying (Petroni et al., 2019; Adolphs et al., 2021; Ali et al., 2021; Onoe et al., 2022; Wang et al., 2020; Radford et al., 2019; Raffel et al., 2019). Advocates of LMs argue that traditional MR approaches relying on KGs built by open relation extraction are prone to errors arising from components like open information extraction and entity linking. In addition to querying LMs directly, it is shown that when relevant context is available and added to the query, the LMs' performance increases significantly (Petroni et al., 2020; Kassner and Schütze, 2020; Chen et al., 2022a). However, while LMs have performed impressively in answering questions on the basis of manually selected contextual documents, their practical usage is limited since automatic retrieval methods do not always return relevant contextual documents to the query.

In this paper, we show that we can leverage directional predicate entailment effectively to alleviate the limitations of both unsupervised approaches to QA. The contributions of this paper are as follows:

(1) We present a comparative analysis of the MR-based and LM-based approaches in multiple QA scenarios. For the MR-based approach, we extract knowledge to construct KGs by parsing a corpus (English Wikipedia in our experiments). For LM-based approach, we follow the previous work in querying the pre-trained LMs. We perform experiments with multiple LMs including BERT (Devlin et al., 2019) and GPT-3.5 (Brown et al., 2020).

Proceedings of the 2nd Workshop in Pattern-based Approaches to NLP in the Age of Deep Learning , pages 75–91
December 6, 2023.

(2) We alleviate the sparsity issues of the MR-based approach by leveraging directional predicate entailments to infer novel assertions for augmenting the parsed KGs.

(3) For LM-based approaches, we propose an unsupervised method to use predicate entailments for more accurate context-document retrieval, showing significant improvements in cloze-style QA tasks.

(4) We propose a novel Boolean QA task to compare the directional inference capabilities of LMs and EGs, presenting evidence that smaller LMs (BERT and RoBERTa) are far behind in inferential capabilities compared to EGs, while larger LMs (GPT-3.5) have similar but complementary capabilities with EGs. Our analysis suggests a role for both EGs and LMs in open-domain QA.

2 Related Work

Open-domain QA with Machine Reading. MR-based approaches aim to extract knowledge from corpora to answer open-domain questions. It is common to express knowledge as a collection of "facts" in the form of triples (subject, relation, object), where subject and object are entities connected by the relations. The extracted KGs store the collection with entities as nodes and relations as edges, which can be used to answer questions.

Semantic parsing is an efficient open-domain information extraction approach for large corpora (Etzioni et al., 2011; Reddy et al., 2014). Harrington and Clark (2007) propose an effective pipeline that extracts facts by utilizing a localized update algorithm, which transfers sentences into syntax structures and generates KGs incrementally. These MR-based approaches are explainable for QA because every answer is supported by source sentences in the text. However, KGs built in this way are limited to exact match between the question form and the triples in the graph. For example, if a triple *(Amon Bazira, be assassinated in, Kenya)* is extracted from the sentence *"Amon Bazira was assassinated in Kenya"*, the KG would not provide an answer to the question *"Where did Amon Bazira die?"* because the training corpus lacks any sentence constituting an exact match, such as *"Amon Bazira died in Kenya"*. As a result, the parsed KG exhibits high precision but low recall on the task.

Using pre-trained LMs as Latent KG. Petroni et al. (2019) claim that pre-trained LMs encode the knowledge presented in large amounts of texts. They query LMs using "fill-in-the-blank" cloze statements, such as *"Amon Bazira was assassinated in [MASK]"*. They report results on Masked Language Models (MLMs) such as BERT, which are optimized to predict the next word in a sequence or fill in masked words. They show promising performance on cloze-style QA tasks. Ali et al. (2021) propose a method for fact extraction based on BERT, using the BERT sentence-encoding algorithm on a corpus already annotated for named entities. Additionally, Petroni et al. (2020) demonstrate the value of retrieved documents in enhancing BERT's performance. Lin et al. (2021); He et al. (2021); Perez et al. (2021) show improved performance for LMs under few-shot settings. Moreover, Alivanistos et al. (2022); Fichtel et al. (2021) propose approaches to train prompt-learning models with supervised datasets, using the generated prompts to enhance LM performance on open-domain QA. Larger LM models, as shown in the works of Brown et al. (2020), demonstrate better performance.

These results suggest that LMs could work as latent KGs by memorizing vast corpora. However, LLMs are expensive to train, and impractical to update for tasks like questions involving recent news events. Smaller neural LMs are faster to retrain, but fail when natural language inference from limited context is required (Petroni et al., 2020). Attempts to fine-tune these LMs with supervision from Natural language inference (NLI) datasets tend to pick up artifacts and show little evidence of learning *directional* common-sense inferences, such as that, *"be assassinated in"* entails *"die in"* but not the reverse (Li et al., 2022a). In this paper, we query LMs for factual knowledge in a zero-shot setting, but show how the LM-based approach could benefit from the MR-based approach and predicate entailment.

Relational Entailment Graphs. Where a KG has entities as nodes and relations as edges, an Entailment Graph (EG) has relations as nodes and directed edges corresponding to the entailment relation. EGs are usually built by first detecting Distributional Inclusion (Dagan et al., 1999; Geffet and Dagan, 2005) among the set of entity tuples involved in pairs of predicates, and then applying global graph learning algorithms (Berant et al., 2010, 2011; Hosseini et al., 2018, 2021). In this paper, we propose methods that utilize EGs to enhance the performance of MR-based and LM-based methods in knowledge completion, leading to significant improvements in open-domain QA.

3 Method

In §3.1, we propose an unsupervised MR-based method that consists of three key steps: A) constructing a KG by semantic parsing (§3.1.1), B) constructing EGs from text (§3.1.2), and C) augmenting the KG with EGs in an unsupervised way to infer latent knowledge (§3.1.3). We then further augment the KG with LM backoff (§3.1.4). In §3.2, we discuss the LM-based approach and propose a method to enhance the performance by extracting highly-relevant contexts using EGs (§3.2.1).

3.1 Machine-Reading Approach

3.1.1 Constructing KG from Corpus

We propose a pipeline to extract KG from corpora with semantic parsing. First, we preprocess the Wikipedia corpus in order to improve the performance of semantic analysis tools by reducing the ambiguity of the raw text. We employ a coreference resolution tool (Lee et al., 2018) to handle coreferences of texts, and then follow Hosseini et al. (2018) and use GraphParser (Reddy et al., 2014) to extract triples from the processed text. GraphParser[1] utilizes a combinatory categorial grammar (CCG) parser (Steedman, 2000) to convert sentences into semantic graphs, which are subsequently transformed into triples. Previous works (Hosseini et al., 2018) show the parser based on CCG performs better than Stanford Open IE (Etzioni et al., 2011; Angeli et al., 2015) in open-domain relation extraction. These extracted triples consist of predicates associated with two arguments. We then assign types to entities by linking them to their corresponding FreeBase IDs using a Named Entity Linking tool, Aidalight (Nguyen et al., 2014). Figure 1 illustrates an example of extracted triples from a raw sentence. After the process, the extracted knowledge is represented in the form of binary predicates and associated entities[2].

3.1.2 Constructing Entailment Graphs

We utilize the EGs extracted from news corpora by Hosseini et al. (2018) as a source of predicate entailments, which is based on the Distributional Inclusion Hypothesis (Dagan et al., 1999; Geffet

[1]The code of GraphParser is available at https://github.com/sivareddyg/graph-parser

[2]The works of KG construction are available at https://github.com/LeonChengg/entGraphQA.git

Steps:

1. Text: Diego is a miniature painter. He was born in Toledo in 1498.

2. Coref: Diego is a miniature painter. Diego was born in Toledo in 1498.

3. Extract facts: <Diego, be born in, Toledo>,
< Diego, be born in, 1498>,
<Diego, be, painter>

4. Entity Linker: <Diego de Arroyo, be born in, Toledo>,
< Diego de Arroyo, be born in, 1498>,
<Diego de Arroyo, be, painter>

Figure 1: The workflow of extracting knowledge from text.

and Dagan, 2005). The EGs construction algorithm consists of two key steps: local learning and global learning.

In the local learning step, we use GraphParser to extract binary relations between a predicate and its arguments from sentences. Subsequently, we compute local distributional similarity scores to learn entailments between predicates with typed arguments. We compute the co-occurrence of predicates associated with the same entities of the same types. Such predicates with matching entities of the same types are assumed to concern the same event or episode. In the global learning step, the EGs learn globally consistent similarity scores based on soft constraints that consider both the structures across typed entailment graphs and inside each graph. In our EGs construction process, we compute the BInc score (Szpektor and Dagan, 2008) as the directional entailment score between predicates and use it as the input to the global graph learning step.[3]

3.1.3 Augmenting KG with EG

To augment the KG, we infer latent facts using the EGs. For every triple (e_i, p, e_j) in the KG, we add triples (e_i, q, e_j) for all q in the EG where p entails q. The additional triples result in a larger augmented KG with reduced sparsity. Figure 2 illustrates an example of adding latent links to a KG. In this example, the EG indicates that the predicate *"be assassinated in"* entails *"die in"* for arguments of types *(person, location)*. Given the fact *(Amon Bazira, be assassinated in, Kenya)* stored in our KG, we add the latent fact *(Amon Bazira, die in, Kenya)*. A query such as *"Where did Amon Bazira die?"* now returns the correct answer. It is crucial to note that the inference is directional. In this in-

[3]We also experimented with two other EGs (Hosseini et al., 2021; Chen et al., 2022b) which resulted in consistent results (Appendix B).

stance, we can not infer *"be assassinated in"* from *"die in"*.

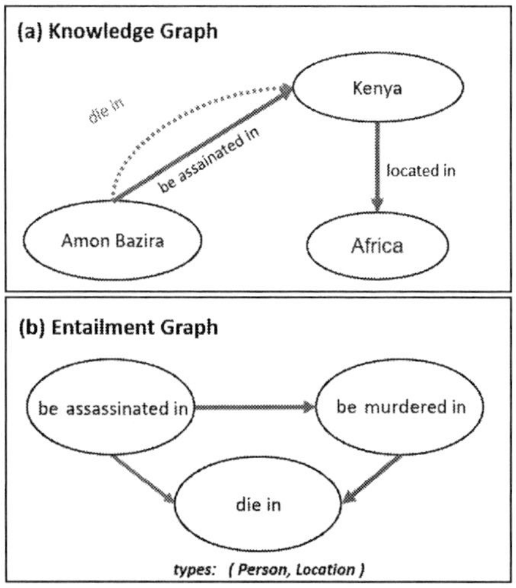

Figure 2: An example of adding latent knowledge. (a) The missing relation *"die in"* is added by using the entailment *"be assassinated in"* entails *"die in"*. (b) Part of the EG for arguments of types *(person, location)*.

If we augment the entire KG extracted from Wikipedia with the EG in an offline manner, the memory requirements for storing the KG becomes prohibitively large. To address this issue, we propose an online approach for KG augmentation for open-domain QA, reducing the storage requirements of the KG without compromising precision. For each query, we simultaneously use both the KG and EGs. If a query *(entity, q, [target entity])* does not yield any results in the KG, it returns *"not found"* even if the target entity could be inferred. To resolve that, we query the EG to get candidate predicates p that entail q. The predicates are sorted based on their entailment scores into a list $P = [p_1, p_2, \dots, p_n]$, where each p_i ($1 \leq i \leq n$) entails q. We start from the beginning of the list and iteratively query the KG with *(entity, p_i, [target entity])*. We return the first matched target entity, or *"not found"* if there is no match.

For instance, if a query such as *(Amon Bazira, die in, [MASK])* does not yield any matching facts in our KG, we search the EG. In the EG, *"suicide in"* and *"be assassinated in"* entail *"die in"*. We sort *"suicide in"* and *"be assassinated in"* based on their entailment scores. First, we replace *"die in"* with *"suicide in"*, generating a modified query *(Amon Bazira, suicide in, [MASK])*. If this query still does not return any facts, we query the KG with *(Amon Bazira, be assassinated in, [MASK])*, which returns an answer *"Kenya"*. This method utilizes the EG as a plug-in without explicitly adding large numbers of triples to the KG.

3.1.4 Backoff augmented KGs with LMs

While the symbolic KGs suffer from sparsity, even when augmented with EGs, LMs return the prediction of a masked token for every question in open-domain QA. To further analyze how we can alleviate the sparsity issues, we evaluate the performance of completing the augmented KG using LMs in QA. For each query, if the augmented KG fails to provide predictions, we utilize the predictions generated by pre-trained LMs to answer it. Both the augmentation method with EGs and the backoff approach with LMs are set up in an unsupervised way to ensure a fair comparison.

3.2 LM-based Approach

In open-domain QA, we utilize pre-trained LMs as latent KGs to provide answers. We explore two conditions when analyzing the prompts of LMs: non-contextual and contextual settings.

Non-Contextual Settings. In this setting, we utilize the original questions as inputs without any additional information. In generative LMs, we directly query the question and consider the returned tokens as the answer. For MLMs, the questions are transformed into "fill-in-blank" statements, where the target tokens are masked and regarded as the answer to be predicted.

Contextual Settings. To analyze the impacts of contexts, we use unsupervised methods to retrieve documents from open-domain corpora. These documents are considered relevant to the questions. For each query, we extract the first paragraph of the most relevant document as the context and concatenate it with the query to generate a new input for LMs.

3.2.1 Retrieving Context with EGs

To measure the enhancements introduced by EGs, we adopt the DrQA (Chen et al., 2017) retriever to extract context from open-domain corpora. This approach enables us to replicate the experimental setup of Petroni et al. (2020), guaranteeing a fair and comparable evaluation. This widely-used and efficient unsupervised retriever relies on term frequency-inverse document frequency (TF-IDF) calculations. However, the limitation of DrQA retriever is lacking inferential capabilities, which results in the omission of relevant documents. For example, when faced with a question like *"Who **played against** Arsenal?"*, the retriever, lacking inferential reasoning, may ignore a relevant document stating *"Manchester City **beat** Arsenal 3-0 to book a place in the Premier League final."*.

To enhance the inferential capabilities of the retriever, we add EGs into the retrieval process. For each question, we extract new predicates from EGs to generate new questions involving the same entity arguments. According to Distributional Inclusion Hypothesis, if the generated question entails the original question, the answers to the generated question can be used to answer the original question. For example, if the original question is *"Who **played against** Arsenal?"*, we can generate a new question *"Who **beat** Arsenal?"* when the predicate *"beat"* entails *"play against"*. The retrieved document *"Manchester City **beat** Arsenal 3-0 to book a place in the Premier League final."* contains information that can answer the original question.

To rank the retrieved documents, we define a new scoring function that combines entailment scores:

$$Score(d_i) = (1-\alpha) * f(q_{ori}, d_i) + \alpha * \sum_{j=1}^{k} f(q_j, d_i) * E(q_j, q_{ori})$$

Where q_{ori} represents the original question, and q_j denotes the j_{th} generated question, ordered by entailment scores. The function $f(q_j, d_i)$ calculates the retriever's score, evaluating the relevance between q_j and the i_{th} document. $E(q_j, q_{ori})$ estimates the probability of q_j entailing q_{ori} using the entailment score from the EG. In our experiments, we set $\alpha = 0.5$ and generate three questions ($k = 3$). By leveraging this scoring function, we concatenate the first paragraph of the most relevant document with the original question as input.

4 Experiment 1: Cloze-style QA

Cloze-style QA aims at answering queries structured as "fill-in-the-blank" cloze statements, which is easy to be evaluated on different LMs without requirements of fine-tuning, especially for MLMs, like BERT-based models. This task has been widely used to measure the capabilities of LMs in memorizing knowledge from the pretraining corpus for open-domain QA. To add both pre-trained Masked LMs and Generative Pre-trained LMs into our analysis of LM-based approaches, we choose this QA task to compare the MR-based and LM-based approaches, and their variants, described in Section 3.

Corpus	Relation	Statistics	
		Facts	**Rel**
Google-RE	Place-of-Birth	2937	1
	Date-of-Birth	1852	1
	Place-of-Death	796	1
	Total	5527	3
T-REx	Total	31051	41

Table 1: Statistics for the test data

4.1 Dataset

4.1.1 Training and Development Data

We use the English Wikipedia and NewsSpike (Zhang and Weld, 2013) corpora as the training dataset to generate the KG and EGs, respectively. We use YAGO3-10 (Rebele et al., 2016) in our experiments as the development set.

Wikipedia: To include all Wikipedia entities in the training set, we use the whole Wikipedia corpus to extract the KG. The Wikipedia corpus contains 5.4M documents[4]. We extract about 158M binary relations using the semantic parser of (Reddy et al., 2014), GraphParser.

NewsSpike: We use the multiple-source NewsSpike corpus to train the EGs. NewsSpike was deliberately built to include different articles from different sources describing identical news events. The corpus scraped RSS news feeds from January–February 2013 and linked them to full stories collected through a Web search of the RSS titles. It contains 550K articles (20M sentences). We extracted 29M binary relations using the same semantic parser, GraphParser[5] . We train the EG on the NewsSpike corpus independently and use it as a plug-in to augment open-domain KGs for QA.

YAGO3-10: YAGO3-10 is a large semantic knowledge base, derived from Wikipedia, WordNet, WikiData, GeoNames, and other data sources. There are 123K entities and 37 relations in the YAGO3-10. We choose YAGO3-10 as the development set because it is derived from multi-sources, containing low overlaps between our test sets.

[4]The dataset utilized in our research is based on a Wikipedia dump from the year 2021.

[5]The constructed EGs contain all relations of the test set.

4.1.2 Test Set

The LAMA probe (Petroni et al., 2019) dataset requires the models to answer cloze-style questions about relational facts. Our evaluation focuses on the Google-RE and T-REx subsets of LAMA, which is aimed at measuring factual knowledge. For each relation, the LAMA probe provides a manual prompt for querying as well as the Wikipedia snippet evidence aligned with questions.

Google-RE: The Google-RE corpus is manually extracted from Wikipedia and contains 5.5K facts. It covers five relations, where three of them are used in the LAMA probe. The query prompts are pre-defined manually, e.g. *"Steve Jobs was born in [Y]"* for relation *"Place-of-Birth"*. Each fact in Google-RE dataset is associated with a manually selected snippet of text from Wikipedia that supports it. These associated snippets are regarded as the golden context in our contextual experiments.

T-REx: The T-REx (Elsahar et al., 2018) knowledge source is a subset of Wikidata triples. The T-REx in LAMA probe has 41 relations with manual prompts for querying and it subsamples at most 1000 facts per relation. In contrast to the Google-RE knowledge source, which is defined manually, the facts in T-REx were associated with an automatically extracted, and hence possibly irrelevant, Wikipedia snippet. Elsahar et al. (2018) report an accuracy of 97.8% for the alignment.

4.2 Baselines

To compare with the results in LAMA probe, we consider the following baselines.

IE: For the relation-based knowledge sources, we consider the pre-trained Information Extraction (IE) model of Sorokin and Gurevych (2017). This model was trained on a subcorpus of Wikipedia annotated with Wikidata relations. It extracts relation triples from a given sentence using an LSTM-based encoder and an attention mechanism. We add this approach to the baselines because it explicitly stores triples, unlike the LMs.

BERT: Petroni et al. (2019) proved the efficacy of pre-trained MLMs in cloze-style QA. The aim of MLMs is learning to fill the word at the masked position. We add BERT-large (Devlin et al., 2019) in our baselines, which employs a Transformer architecture and trains it on the BookCorpus (Zhu et al., 2015) as well as a crawl of English Wikipedia. The training corpus contains the Wikipedia articles employed in LAMA probe.

	Models	Precision@1	Recall
Single Model	KG	**58.8**	8.5
	BERT	10.5	10.5
	GPT-3.5	19.0	19.0
Augmented Models	KG+EG	**41.7**	17.0
	KG+BERT	20.2	20.2
	KG+GPT	24.3	24.3
	KG+EG+BERT	23.5	23.5
	KG+EG+GPT	26.0	**26.0**

Table 2: We show the Precision@1 and Recall of parsed-KG, BERT-large, GPT-3.5, EG-augmented KG and the EG-augmented KG with LM backoff in non-contextual settings[7].

GPT-3.5: Large Language Models (LLMs), like GPT series models, have shown impressive capabilities in QA. To analyze the performance on LLMs, we take text-davinci-003 (GPT-3.5) as the baseline of evaluation, as it is the largest and best-aligned version[6]. Unlike BERT, the GPT-3.5 is generative. We manually transfer the LAMA probe cloze-style prompts to natural questions for GPT-3.5, like using "where was Steve Jobs born?" instead of "Steve Jobs was born in [MASK]". All prompts for GPT-3.5 are shown in Appendix H.

4.3 Results: Cloze-style QA

The performance of parsed-KGs (MR-based approaches) and LM-based approaches in cloze-style QA is evaluated under two settings: non-contextual and contextual.

Table 2 demonstrates the precision@1 and recall of different models under non-contextual settings. The parsed KG exhibits impressive precision performance due to its high proportion of exact matches but is limited in recall by its sparsity. After being augmented with EGs, the recall improves significantly and the precision is much higher than other combinations (e.g. see KG+EG vs KG+GPT, and KG+EG vs KG+BERT). It demonstrates that EGs perform stronger capabilities of inferring latent knowledge to alleviate the sparsity of parsed KGs. This experiment shows that the MR-based approaches exhibit significantly higher precision compared to LM-based approaches. Additionally, the augmentation of KGs with EGs effectively addresses the recall limitation, still outperforming LMs and their combinations in precision.

[6] In our experiment, we evaluate GPT-3.5 model via the OpenAI API (https://platform.openai.com/), with the temperature setting fixed as 0.

[7] In LAMA probe, there are no negatives so the recall is same as Precision@1 when LMs return prediction for every query.

Dataset	Rel	Single Model: IE	KG	BERT	GPT-3.5	EG-Augmented KG: KG+EG	EG-Augmented KG with LM backoff: KG+EG+BERT	KG+EG+GPT
Google-RE	*PoB*	13.8	19.9	16.1	30.3	27.7	30.7	37.0
	DoB	1.9	7.7	1.0	2.0	8.5	9.9	11.3
	PoD	7.2	14.6	14.0	24.7	26.0	29.6	29.7
	Average	7.6	14.0	10.5	19.0	20.7	23.5	**26.0**
TREx	Average	33.8	29.2	31.5	59.1	35.1	64.7	**79.3**

Table 3: Main results on cloze-style QA without context. This table shows the F-score on BERT-large, GPT3, parsed-KG and its augmented versions across the set of evaluation corpora.

	Dataset	BERT-large	GPT-3.5	KG+EG
context_{NULL}	Google-RE	10.5	19.0	20.7
	TREx	31.5	59.1	35.1
context_{DrQA}	Google-RE	40.8	72.1	20.7
	TREx	43.1	81.7	35.4
$\text{context}_{DrQA+EG}$	Google-RE	59.9	**84.0**	20.7
	TREx	54.2	**80.6**	35.4
context_{Golden}	Google-RE	78.0	**98.4**	29.6
	TREx	62.6	**95.1**	38.0

Table 4: The F-score of different models in cloze-style QA when context documents are provided, with subscripts "Golden", "DrQA", and "DrQA+EG", indicating the context extraction methods from original snippets, the DrQA retriever, and the version with EGs, respectively.

To further analyze the impact of introducing EGs to various models on F-scores, we present the non-contextual results of cloze-style QA across a range of corpora in Table 3. Among the single models without EGs, GPT-3.5 outperforms other methods, and the parsed KG exhibits better performance compared to BERT. Furthermore, KG+EG presents that augmenting the KGs with EGs leads to an improvement in F-scores. Moreover, the incorporation of LM backoff yields additional improvements in EG-augmented KGs, as shown in the comparison between KG+EG+GPT and KG+EG. The combination of EG-augmented KGs with the GPT-3.5 model backoff (KG+EG+GPT) demonstrates the highest level of performance in terms of F-scores among all combinations. This combination utilizes the high precision benefits provided by EG-augmented KGs while effectively addressing the low recall limitations through the use of LLMs.

Table 4 presents the performance of LMs and KG when provided with contexts. LM-based methods show significant improvement with context, but the impact of context on the KG is limited. This finding indicates that contexts have a more significant impact on LMs compared to parsed KGs. Furthermore, the experiments show that the contexts retrieved by DrQA+EGs outperform those retrieved by the DrQA retriever alone, highlighting the importance and complemantary roles of entailment in retrieving highly relevant contexts for QA. EGs introduce entailment between questions and documents in the retrieval process, contributing to this improved performance.

Models		Google-RE: *infrequent*	*frequent*
MR-based	KG	**15.1**	14.7
	KG+EG	18.7	**19.2**
LM-based	BERT	6.7	**11.2**
	GPT-3.5	16.2	**20.6**

Table 5: The table shows F-scores for subsets of the Google-RE dataset categorized based on frequency.

In order to compare the performance of different EGs trained on different corpora and score functions, we report the results of different EGs in Appendix B. and report the error analysis in Appendix A.

We also analyze the impact of query frequency on LM-based approaches. We run experiments on two subsets of Google-RE queries: the 5% least frequent (*infrequent*) queries by calculating the mentioned entities occurrence in the NewsCrawl corpus (Barrault et al., 2019), and the 5% most frequent queries (*frequent*). As shown in Table 5, LM-based approaches achieve higher F-scores for frequent queries compared to infrequent queries. However, the question frequency appears to have less impact on parsed KG. The results show that LM is limited in effectively answering queries involving infrequent entities, indicating the challenges faced by LM in handling long-tail scenarios.

In conclusion, MR-based approaches reach higher precision but suffer from sparsity, causing low recall in QA. On the other hand, the quality of retrieved contexts is the main limitation of LMs. The contexts extracted by various unsupervised approaches exhibit significant improvements in the LM-based methods, but these approaches show different capabilities in contextual extraction. EGs can enhance both approaches by utilizing tex-

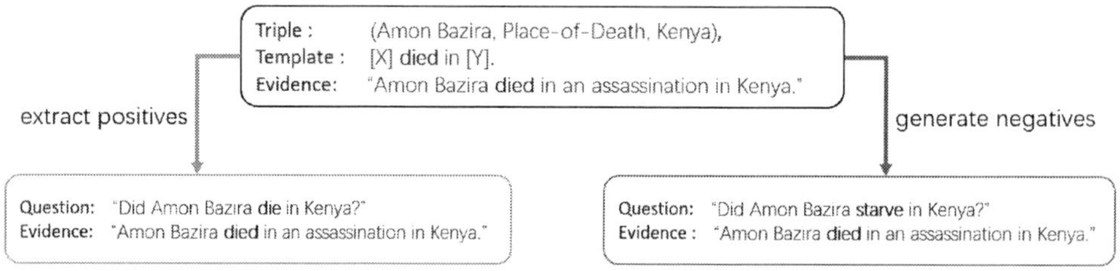

Figure 3: Constructing Boolean QA data by Google-RE and T-REx. (a) The left part shows we extract positives from LAMA probe. (b) We generate the negatives by using the hyponyms to replace the predicate.

tual entailment between common-sense in questions and open-domain corpora. EGs augment the parsed KG by inferring latent knowledge through the entailment between common-sense, enhancing the performance of MR-based methods. For LM-based methods, EGs provide ways to retrieve highly-relevant contexts for questions, by inferring common sense from original questions to latent related documents.

5 Experiment 2: Boolean QA

The LAMA probe is basically an intrinsic evaluation dataset for measuring the capabilities of LMs in extracting knowledge for QA, but it has limitations for evaluating inferential capability (Rogers et al., 2020). One such limitation is that the LAMA probe is derived from the Wikipedia corpus, which is likely to have been included in LMs training data. The LMs tend to choose as answer those triples in the evidence that are similar to those seen in the training data, minimizing dependency on inference, and leading to overestimation of the capabilities of LMs in cloze-style QA. As a consequence, the LAMA probe task fails to evaluate the sensitivity of LMs to directionality of entailment from evidence to the answer to the question.

We propose a Boolean QA task, which adds negative test items to the positive items in the original Google-RE and T-REx datasets (in §4.1.2). We follow McKenna et al. (2021) in automatically generating questions whose answer is not entailed by the original evidence by replacing the relation in the original question by a WordNet hyponyms (Miller, 1998—see figure 3). Such questions are likely to appear to the LMs to be similar to propositions in the evidence, despite not being entailed. The Boolean QA task thereby measures the models' sensitivity to the direction of entailment, as well as the extent to which the EG improves cloze-style QA.

5.1 Boolean QA Data

5.1.1 Extracting Positives

Each instance in Google-RE and T-REx is formed as a triple, like the one shown in Figure 3(a). We transform the fact *(Amon Bazira, die in, Kenya)* into a natural boolean question, such as *"Did Amon Bazira die in Kenya?"*. Then we use the associated Wikipedia snippets from the LAMA probe as the evidence. Since these snippets are provided in the Google-RE and T-REx data, we know that these questions are answerable by the snippets.

5.1.2 Generating Negatives

Negative questions are generated from the positive questions by identifying a hyponym of the relevant predicate using WordNet. Hyponyms usually entail that predicate but are not entailed by it. Therefore it is unlikely that the Google-RE evidence snippet supports the hyponym relation[8]. Such negative questions are difficult for LMs to reject because they are similar to the positive and hence to the text in the evidential snippet.

Figure 3(b) demonstrates an example of negatives generation. In this example, we identify "**starve**" as the hyponym of "**die**" using WordNet. Then a negative *"Did Amon Bazira* ***starve*** *in Kenya?"* will be generated from the positive question *"Did Amon Bazira* ***die*** *in Kenya?"*. The performance in Boolean QA presents the capabilities of directional common-sense inferences, which is crucial for inferring latent knowledge from texts.

5.2 Evaluation on Boolean QA

BERT, RoBERTa (Liu et al., 2019), and GPT-3.5 are the baselines for this task. We evaluate the BERT and RoBERTa by computing cosine similarity between the predicate vector in the question and

[8]We manually checked 100 random samples of generated negatives, and found only 4 cases where a positive answer would be appropriate.

Models	Dataset	
	Google-RE	T-REx
BERT	64.0	47.2
RoBERTa	61.9	49.5
GPT-3.5	87.6	68.1
EG	85.3	67.7
EG+BERT	85.3	71.2
EG+GPT-3.5	**88.5**	**75.0**

Table 6: The F-score in Boolean QA task

the predicate vector in the answer, following the evaluation of McKenna et al. (2021).

For GPT-3.5, we convert the token probability from its outputs using the following mapping:

$$\begin{aligned} score = 0.5 + 0.5 * \mathbb{I}[(\text{output} = True)] * S_{\text{output}} \\ -0.5 * \mathbb{I}[(\text{output} = False)] * S_{\text{output}} \end{aligned}$$

In the equation, $\mathbb{I}$ represents the indicator function. $score$ estimates the probability of positive classification based on the textual model output probability S_{output}, using a linear transformation, which preserves the ordering of model confidences. Note that we add an offset 0.5 to ensure that $0 \leq S_{\text{output}} \leq 1$.

We evaluate EGs by looking for entailment scores between predicates, which are defined on a scale of 0 to 1. For fairness, our EGs are trained on the NewsSpike corpus, which is independent of the evaluation datasets, Google-RE and T-REx. If the predicate in answers is absent from EGs, the model returns the answer as false.

5.3 Results: Boolean QA

To compare the capabilities of directional inference, we report the F-score of Boolean QA in Table 6. The results demonstrate that the EGs and GPT-3.5 perform at a similar level, and they significantly outperform BERT and RoBERTa. We combine the score of EG and LMs with a linear function and show improvement in Boolean QA. The experiments suggest that EGs exhibit stronger capabilities of directional common-sense inference than BERT and achieve a similar level to LLMs, like GPT-3.5, with less training resources and more efficient computation (shown in Appendix E).

Furthermore, the results also prove EGs can identify the directional inference between questions and documents, presenting evidence to explain why EGs can augment the pre-parsed KG and retrieve high-quality contexts for LMs. The successful augmentation explains the efficient enhancement of the parsed KG using EGs in cloze-style QA. The limitation of LMs in directional inference indicates that LMs tend to exhibit a propensity for memorization of factual knowledge rather than a reliance on inferential reasoning in QA scenarios, potentially constraining the practical utility of LMs in QA applications.

6 Conclusion

In this paper, we have conducted a comprehensive analysis of the limitations of Machine-Reading and LM-based approaches in QA. We propose a novel method that utilizes entailment graphs to infer directional relations, addressing the sparsity issue and low relevance of retrieved contexts. Additionally, we have introduced an open-domain Boolean QA task to evaluate the capabilities of directional inference. In Boolean QA, the entailment graphs present stronger capabilities in directional inference than BERT and RoBERTa, achieving comparable performance to GPT-3.5. These results demonstrate the effectiveness of the entailment graphs in enhancing performance under both unsupervised approaches, by making common-sense inference available to open-domain QA.

7 Limitations

We analyze the performance of MR-based and LM-based approaches in QA, and we propose to utilize the directional inference capabilities of EGs to enhance both approaches, showing improvement in QA. A limitation in this work is that it focuses on open-domain cloze-style QA only in English. We have not evaluated our methods on multi-lingual QA tasks, although Li et al. (2022b) have built a large entailment graph for Chinese, which could be applied. The parser, entity typing method used in the entailment graphs, the Boolean QA dataset which is constructed using WordNet, and the LMs, are only language-dependent components. In addition, the parsed KG is extracted from the whole English Wikipedia corpus. Although we can construct the KG incrementally, the program still requires large amounts of memory to run on large corpora. We were not able to construct KGs on more amount of text with our computational resources.

8 Acknowledgements

This research was supported by ERC Advanced Fellowship GA 742137 SEMANTAX, the University of Edinburgh Huawei Laboratory.

References

Leonard Adolphs, Shehzaad Dhuliawala, and Thomas Hofmann. 2021. How to Query Language Models? *arXiv preprint arXiv:2108.01928*.

Manzoor Ali, Muhammad Saleem, and Axel-Cyrille Ngonga Ngomo. 2021. Unsupervised Relation Extraction Using Sentence Encoding. In *ESWC2021 Poster and Demo Track*.

Dimitrios Alivanistos, Selene Báez Santamaría, Michael Cochez, Jan-Christoph Kalo, Emile van Krieken, and Thiviyan Thanapalasingam. 2022. Prompting as Probing: Using Language Models for Knowledge Base Construction. *arXiv preprint arXiv:2208.11057*.

Gabor Angeli, Melvin Jose Johnson Premkumar, and Christopher D Manning. 2015. Leveraging linguistic structure for open domain information extraction. In *Proceedings of the 53rd Annual Meeting of the Association for Computational Linguistics and the 7th International Joint Conference on Natural Language Processing (Volume 1: Long Papers)*, pages 344–354.

Loïc Barrault, Ondřej Bojar, Marta R. Costa-jussà, Christian Federmann, Mark Fishel, Yvette Graham, Barry Haddow, Matthias Huck, Philipp Koehn, Shervin Malmasi, Christof Monz, Mathias Müller, Santanu Pal, Matt Post, and Marcos Zampieri. 2019. Findings of the 2019 conference on machine translation (WMT19). In *Proceedings of the Fourth Conference on Machine Translation (Volume 2: Shared Task Papers, Day 1)*, pages 1–61, Florence, Italy. Association for Computational Linguistics.

Jonathan Berant, Ido Dagan, and Jacob Goldberger. 2010. Global Learning of Focused Entailment Graphs. In *Proceedings of the 48th Annual Meeting of the Association for Computational Linguistics*, pages 1220–1229.

Jonathan Berant, Ido Dagan, and Jacob Goldberger. 2011. Global Learning of Typed Entailment Rules. In *Proceedings of the 49th Annual Meeting of the Association for Computational Linguistics: Human Language Technologies*, pages 610–619.

Eric Brill, Susan Dumais, and Michele Banko. 2002. An analysis of the AskMSR question-answering system. In *Proceedings of the 2002 Conference on Empirical Methods in Natural Language Processing (EMNLP 2002)*, pages 257–264. Association for Computational Linguistics.

Tom Brown, Benjamin Mann, Nick Ryder, Melanie Subbiah, Jared D Kaplan, Prafulla Dhariwal, Arvind Neelakantan, Pranav Shyam, Girish Sastry, Amanda Askell, et al. 2020. Language Models are Few-Shot Learners. *Advances in neural information processing systems*, 33:1877–1901.

Danqi Chen, Adam Fisch, Jason Weston, and Antoine Bordes. 2017. Reading Wikipedia to Answer Open-Domain Questions. In *Proceedings of the 55th Annual Meeting of the Association for Computational Linguistics (Volume 1: Long Papers)*, pages 1870–1879.

Yanda Chen, Ruiqi Zhong, Sheng Zha, George Karypis, and He He. 2022a. Meta-learning via Language Model In-context Tuning. In *Proceedings of the 60th Annual Meeting of the Association for Computational Linguistics (Volume 1: Long Papers)*, pages 719–730.

Zhibin Chen, Yansong Feng, and Dongyan Zhao. 2022b. Entailment Graph Learning with Textual Entailment and Soft Transitivity. In *Proceedings of the 60th Annual Meeting of the Association for Computational Linguistics (Volume 1: Long Papers)*, pages 5899–5910.

Ido Dagan, Lillian Lee, and Fernando CN Pereira. 1999. Similarity-Based Models of Word Cooccurrence Probabilities. *Machine learning*, 34(1):43–69.

Jacob Devlin, Ming-Wei Chang, Kenton Lee, and Kristina Toutanova. 2019. BERT: Pre-training of Deep Bidirectional Transformers for Language Understanding. In *NAACL-HLT (1)*.

Hady Elsahar, Pavlos Vougiouklis, Arslen Remaci, Christophe Gravier, Jonathon Hare, Frederique Laforest, and Elena Simperl. 2018. T-REx: A Large Scale Alignment of Natural Language with Knowledge Base Triples. In *Proceedings of the Eleventh International Conference on Language Resources and Evaluation (LREC 2018)*.

Oren Etzioni, Anthony Fader, Janara Christensen, Stephen Soderland, and Mausam Mausam. 2011. Open Information Extraction: the Second Generation. In *Proceedings of the Twenty-Second international joint conference on Artificial Intelligence-Volume Volume One*, pages 3–10.

David Ferrucci, Eric Brown, Jennifer Chu-Carroll, James Fan, David Gondek, Aditya A Kalyanpur, Adam Lally, J William Murdock, Eric Nyberg, John Prager, et al. 2010. Building Watson: An Overview of the DeepQA project. *AI magazine*, 31(3):59–79.

Leandra Fichtel, Jan-Christoph Kalo, and Wolf-Tilo Balke. 2021. Prompt Tuning or Fine-Tuning-Investigating Relational Knowledge in Pre-Trained Language Models. In *3rd Conference on Automated Knowledge Base Construction*.

Maayan Geffet and Ido Dagan. 2005. The Distributional Inclusion Hypotheses and Lexical Entailment. In *Proceedings of the 43rd Annual Meeting of the Association for Computational Linguistics (ACL'05)*, pages 107–114.

Brian Harrington and Stephen Clark. 2007. ASKNet: Automated Semantic Knowledge Network. In *AAAI*, pages 1862–1863.

Tianxing He, Kyunghyun Cho, and James Glass. 2021. An Empirical Study on Few-shot Knowledge Probing for Pretrained Language Models. *arXiv preprint arXiv:2109.02772*.

Mohammad Javad Hosseini, Nathanael Chambers, Siva Reddy, Xavier R Holt, Shay B Cohen, Mark Johnson, and Mark Steedman. 2018. Learning Typed Entailment Graphs with Global Soft Constraints. *Transactions of the Association for Computational Linguistics*, 6:703–717.

Mohammad Javad Hosseini, Shay B Cohen, Mark Johnson, and Mark Steedman. 2021. Open-Domain Contextual Link Prediction and its Complementarity with Entailment Graphs. In *Findings of the Association for Computational Linguistics: EMNLP 2021*, pages 2790–2802.

Nora Kassner and Hinrich Schütze. 2020. BERT-kNN: Adding a kNN Search Component to Pretrained Language Models for Better QA. In *Findings of the Association for Computational Linguistics: EMNLP 2020*, pages 3424–3430.

Tushar Khot, Ashish Sabharwal, and Peter Clark. 2017. Answering Complex Questions Using Open Information Extraction. In *Proceedings of the 55th Annual Meeting of the Association for Computational Linguistics (Volume 2: Short Papers)*, pages 311–316.

Kenton Lee, Luheng He, and Luke Zettlemoyer. 2018. Higher-order coreference resolution with coarse-to-fine inference. In *Proceedings of the 2018 Conference of the North American Chapter of the Association for Computational Linguistics: Human Language Technologies, Volume 2 (Short Papers)*, pages 687–692, New Orleans, Louisiana. Association for Computational Linguistics.

Tianyi Li, Mohammad Javad Hosseini, Sabine Weber, and Mark Steedman. 2022a. Language Models Are Poor Learners of Directional Inference. In *Findings of the Association for Computational Linguistics: EMNLP 2022*, pages 903–921, Abu Dhabi, United Arab Emirates. Association for Computational Linguistics.

Tianyi Li, Sabine Weber, Mohammad Javad Hosseini, Liane Guillou, and Mark Steedman. 2022b. Cross-lingual Inference with A Chinese Entailment Graph. In *Findings of the Association for Computational Linguistics: ACL 2022*, pages 1214–1233.

Xi Victoria Lin, Todor Mihaylov, Mikel Artetxe, Tianlu Wang, Shuohui Chen, Daniel Simig, Myle Ott, Naman Goyal, Shruti Bhosale, Jingfei Du, et al. 2021. Few-shot Learning with Multilingual Language Models. *arXiv preprint arXiv:2112.10668*.

Yinhan Liu, Myle Ott, Naman Goyal, Jingfei Du, Mandar Joshi, Danqi Chen, Omer Levy, Mike Lewis, Luke Zettlemoyer, and Veselin Stoyanov. 2019. RoBERTa: A Robustly Optimized BERT Pretraining Approach. *arXiv:1907.11692 [cs]*. ArXiv: 1907.11692.

Nick McKenna, Liane Guillou, Mohammad Javad Hosseini, Sander Bijl de Vroe, Mark Johnson, and Mark Steedman. 2021. Multivalent Entailment Graphs for Question Answering. In *2021 Conference on Empirical Methods in Natural Language Processing*, pages 10758–10768. ACL Anthology.

Yuanliang Meng, Anna Rumshisky, and Alexey Romanov. 2017. Temporal Information Extraction for Question Answering Using Syntactic Dependencies in an LSTM-based Architecture. In *Proceedings of the 2017 Conference on Empirical Methods in Natural Language Processing*, pages 887–896.

George A Miller. 1998. *WordNet: An Electronic Lexical Database*. MIT press.

Dan Moldovan, Sanda Harabagiu, Marius Pasca, Rada Mihalcea, Roxana Girju, Richard Goodrum, and Vasile Rus. 2000. The Structure and Performance of an Open-Domain Question Answering System. In *Proceedings of the 38th annual meeting of the Association for Computational Linguistics*, pages 563–570.

Dat Ba Nguyen, Johannes Hoffart, Martin Theobald, and Gerhard Weikum. 2014. AIDA-light: High-throughput Named-entity Disambiguation. In *Workshop on Linked Data on the Web 2014*, pages 1–10. CEUR-WS. org.

Yasumasa Onoe, Michael JQ Zhang, Eunsol Choi, and Greg Durrett. 2022. Entity Cloze By Date: What LMs Know About Unseen Entities. *arXiv e-prints*, pages arXiv–2205.

Ethan Perez, Douwe Kiela, and Kyunghyun Cho. 2021. True Few-Shot Learning with Language Models. *Advances in Neural Information Processing Systems*, 34:11054–11070.

Fabio Petroni, Patrick Lewis, Aleksandra Piktus, Tim Rocktäschel, Yuxiang Wu, Alexander H. Miller, and Sebastian Riedel. 2020. How Context Affects Language Models' Factual Predictions. In *Automated Knowledge Base Construction*.

Fabio Petroni, Tim Rocktäschel, Sebastian Riedel, Patrick Lewis, Anton Bakhtin, Yuxiang Wu, and Alexander Miller. 2019. Language Models as Knowledge Bases? In *Proceedings of the 2019 Conference on Empirical Methods in Natural Language Processing and the 9th International Joint Conference on Natural Language Processing (EMNLP-IJCNLP)*, pages 2463–2473.

Alec Radford, Jeffrey Wu, Rewon Child, David Luan, Dario Amodei, Ilya Sutskever, et al. 2019. Language Models are Unsupervised Multitask Learners.

Colin Raffel, Noam Shazeer, Adam Roberts, Katherine Lee, Sharan Narang, Michael Matena, Yanqi Zhou, Wei Li, and Peter J Liu. 2019. Exploring the Limits of Transfer Learning with a Unified Text-to-Text Transformer. *arXiv preprint arXiv:1910.10683*.

Thomas Rebele, Fabian Suchanek, Johannes Hoffart, Joanna Biega, Erdal Kuzey, and Gerhard Weikum. 2016. YAGO: a Multilingual Knowledge Base from Wikipedia, Wordnet, and Geonames. In *The 15th International Semantic Web Conferenece*.

Siva Reddy, Mirella Lapata, and Mark Steedman. 2014. Large-scale Semantic Parsing without Question-Answer Pairs. *Transactions of the Association for Computational Linguistics*, 2:377–392.

Anna Rogers, Olga Kovaleva, Matthew Downey, and Anna Rumshisky. 2020. Getting Closer to AI Complete Question Answering: A Set of Prerequisite Real Tasks. In *Proceedings of the AAAI conference on artificial intelligence*, volume 34, pages 8722–8731.

Taylor Shin, Yasaman Razeghi, Robert L Logan IV, Eric Wallace, and Sameer Singh. 2020. Autoprompt: Eliciting Knowledge from Language Models with Automatically Generated Prompts. In *Proceedings of the 2020 Conference on Empirical Methods in Natural Language Processing (EMNLP)*, pages 4222–4235.

Daniil Sorokin and Iryna Gurevych. 2017. Context-Aware Representations for Knowledge Base Relation Extraction. In *Proceedings of the 2017 Conference on Empirical Methods in Natural Language Processing*, pages 1784–1789.

Mark Steedman. 2000. *The Syntactic Process*. MIT Press, Cambridge, MA.

Idan Szpektor and Ido Dagan. 2008. Learning entailment rules for unary templates. In *Proceedings of the 22nd International Conference on Computational Linguistics (Coling 2008)*, pages 849–856, Manchester, UK. Coling 2008 Organizing Committee.

Hugo Touvron, Thibaut Lavril, Gautier Izacard, Xavier Martinet, Marie-Anne Lachaux, Timothée Lacroix, Baptiste Rozière, Naman Goyal, Eric Hambro, Faisal Azhar, Aurelien Rodriguez, Armand Joulin, Edouard Grave, and Guillaume Lample. 2023. LLaMA: Open and Efficient Foundation Language Models.

Chenguang Wang, Xiao Liu, and Dawn Song. 2020. Language Models are Open Knowledge Graphs. *arXiv preprint arXiv:2010.11967*.

Congle Zhang and Daniel S Weld. 2013. Harvesting Parallel News Streams to Generate Paraphrases of Event Relations. In *Proceedings of the 2013 Conference on Empirical Methods in Natural Language Processing*, pages 1776–1786.

Yukun Zhu, Ryan Kiros, Rich Zemel, Ruslan Salakhutdinov, Raquel Urtasun, Antonio Torralba, and Sanja Fidler. 2015. Aligning Books and Movies: Towards Story-like Visual Explanations by Watching Movies and Reading Books. In *Proceedings of the IEEE international conference on computer vision*, pages 19–27.

A Error Analysis of MR-based Approaches

We manually analyze 150 samples for the Machine-Reading approach. About 23% of them are caused by GraphParser and are cases where it returns wrong relations from text. Most of them are caused by non-standard sentences in Wikipedia documents. For example, *"Norman MacLeod (c. 1731 – 1796) was a British army officer, merchant, and official of the British Indian Department."*, the parser cannot extract the fact *(Norman MacLeod, bear in, 1731)* from the sentence because it cannot analyze "(c. 1731 – 1796)". It also leads to bad performance in the relation *"Date-of-Birth"*.

20% of the errors in the KG are due to entity linking returning wrong entities or types, caused by ambiguity in Google-RE and T-REx. For example, a sentence in Googe-RE is *"Jason then continued to Sparta, where he died and was buried"* and the fact in Google-RE is *(Jason, Place-of-Death, Sparta)*. But in evaluation, *"Jason"* is linked to *"Jason Hu"*, who is a modern politician.

About 44% are caused by the mismatch between training and test corpora. For example, the relation *"is connected to"* describes the connections between airports, but we cannot get the knowledge from the training corpus, Wikipedia.

The rest of the errors (13%) are because of other reasons including entailment graphs errors, that are mainly caused by the ambiguity of some high-frequency predicates. For example, predicate *"bear in"* entails predicate *"be from"*. These predicates, like *"be from"*, are common in sentences. If the relation of the query contains these predicates, the KG will return wrong answers easily. When we use the predicate *"be from"* for querying the KG, it will return false results because the predicate has too many meanings. e.g., in the sentence *"Shane Doan is from Arizona"* may mean *"Shane comes from Arizona"*, not the Place-of-Birth. In our experiment, some entailment graphs errors are caused by spurious correlations. For example, there are many documents in Wikipedia like *"Steve Jobs was born on February 24, 1955, in California, ..., Jobs died at his Palo Alto, California home around 3 p.m."*. From these sentences, we may extract facts like *(Steve Jobs, bear in, California)* and *(Steve Jobs, die in, California)*. These predicates link the same entities. It is likely to incorrectly give the entailment relationship between the two predicates.

B Different Entailment Graphs on cloze-style QA

EGs play a crucial role in capturing the relationships between typed predicates, utilizing a score function to measure the probability of one predicate entailing another. Some works introduced various models for generating EGs with improved quality in NLI datasets. Hosseini et al. (2021) proposed the Contextualized and Non-Contextualized Embeddings (CNCE) model, which leverages contextual link prediction to calculate a novel relation entailment score. Similarly, Chen et al. (2022b) introduced the Entailment Graph with Textual Entailment and Transitivity (EGT2) method, demonstrating promising performance on Recognizing Textual Entailment (RTE) tasks.

To evaluate the performance of state-of-the-art (SOTA) entailment graphs in cloze-style QA, we compare their performance in augmenting parsed KGs. We specifically investigate the impact of different training sets by training the entailment graphs on three distinct corpora: Wikipedia, NewsSpike, and NewsCrawl (Barrault et al., 2019). We present the summarized results of the different entailment graphs in Table 7.

	P@1	R	F
BERT-large	10.5	-	10.5
RoBERTa	4.8	-	4.8
Transformer-XL	1.6	-	1.6
GPT-3.5	19.0	-	19.0
KG	**58.8**	8.5	14.0
KG+EG$_{wiki_binc}$	43.8	12.3	17.4
KG+EG$_{ns_binc}$	41.7	15.0	20.7
KG+EG$_{ns_cnce}$	40.7	**16.2**	**21.0**
KG+EG$_{ns_egt2}$	56.6	9.6	18.7
KG+EG$_{nc_binc}$	42.6	14.6	19.6
KG+EG$_{nc_cnce}$	44.9	15.1	20.7

Table 7: Results of different entailment graphs on Google-RE in cloze-style QA. This table presents the mean average precision at one (P@1), recall, and F-score of Google-RE. The result shows the average per number of relations in Google-RE. In this table, the subscripts *wiki*, *ns* and *nc* means the entailment graphs are trained on Wikipedia, NewsSpike and NewsCrawl (Barrault et al., 2019). Subscripts *binc* means EGs constructed using the approach of Hosseini et al. (2018). Subscripts *cnce* and *egt2* means the entailment graphs are trained on CNCE and EGT2.

We notice that the entailment graphs trained on NewsSpike (EG$_{ns_binc}$) outperform the entailment graphs trained on Wikipedia (EG$_{ns_wiki}$). Dif-

	KG	KG + EG_{wiki_binc}		KG + EG_{ns_binc}		KG + EG_{nc_binc}	
		local	global	local	global	local	global
P@1	**58.8**	43.2	43.8	42.0	41.7	41.7	42.6
R	8.5	12.3	12.3	13.7	**15.0**	14.3	14.6
F	14.0	16.9	17.4	18.0	**20.7**	19.1	19.6

Table 8: Knowledge graph combined with different entailment graphs. global means the entailment graph is based on global BInc score, local means the entaiment graph with local BInc score.

Corpus	BERT-large	GPT-3.5	KG_{corpus}	$KG_{document}$	KG_{corpus}+EG	$KG_{document}$+EG
Google-RE	10.5	19.0	14.0	12.9	**20.7**	20.3
T-REx	31.5	**59.1**	29.2	27.8	35.1	33.9

Table 9: The F-scores of different KGs. KG_{corpus} and $KG_{document}$ means the KG is constructed using the whole Wikipedia corpus or retrieved documents.

ferent from the Wikipedia corpus, the articles in NewsSpike mainly describe the same news events by multiple authors. Hence, the predicates in NewsSpike have stronger relevance, which reduces sparsity issues. We analyze the performance of EGs trained by different approaches, EG_{ns_binc}, EG_{ns_cnce} and EG_{ns_egt2}. We notice the edges in EG_{ns_egt2} are fewer than the EG_{ns_cnce} and EG_{ns_binc}. Although the EG_{ns_egt2} shows impressive performance on RTE tasks, it is limited in sparsity, resulting in bad performance on the QA task. The experiments suggest that the main limitation of augmented KG is the sparsity of EGs in QA.

In order to analyze the effects of global learning, we show the entailment graphs on local and global scores in cloze-style QA in Table 8. The entailment graph based on global scores performs better than entailment graphs just trained on local scores.

C Different Approaches of Open-domain KG Construction

We propose two approaches to construct the open-domain KG in the MR-based method: using the whole Wikipedia corpus (*corpus-based*) or using retrieved documents (*document-based*) to extract knowledge. We analyze the performance of different KG and show the results in Table 9. The document-based KGs require less memory with sacrificing a little performance.

D Analyzing the Impact of Prompts

Petroni et al. (2019) propose the MLM could work as a latent knowledge base for zero-shot cloze-style QA with manual prompts during querying.

Relation	$Prompts_{LAMA}$	$Prompt_{re-written}$
Google-RE	10.5	5.4
T-REx	32.3	16.3

Table 10: Precision of BERT-large querying by different prompts.

We notice some prompts in the LAMA probe are the high-frequency sentences chosen from the test set, Wikipedia. For example, the relation "Date-of-Birth" are labeled with the prompt "[S] (born [O])" for querying. This expression is common in Wikipedia but is not a natural sentence.

To analyze the effects of prompts on MLMs, we evaluate BERT-large on the cloze-style QA with automatic re-written prompts, like replacing the LAMA probe's prompt "[S] (born [O])" with a natural sentence "[S] was born on [O]". The precision of BERT-large is shown on Tabel 10. From the table, if we change the pre-defined manual prompts in the LAMA probe, the precision will decrease significantly. It indicates the LMs attempt to memorize the expression of training data for answering questions, instead of inferring knowledge. High-frequency pre-defined query prompts will improve the performance of LMs but will be limited for practical applications.

E Computational Costs

The KG construction process (MR-based approach) involves two steps: text preprocessing and knowledge extraction. In offline construction, the entire Wikipedia corpus is processed, which requires approximately 6 days when utilizing 20 CPU threads (Intel(R) Xeon(R) CPU E5-2697 v4 @ 2.30GHz). However, by leveraging GPUs (GeForce RTX 2080 Ti) for coreference resolution during the preprocessing step, the processing time can be reduced to 36 hours with the use of 4 GPUs. The knowledge extraction step takes approximately 24 hours. Compared to the computational resources required for training GPT-3.5 or BERT-large, the MR-based approach necessitates fewer resources. Furthermore, the parsed KG can be constructed incrementally by adding more documents, and it does not need to load the whole model in KG construction. In online construction, we can dynamically parse the KG based on the retrieved documents.

In our experiments, the training of EGs on the NewsSpike corpus uses 220G of CPU resources over a period of 6 days. Notably, this resource requirement is significantly lower compared to the training of LLMs such as GPT3.5. When it comes to inference, GPT-3.5 necessitates online execution, whereas the augmented KG can be utilized on a local machine. We also experimented with other LLMs like LLaMA-65B (Touvron et al., 2023), which exhibited a response generation time of approximately 1.5 minutes using 4 x A100 (80G) GPUs. This extended response time renders it impractical for use in real-world QA system scenarios.

F Samples of Predicates in Entailment Graph

When querying with the relations from Google-RE, *"Place-of-Birth"*, *"Date-of-Birth"*, *"Place-of-Death"*, we show the samples ranked by the entailment score in EG. The top five predicates in the entailment graphs are shown in Table 11.

Predicate	Types	Top 5 predicates in EG
		grow.up.in
		be.in
bear.in	**person-location**	native.of
		live.in
		carry
		name.in
		address.in
bear.in	**person-time**	have.in
		be.in
		live.in
		die.at.home.in
		die.at
die.in	**person-location**	dead.found.in
		suicide.in
		kill.in

Table 11: Top 5 predicates in entailment graphs

G Additional Implementation Details

In KG construction, we do not perform any hyper-parameter tuning when generating KG. We followed the configs of Hosseini et al. (2018) in training entailment graphs, which sets the minimum number of predicates (for each argument-pair), and the minimum number of argument-pairs (for each predicate) to 3. In the evaluation of Boolean QA, we utilize a linear function to combine EG with BERT and GPT-3.5. For the EG+BERT combination, we assign a weight of 0.94 to the EG and 0.06 to BERT. In the EG+GPT-3.5 combinations, the weight assigned to the EG is 0.42.

H Cloze-style Prompts to Natural Question

Questions in LAMA probe are manually formulatd as "fill-in-the-blank" cloze statements. The prompts in LAMA probe are designed for MLM, like BERT. We manually change the cloze-style prompts to natural questions for the generative model such as GPT-3.5, as shwon in Table 12. We conducted a series of experiments involving the utilization of AutoPrompt (Shin et al., 2020) for the automatic generation of prompts for GPT-3.5. However, the performance of prompts generated through this automated process was found to be inferior to those manually curated and labeled. In order to perform a comprehensive analysis of the LMs and make a valid comparison against MR-based approaches, we present the results based on the utilization of manually generated prompts.

I Generating Prompts for Query Automatically

Unlike queries in Google-RE and T-REx using manual-labeld cloze-style prompts, we automatically generate a query for each triple in YAGO3-10 by concatenating the relation names and entities. For example, when querying the triple *(Kobe Bryant, playsFor, Los Angeles Lakers)*, it will be generated as the sentence *"Kobe Bryant plays for [MASK]"* for LMs.

Dataset	Relation Names	Cloze-Style Prompts from LAMA probe	Generated Natural Questions
Google-RE	place of birth	[X] was born in [Y] .	Where was [X] born?
	place of death	[X] died in [Y] .	Where did [X] die?
	date of birth	[X] (born [Y]).	When was [X] born?
T-REx	place of birth	[X] was born in [Y] .	Where was [X] born?
	place of death	[X] died in [Y] .	Where did [X] die?
	subclass of	[X] is a subclass of [Y] .	[X] is a subclass of what?
	official language	The official language of [X] is [Y] .	What is the official language of [X]?
	position played on team / speciality	[X] plays in [Y] position .	What position does [X] play?
	original network	[X] was originally aired on [Y] .	Where was [X] originally aired?
	shares border with	[X] shares border with [Y] .	[X] shares border with whom?
	named after	[X] is named after [Y] .	What is [X] named after?
	original language of film or TV show	The original language of [X] is [Y] .	What is the original language of [X]?
	member of	[X] is a member of [Y] .	[X] is a member of what?
	field of work	[X] works in the field of [Y] .	What field does [X] work in?
	occupation	[X] is a [Y] by profession .	[X] is a what by profession?
	has part	[X] consists of [Y] .	What does [X] consist of?
	diplomatic relation	[X] maintains diplomatic relations with [Y] .	Which conutry does [X] maintain diplomatic relations with?
	manufacturer	[X] is produced by [Y] .	Who produced [X]?
	country of citizenship	[X] is [Y] citizen .	What is the country of [X]?
	language of work or name	[X] was written in [Y] .	Which language was [X] written in?
	continent	[X] is located in [Y] .	Where is [X] located in?
	developer	[X] is developed by [Y] .	Who developed [X]?
	capital of	[X] is the capital of [Y] .	[X] is the capital of what?
	located in the administrative territorial entity	[X] is located in [Y] .	Where is [X] located in?
	languages spoken, written or signed	[X] used to communicate in [Y] .	Which language did [X] use to communicate in?
	employer	[X] works for [Y] .	Who does [X] work for?
	genre	[X] plays [Y] music .	What music does [X] play?
	country	[X] is located in [Y] .	Where is [X] located in?
	position held	[X] has the position of [Y] .	What position does [X] have?
	record label	[X] is represented by music label [Y] .	[X] is represented by what music label?
	location	[X] is located in [Y] .	Where is [X] located in?
	work location	[X] used to work in [Y] .	Where did [X] work?
	religion	[X] is affiliated with the [Y] religion .	[X] is affiliated with the what religion?
	instrument	[X] plays [Y] .	What does [X] play?
	owned by	[X] is owned by [Y] .	Who owns [X]?
	native language	The native language of [X] is [Y] .	What is the the native language of [X]?
	twinned administrative body	[X] and [Y] are twin cities .	Which city and [X] are twin cities?
	applies to jurisdiction	[X] is a legal term in [Y] .	[X] is a legal term in what?
	instance of	[X] is a [Y] .	[X] is a what ?
	country of origin	[X] was created in [Y] .	Where was [X] was created?
	headquarters location	The headquarter of [X] is in [Y] .	Where is the headquarter of [X]?
	capital	The capital of [X] is [Y] .	Where is the capital of [X]?
	location of formation	[X] was founded in [Y] .	Where was [X] founded?
	part of	[X] is part of [Y] .	[X] is part of what?

Table 12: For generative LMs, we generate the natural questions from the cloze-style prompts in LAMA probe. The table shows the mapping between manual prompts and generated questions.

Rels in YAGO	Generated prompts	Examples	
		Query	Answer
isLocatedIn	[X] is loctaed in [Y]	The Safety of Objects is located in [MASK]	United Kingdom
diedIn	[X] died in [Y]	Jean Genet died in [MASK]	Paris
wasBornIn	[X] was born in [Y]	Peter Creamer was born in [MASK]	Hartlepool
hasGender	[X] has gender [Y]	Robert Bly has gender [MASK]	male
playsFor	[X] plays for [Y]	Edgardo Abdala plays for [MASK]	Huachipato
actedIn	[X] acted in [Y]	Charles Durning acted in [MASK]	Tootsie
happenedIn	[X] happened in [Y]	Operation Anaconda happened in [MASK]	Afghanistan
isAffiliatedTo	[X] is affiliated to [Y]	Toni Kuivasto is affiliated to [MASK]	Helsingin Jalkapalloklubi
directed	[X] directed [Y]	Charles Walters directed [MASK]	Lili
isPoliticianOf	[X] is politician of [Y]	Mario Monti is politician of [MASK]	Italy
isCitizenOf	[X] is citizen of [Y]	Nusrat Bhutto is citizen of [MASK]	Iran
dealsWith	[X] deals with [Y]	Togo deals with [MASK]	France
hasOfficialLanguage	[X] has official language [Y]	Guntur has official language [MASK]	Urdu
edited	[X] edited [Y]	V. T. Vijayan edited [MASK]	Saamy
hasCapital	[X] has capital[Y]	Jharkhand has capital [MASK]	Ranchi
hasNeighbor	[X] has neighbor [Y]	Poland has neighbor [MASK]	Lithuania
created	[X] created [Y]	Ilaiyaraaja created [MASK]	Manassinakkare
livesIn	[X] lives in [Y]	Bradley Walsh lives in [MASK]	Essex
wroteMusicFor	[X] wrote music for [Y]	Johnson (composer) wrote music for [MASK]	Thazhvaram
isMarriedTo	[X] is married to [Y]	Livia is married to [MASK]	Augustus
isConnectedTo	[X] is connected to [Y]	Manas International Airport is connected to [MASK]	Kyrgyzstan
participatedIn	[X] participated in [Y]	United States Army participated in [MASK]	Marinduque
hasChild	[X] has child [Y]	William Hague has child [MASK]	Ron Davies
isInterestedIn	[X] is interested in [Y]	Muhammad Taqi Usmani is interested in [MASK]	Tafsir
hasWebsite	[X] has website [Y]	Rural Municipality of Frontier No. 19 has website [MASK]	www.mds.gov.sk.ca/app
isLeaderOf	[X] is leader of [Y]	Xi Jinping is leader of [MASK]	China
hasWonPrize	[X] has won prize [Y]	Philip Hall has won prize [MASK]	De Morgan Medal
influences	[X] influences [Y]	James M. Buchanan influences [MASK]	Elinor Ostrom
isKnownFor	[X] is known for [Y]	Friedrich Engels is known for [MASK]	Marxism
owns	[X] owns [Y]	The Walt Disney Company owns [MASK]	Walt Disney World
worksAt	[X] works at [Y]	Nicholas Kemmer works at [MASK]	University of Edinburgh
graduatedFrom	[X] graduated from [Y]	Ann Richards graduated from [MASK]	Baylor University
exports	[X] exports [Y]	Paraguay exports [MASK]	electricity
hasCurrency	[X] has currency [Y]	Portugal has currency [MASK]	Euro sign
hasMusicalRole	[X] has musical role [Y]	Danny Goffey has musical role [MASK]	piano
hasAcademicAdvisor	[X] has academic advisor [Y]	Robert Lee Moore has academic advisor [MASK]	Oswald Veblen
imports	[X] imports [Y]	Puerto Rico imports [MASK]	fish

Table 13: The queries generated from YAGO3-10

Controlled Data Augmentation for Training Task-Oriented Dialog Systems with Low Resource Data

Sebastian Steindl and **Ulrich Schäfer**
Ostbayerische Technische Hochschule
Amberg-Weiden, Germany
{s.steindl,u.schaefer}@oth-aw.de

Bernd Ludwig
University Regensburg,
Germany
bernd.ludwig@ur.de

Abstract

Modern dialog systems rely on Deep Learning to train transformer-based model architectures. These notoriously rely on large amounts of training data. However, the collection of conversational data is often a tedious and costly process. This is especially true for Task-Oriented Dialogs, where the system ought to help the user achieve specific tasks, such as making reservations. We investigate a controlled strategy for dialog synthesis. Our method generates utterances based on dialog annotations in a sequence-to-sequence manner. Besides exploring the viability of the approach itself, we also explore the effect of constrained beam search on the generation capabilities. Moreover, we analyze the effectiveness of the proposed method as a data augmentation by studying the impact the synthetic dialogs have on training dialog systems. We perform the experiments in multiple settings, simulating various amounts of ground-truth data. Our work shows that a controlled generation approach is a viable method to synthesize Task-Oriented Dialogs, that can in turn be used to train dialog systems. We were able to improve this process by utilizing constrained beam search.

1 Introduction

The current success of Large Language Models (LLMs) is the result of multiple factors. One of them is the availability of high-quality data in large amounts. Specifically, the prospering adoption of these LLMs as chatbots, as pioneered by ChatGPT (OpenAI, 2022), was made possible due to the usage of human feedback during training in the RLHF framework (Christiano et al., 2017).

The category of Task-Oriented Dialog (TOD) systems describes a specific kind of chatbot that aims to help users achieve tasks, such as booking hotels or making reservations, using external services. It can therefore be seen as a language-based interface to these services.

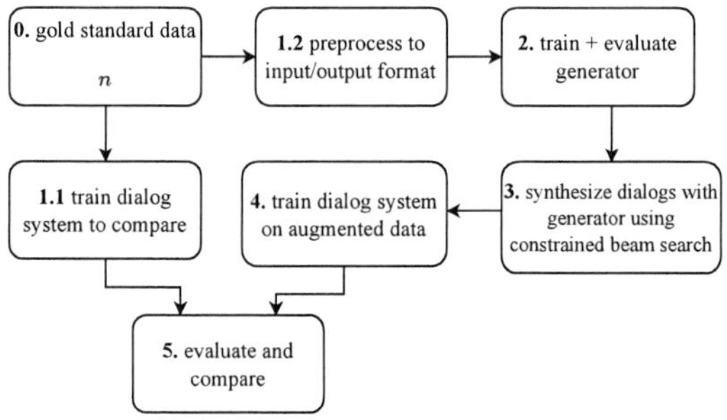

Figure 1: The general setup of the study. We use n gold standard dialogs to train a generator, which synthesizes dialogs that are in turn used to train a dialog system (steps 1.2 to 4.). To evaluate the improvement (step 5), we compare the performance of the dialog system to the baseline, where we only use the n dialogs for training (step 1.1).

In the recent past, different model architectures have been proposed to solve this problem. To evaluate them, the original MultiWOZ (Budzianowski et al., 2018) dataset and its successors are widely used as benchmarks. It contains more than ten thousand dialogs spanning multiple domains (e.g., attraction, hotel and restaurant), paving the way for the adoption of large end-to-end models.

While this benchmark allows for useful comparisons of different architectures and approaches, we deem this scenario of having multiple thousand dialogs to be infeasible for most real-life TOD use cases, where usually not nearly as many dialogs are available. This is due to the fact that the types of dialog needed to train a TOD system are different from those used to train, e.g., a social chatbot, since the TOD conversations need to include the usage of the external systems. Therefore, it is typically not only necessary to have two users (while using the Wizard-of-Oz technique; Kelley, 1984), but to have at least one of them interact with the external service to provide the necessary information to achieve the task.

Proceedings of the 2nd Workshop in Pattern-based Approaches to NLP in the Age of Deep Learning, pages 92–102
December 6, 2023. ©2023 Association for Computational Linguistics

We therefore investigate the synthesis of suitable utterances from given annotations to train TOD systems. We call this method "Controlled Generation for Training" (CG4T). For this, we simulate lower resource scenarios based on the MultiWOZ dataset, allowing us to both evaluate the models on this common benchmark and also to test the method in different, more realistic settings.

With the objective of ensuring that the generated utterances contain the entities defined in the annotation, we additionally investigate the effect of constrained beam search during the generation phase. To sum up, in our work, we aim to answer four research questions (RQ):

- RQ 1: Can a pretrained sequence-to-sequence model be fine-tuned to generate synthetic dialogs based on annotations?
- RQ 2: Can constraining the beam search improve the decoding in comparison to a normal beam search?
- RQ 3: Can the synthetic data be used to train and improve the performance of a TOD system?
- RQ 4: What is the relation between the amount of real data and the usefulness of synthetic data generated this way?

2 Background and Related Work

Controlled Generation. The main goal of the approach presented in this paper is to generate text that fulfills certain requirements, i.e., fitting the annotations it is based on. The general problem of steering generation has been addressed in the young research field of Controllable Text Generation (CTG). The root motivation behind this is to have a Natural Language Generation (NLG) system be controllable by human-defined parameters, which becomes especially important due to their black-box character (Zhang et al., 2022). Some of the applications of CTG include NLG that adheres to a specific topic, emotion, formulating text from structured data (e.g., tables), and data augmentation (Zhang et al., 2022). For example, Keskar et al. (2019) train a model with control codes that allow to influence the generation by prepending them to the prompt.

In similar spirit is the research in so called model alignment. The alignment of a model describes its fine-tuning with the goal of increasing the probability of desired outputs, i.e., those aligning with the intended use and human preferences, and decreasing the chance of undesired outputs. This has recently been achieved both with the RLHF framework (Ouyang et al., 2022) and standard supervised training (Zhou et al., 2023).

TOD Systems and the MultiWOZ Dataset. Since the publication of the original MultiWOZ (Budzianowski et al., 2018) dataset, there have been multiple updated versions, mostly to fix label noise (Eric et al., 2020; Zhang et al., 2022; Ye et al., 2022). The setting introduced by the dataset allows for two types of evaluation: Dialog State Tracking (DST) and Response Evaluation. Since recent publications manage to get near-perfect results for the Response Evaluation as measured by the inform and success metric (Cheng et al., 2022), we decide to focus on the DST task.

There has been varied research (e.g., Bang et al., 2023; Zhao et al., 2022; He et al., 2022) on specific model architectures, using distinct approaches to solve the DST task. Kim et al. (2020) propose SOM-DST, which uses an explicit state memory and predicts the operation to perform for each slot at every turn, e.g., carryover or update. On the other hand, STAR (Ye et al., 2021) tries to leverage the correlations between the slots with a slot self-attention mechanism.

Constrained Beam Search. When generating outputs with an NLG model, the goal of exhaustively finding the sequence with the highest probability is infeasible in most cases. Since for a sequence of length m over a vocabulary with length v, the computational cost would be $\mathcal{O}(v^m)$. Accordingly, beam search is commonly adopted as an approximation and used to create output sequences with a trained LLM. Performing a beam search with a beam size of b consists of keeping b candidates, for which a greedy search is continued, and finally the candidate sequence with the highest probability is picked as the prediction. The constrained beam search (CBS; Kim, 2022) is a variant of this method, which tries to enforce the existence of specific words, so-called constraints, in the output. Since for the DST task it is important to have utterances containing the entities exactly as given in the annotation, we hope that adopting the CBS scheme in our method will increase the amount of annotations appearing in the generated utterances.

Synthetic Data Generation. The proposed ap-

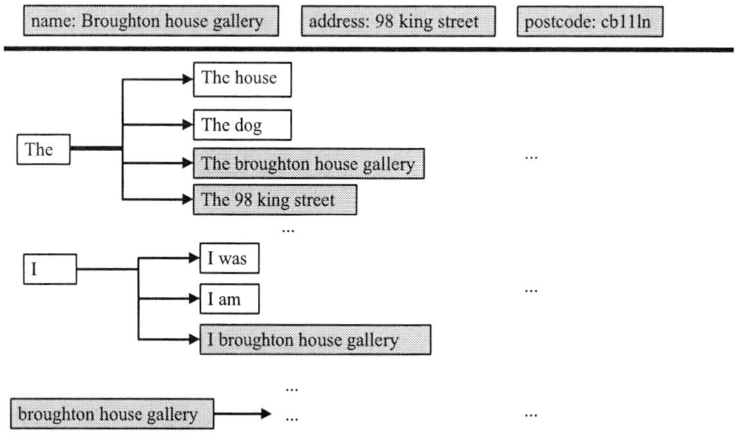

Figure 2: Simplified example step of the constrained beam search principle with three beams. Constraints marked with gray background, all constraints indicated on upper part.

proach is related to that of *bootstrapping*, which predates the Deep Learning era and is based on the triad of annotation a small amount of seed data, training a model and finally applying the model to unlabeled data, thereby generating silver-standard data (Tang and Surdeanu, 2023). Bootstrapping has recently been researched in Machine Learning applications, e.g., Tang and Surdeanu (2023); Eyal et al. (2021). The research into the generation of synthetic data in the form of dialogs has recently gained some interest, amplified by the advances in pretrained LLMs. Kim et al. (2022) distill a dataset containing 1.5 million social dialogs from a LLM. They use the LLM to first derive a short narrative and then again prompt the LLM to infer a dialog based on it. A similar approach has been studied by Miyazaki (2023), who address dialog generation based on story plots. To this end, they also investigate the prompting of LLMs. The synthesis of social dialogs via prompting LLMs was furthermore studied by Chen et al. (2023). They also extend this from dyadic conversations to multiparty dialogs, that contain more than two speakers.

3 Proposed Method and Materials

We use the MultiWOZ 2.4 (Ye et al., 2022) dataset as the basis for all of our experiments. This dataset is the result of multiple corrective iterations of the original MultiWOZ data (Budzianowski et al., 2018). It contains roughly ten thousand dialogs, of which two thousand in total are reserved as validation and test data. We make use of the official split between training, validation and test data. The dialogs were created with the Wizard-of-Oz (WOZ) technique (Kelley, 1984), where the interaction with a dialog system was imitated. While these can therefore be regarded as gold-standard data, the collection process is laborious and costly. To simulate a more realistic setting, we therefore randomly sample n dialogs from the training data and proceed with them as if they were the only collected conversations.

The goal of our method is to synthesize a large amount of dialogs based on a small amount of collected data. Instead of generating the whole dialog in one pass, we predict each utterance one after another based on the turn annotations with a sequence-to-sequence generator model. This can be described as using the annotations as a *blueprint* for the dialog.

The main steps of the method are given as 1.2, 2, 3, and 4 in Fig. 1. They first include the preprocessing of the data, so they fit a specified input/output format (x, y) for the sequence-to-sequence model (1.2). This format is depicted in Fig. 3. With this, we train a sequence-to-sequence model (2.) as the generator $\hat{y} = g_{CBS}(x)$. We write a generator model that uses the constrained beam search as its decoding strategy as $g_{CBS}(x)$. Using the trained $g_{CBS}(x)$ we perform the data augmentation by synthesizing dialogs using CBS (3.), and finally train the TOD system on this augmented data (4.). These steps are described in more detail below.

3.1 Input and Output of the Generator

Our generator model $\hat{y} = g(x)$ maps an input string x_i to an output utterance $\hat{y}_i$. An example of the input to and output of the generator is

in (x)	**<b_ctx> <b_bs>** train-leaveat: dontcare **<e_bs>** **<b_lbl>** train-leaveat: dontcare **<e_lbl>** **<b_pos>** 6 **<e_pos> <e_ctx>** Bot: there are 7 trains that can get you there , the earliest is levaing at 05:19 , the latest at 08:19 . do you have a time you would like to leave the station ? User:
out (y)	no , i do not care what time it leaves as long as it arrives in cambridge by 9:30 .
$\hat{y}$	i do not have a time to leave .

Figure 3: An example of the input x and output y that make up the training data as well as the output $\hat{y}g_{CBS}(x)$ of the trained generator with $n = 2500$. The typo at "levaing" is part of the dataset.

given in Fig. 3. Each x is made up of some meta-information, which we will call context, and the previous utterance. Thus, for an utterance y_i, the input is constructed as the concatenation of the context, the previous speaker and their utterance, and the speaker of y_i.

The context is constructed from

- the belief state (e.g., "train-leaveat: dontcare" in Fig. 3),
- the turns labels (e.g., the second "train-leaveat: dontcare" in Fig. 3 or "restaurant-name: the missing sock" as an example from a different utterance) and
- the turns index within the dialog (i.e., 6 in Fig. 3).

If the current utterance y_i is a system utterance, we also add the system act (e.g., "arrive: ?", if the system asks the user when he wants to arrive) to the context.

We introduce special tokens that indicate the start and end of a certain part of meta-information within the context. These markers are of the form *<b_META>* ... *<e_META>*, with META $\in$ {ctx, bs, lbl, pos, sysact} for context, belief state, label, position and system act, respectively.

To simulate the low resource settings, we randomly sample n dialogs from all train data X in the official MultiWOZ split to create a new training set X^n. We define $X^{\bar{n}} = X \setminus X^n$ to be the *blueprints* which we will use for the data augmentation.

3.2 Constrained Beam Search

With the aim of improving the inclusion of the annotations into the generated dialogs, we evaluate the effect of constrained beam search, which is implemented in the transformers library (Wolf et al., 2020). The main idea of CBS is to consider at every decoding step not only the highest-probability tokens, but also those defined as constraints. In our case, the constraints are the entities or strings contained in the annotations.

To avoid trivial but nonsensical outputs that simply concatenate the constraints, beams that do not (yet) fulfill the constraints are also kept in consideration during the decoding process. The implementation groups all candidates into so-called banks, depending on how close they are to fulfilling the constraint. Through a round-robin selection, b candidates, sourced from all banks, are preserved. Therefore, both outputs that are already closer to fulfilling the constraints, and those that are more sensible while being further from the constraints, are being considered. An example step of this constrained beam search generation is shown in Fig. 2. In this example, an undesired sequence that could be generated without the banks would be simply concatenating the annotation to output "broughton house gallery 98 king street cb11ln".

3.3 Data Augmentation Process

During the data augmentation process, we generate synthetic dialogs by creating each utterance within the dialog one after another. This is visualized in Fig. 4. The input string x, consisting of context and previous utterance, is created from the annotations of the current utterance and the previous utterance. During the training of the generator $g(x)$ or $g_{CBS}(x)$ (cf. step 2 in Fig. 1), we use the ground-truth previous utterance, since these come from available dialogs. The example output in 3 shows that the model correctly interprets the input x and generates an utterance $\hat{y}$ that contains the information that the user does not have to leave by a specific time. However, the information that the user has to arrive by a certain time was not given in the input (since it is missing in the annotation) and thus is also not represented in $\hat{y}$.

During the augmentation of the data, i.e., synthesizing new dialogs with the generator (cf. step 3 in Fig. 1), we use the previously model-generated utterance to keep the scenario realistic. Therefore, the evaluation of the models trained on the augmented data, does not rely on any ground-truth utterances.

In a real-world situation, the annotation for these

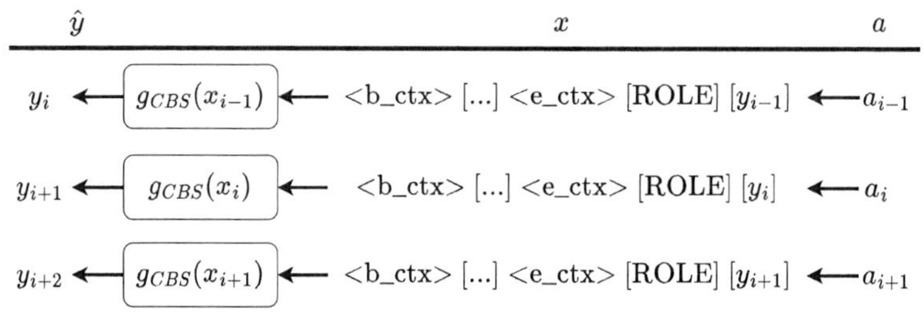

Figure 4: Visualization of the data augmentation process. The generator $g(x)$ creates the utterance predictions $\hat{y}$ from the input x, which is constructed based on the annotations a.

unknown dialogs $X^{\bar{n}}$, that we take from the unused MultiWOZ dialogs in the train split, will in general not be readily available. But the method needs annotations to be provided to the model as a *blueprint*. A solution to this is to have the dialog annotations created algorithmically. This is much simpler to do with traditional methods, which can be pattern-based, than to generate the dialog itself.

3.4 Training the TOD system

Once we have augmented the data by synthesizing all utterances for the dialogs in $X^{\bar{n}}$, we can train the TOD systems on this data. To this end, we keep the structure and annotations of the MultiWOZ train dataset but for all dialogs in $X^{\bar{n}}$, we replace the ground-truth utterance with the synthetic one, i.e., we set $y_i := g_{CBS}(x_i) \; \forall \, x_i \in x, \; \forall \, x \in X^{\bar{n}}$.

4 Experiments

Our experiments can be divided into two stages. The first stage consists of studying the generator and relates to RQ 1 (feasibility) and RQ 2 (constrained beam search). The second focuses on the dialog system and aims to answer RQ 3 (effectiveness). To evaluate the proposed method, we look at four different, simulated low(er) resource settings to answer RQ 4 (magnitude of data). In each of those, we assume that a certain amount n of annotated dialogs have been collected, which will be used for the CG4T approach. Concretely, we use $n \in \{150, 750, 1000, 2500\}$ in an attempt to understand the effect different magnitudes of data have.

4.1 Experiments on the Generator

To train our generator models, we randomly split X^n into a train, validation and test set, using a 70-10-20 split for each n, respectively. We further filter the training data so that it contains only utterances that have annotations. This has shown to be beneficial in preliminary experiments. Therefore, in each setting, the generator itself is trained and evaluated with a different amount of data. This is a necessary condition to realistically simulate the different settings. We chose the BART Base (Lewis et al., 2020) model as the architecture for our generator and used the pretrained checkpoint provided by the transformers library (Wolf et al., 2020).

We trained each generator model on its respective training data for 50 epochs using the Cross Entropy Loss, only saving the model with the lowest loss on the validation set. This was consistently achieved around the tenth epoch, after which the model started overfitting. An example of a completely synthesized conversation is given in Fig. 5.

User: i am looking for a train that leaves from cambridge on wednesday.
Bot: there are 5 trains peterborough on wednesday.
User: i need to leave peterborough after 12:45.
Bot: tr1879 leaves at 13:06 on wednesday.
User: i am also looking for a train.
Bot: i have a train that will get you to peterborough by 13:56. it will cost 16.50 pounds per ticket.
User: can you book that for 1 person?
Bot: yes, please.
User: i am also looking for a museum in the centre of town.
Bot: broughton house gallery is located at 98 king street, postcode cb11ln.
User: thanks.
Bot: you're welcome, i hope you enjoy your time in cambridge!

Figure 5: An example of a dialog synthesized by the generator. The ground-truth dialog is shown in Fig. 6 in the appendix A. Speaker roles are added in bold to improve readability.

To evaluate the generators, we investigate their language generation capabilities as well as their task completion, which we define as adhering to the annotation. We use BERTScore (Zhang et al.,

2019), which is especially suited to measure semantic similarity, to evaluate the text generation. This metric uses contextual BERT embeddings to calculate the similarity between the generated sentence and the ground-truth reference.

To measure the task-completion, we define the mean annotation metric as

$$Annot = \frac{1}{k}\sum_{j=1}^{k}(\frac{1}{l}\sum_{i=1}^{l}z(a_i, y_j)), \quad (1)$$

with a_i being one annotation of all l annotations a, y_j is one of all k utterances and

$$z(a_i, y_j) = \begin{cases} 1 & a_i \text{ is in } y_j, \\ 0 & a_i \text{ is not in } y_j. \end{cases} \quad (2)$$

In other words, we calculate the mean percentage of annotations that are part of the generated utterance. We define an annotation a_i as consisting of both the slot name and the slot value, since depending on the concrete utterance, containing the slot name can be desirable. However, the annotations are rather diverse, and the slot values do not only contain information entities, e.g., restaurant names or reservation times. So while in most cases we expect the text to contain exactly the slot value, there are also annotations where a slot has, for example, a boolean value. E.g., the slot "parking" for the domain hotel might have the value "yes". In this case, we do not necessarily want the utterance to contain the slot value but rather the slot name. Therefore, we check both the slot name and its value for occurrence. Still, it is possible that neither the slot name nor its value are supposed to be part of the utterance as-is. Take as an example the annotation "train-leaveat: dontcare". Therefore, to improve the meaningfulness of the metric, we also report it in proportion to the $Annot$ of the test dataset utterances (cf. Tab. 4). We write this as $Annot_R$.

4.2 Experiments on the Data Augmentation

The second stage of the experiments investigates if the synthetic dialogs generated in the previous experiments can improve the performance of TOD systems by means of data augmentation. Since the experiments on the constrained beam search have shown positive results, we adopted this method during the data augmentation.

That is, with $g_{CBS}(x)$ we synthesize dialogs for all $x \in X^{\bar{n}}$. To this end, we train two distinct recent model architectures, where the publications include an open-source code base. SOM-DST[1] (Kim et al., 2020) is an approach using explicit state memory and predicting the operation to perform for each slot at every turn. The second architecture is called STAR[2] (Ye et al., 2021), which introduces a slot self-attention mechanism to learn the correlations between the slots. This method predicts the slot-value-combination with the highest likelihood and can thus be classified as ontology-based, while SOM-DST can be classified as open-vocabulary, using only the dialog context (Ye et al., 2022). We trained both approaches with the hyperparameter setup provided by their authors.

We utilize the Joint Goal Accuracy (JGA) (Nouri and Hosseini-Asl, 2018) as a metric for this second stage of experiments. JGA is commonly used to evaluate models in the DST task. This metric measures, for each utterance, if the value for each slot is exactly and correctly predicted. Hence, the JGA is a rather strict evaluation metric. The results are reported in Tab. 5.

4.3 Descriptive Statistics of the Generated Data

We calculate the mean length and its standard deviation of the generated utterances and compare them to the ground-truth statistics in Tab. 1. These results show a trend of higher standard deviation with larger n. This makes sense, as it shows that a generator that was provided with more training data is capable of synthesizing utterances with higher diversity. The data at hand also shows that the system utterances are longer on average in every setting, including ground-truth. The average length of synthesized texts stays roughly the same in all n-scenarios for user and system utterances, respectively.

However, in all of these settings, they are shorter than in the ground-truth data. This can be explained by the absence of, e.g., fill words or additional information that does not concern the slots since the utterances are more tailored towards the annotation and are less likely to contain additional words. An example of this can be seen in the ground-truth dialog in Fig. 6 in the appendix A. The user says "i would like to go to peterborough and leave after 12:45, i have to attend a meeting beforehand", while in the generated utterance (cf. Fig. 5), the user says "i need to leave peterborough after 12:45".

[1]https://github.com/clovaai/som-dst

[2]https://github.com/smartyfh/DST-STAR

n	Length User	Length System
150	48.37 ± 17.56	55.35 ± 22.90
750	44.03 ± 20.55	56.89 ± 28.88
1000	40.11 ± 22.73	56.83 ± 28.45
2500	44.57 ± 23.90	61.79 ± 34.07
gt	61.99 ± 29.04	89.22 ± 38.68

Table 1: $\mu \pm \sigma$ of the length of user and system utterances for different n, where $n =$ gt shows the statistics of the ground-truth training data X. The length is measured as the number of characters including punctuation and white spaces.

	RTTR		MTLD	
n	User	System	User	System
150	2.29	3.02	26.18	36.07
750	2.42	4.09	32.08	43.76
1000	2.71	4.57	37.36	46.35
2500	3.33	6.17	46.10	55.67
gt	4.32	10.73	63.56	65.71

Table 2: Lexical richness measured as RTTR and MTLD of user and system utterances for different n, where $n =$ gt shows the statistics of the ground-truth training data X.

Besides the mix-up of departure and destination, the information about the user having to attend a meeting is also left out. This is to be expected, as the annotation does not track this information.

This can be seen as both a positive and a negative effect. On the one hand, the generator fails to imitate the length of the utterances. On the other hand, the synthesized texts are more concise.

We do not report the statistics on the number of turns since, due to the generation process, where we generate an utterance for each utterance-annotation existing in the data, the number of turns in all n-scenarios is the same as for the ground-truth data.

Furthermore, we evaluate the lexical diversity of the generated utterances using the root type-token ratio (RTTR; Guiraud, 1958) and the measure of textual lexical diversity (MTLD; McCarthy and Jarvis, 2010) with a threshold of 0.72. Both were computed with the LexicalRichness library[3]. The results, depicted in Tab. 2, are analogous to the findings regarding the utterance length. A higher n of available data consistently lead to higher lexical richness for both user and system utterances, as measured by both metrics. However, even in the setting of $n = 2500$, the utterances do not reach the lexical diversity of the ground-truth utterances. The fact that system utterances invariably show higher diversity can be explained by the usual course the dialogs have, in that the system provides slot values, which can be expected to have more lexical variance than the rest of the utterance since they contain, e.g., restaurant names or booking references.

5 Qualitative Error Analysis

To better understand the weaknesses of the generator, we performed a qualitative error analysis by comparing generated dialogs to their ground-truth. In the following, we will reference the errors with regard to the generated dialog in Fig. 5 and its ground-truth in Fig. 6 in the appendix A.

First, errors in the annotation will naturally be replicated in the generated utterance. As an example, while in the ground-truth the user requests the reference number for the ticket and the system delivers it, the generated dialog does not mention the reference number at all. However, since the annotation does not contain the reference number either, we cannot expect it to be generated. Second, we can see that sometimes the speaker role seems to not be completely taken into account, leading to formulations that are unexpected for the dialog system, such as the "yes, please" response the system gave to the user's request to book a train ticket. Lastly, while the concrete text of the slot values will in general be correct due to the constrained beam search, the embedding of them into context still contains errors, both semantically and syntactically. An example we can see in the generated dialog is first that the chatbot produces a faulty utterance "there are 5 trains peterborough on wednesday". Thus, at the same time, prematurely giving the number of trains for the destination but also not specifying it is the destination. The premature destination mention is due to it already being part of the belief state annotation for this turn.

To sum up, while the model in general achieves decent results, there are still multiple caveats, and the error analysis emphasizes the importance of the annotations.

6 Results and Discussion

Our experiments show that the model is able to generate utterances based on the provided annotations. These utterances resemble the language defined by

[3] https://github.com/LSYS/LexicalRichness

	F1		Precision		Recall	
n	$g_{CBS}(x)$	$g(x)$	$g_{CBS}(x)$	$g(x)$	$g_{CBS}(x)$	$g(x)$
150	87.84	**89.27**	89.12	**91.05**	86.65	**87.60**
750	89.41	**89.75**	91.36	**91.90**	**87.76**	**87.76**
1000	89.25	**89.60**	91.09	**91.77**	87.54	**87.60**
2500	89.56	**89.90**	91.44	**91.99**	87.81	**87.98**

Table 3: F1, Precision and Recall of the BERTScore for the different scenarios *with* and *without* constrained beam search as indicated by $g_{CBS}(x)$ and $g(x)$, respectively. Better marked in bold for each metric and n, respectively.

the training data, as is shown by the BERTScore (cf. Tab. 3). The improvements with increased n are negligible for this metric. This can be attributed to the fact that, due to fine-tuning a pretrained LLM, the model already had good general language generation capabilities to begin with. However, with regard to the average utterance length (cf. Tab. 1) and lexical richness (cf. Tab. 2), the generated text does not perfectly align with the training data. Nevertheless, we consider the model to have a good, but not perfect, language generation capability for this specific task. Besides language generation, RQ 1 also tends to the task-completion, which in this case is adhering to the annotations.

We report the results for the $Annot_R$ metric in Tab. 4. These show that the model is also capable of generating utterances that adhere to the annotations. The performances for the different n-scenarios are comparable. It is an important insight that the $Annot_R$ metric is more expressive. This makes up for a weakness of the metric, which stems from the different kind of annotations that exist.

The dialog in Fig. 5 shows that when few annotations are provided for an utterance, the generation can lead to an unfitting utterance. For example, when the user asks to book the train ticket for one person, the system answers with "yes, please". From the usual dialog flow the MultiWOZ conversations have, it is clear that this utterance usually belongs to a user and not the system. The generator mistakenly used this as a confirmation, even though it is unfitting for this speaker in this scenario.

Since both the language generation and the task-completion capabilities are sufficient, we answer RQ 1 positively: We successfully used a pretrained sequence-to-sequence model to generate synthetic dialogs based on annotations.

The effect of the constrained beam search is also shown in tables Tab. 3 and Tab. 4. As is to be expected from the method, constraining the generation led to slightly worse results in the BERTScore metrics. This is consistent over all n. However, regarding the $Annot$ metric, the constrained beam search improved the outcome substantially. With it, the $Annot_R$ relative to the test data was near-perfect over all n. A special case is $n = 150$, where $Annot_R > 1$. This means that on average, the utterances predicted by the generator model contained more annotations than the actual test data. This effect can be explained by the small sample size, as well as the fact that the ground-truth $Annot$ of the test data over all n is roughly 0.73. The large increase in $Annot$ score with a small decline in BERTScore metrics suggests that CBS is useful for annotation-based generation, which leads us to answer RQ 2 positively.

As a result, we utilized constrained beam search for the second stage of experiments. Tab. 5 shows the results for the selected TOD system architectures for the n-scenarios. We report both the results of using only these n dialogs, and additionally using the synthetic dialogs, i.e., with CG4T.

The first finding is that for all n and both architectures, CG4T did improve the JGA, therefore showing that the synthetic dialogs generated from annotations can indeed increase the performance of both open-vocabulary and ontology-based TOD systems. Consequently, we answer RQ 3 positively as well. Still, the results show that with larger n, the benefit gained through the usage of CG4T decreases. This is to be expected given the nature of the method, which led us to pose RQ 4. Finally, Tab. 5 demonstrates the significant differences in JGA between the two approaches.

Regarding RQ 4 we evaluate the combined results from experiments in stages one and two. Stage one showed that only a few gold standard dialogs are needed to get good language generation capability. Moreover, thanks to CBS, we can also attain satisfying results for task-completion. The second stage showed that the more dialogs available, the lesser the improvement. From this we conclude that a) the less data one has, the more sense it makes to use this method and b) for this concrete scenario, the method is nonessential past a magnitude of 2500 dialogs.

	Annot		*Annot*$_R$	
n	$g_{CBS}(x)$	$g(x)$	$g_{CBS}(x)$	$g(x)$
150	**0.76**	0.69	**1.04**	0.94
750	**0.72**	0.63	**0.99**	0.87
1000	**0.71**	0.62	**0.98**	0.85
2500	**0.72**	0.61	**0.99**	0.84

Table 4: *Annot* and *Annot*$_R$ in relation to the test data for the different scenarios *with* and *without* constrained beam search as indicated by $g_{CBS}(x)$ and $g(x)$, respectively. Better marked in bold for each metric and n, respectively.

	STAR		**SOM-DST**	
n	**as is**	**CG4T**	**as is**	**CG4T**
150	3.50	**42.40**	1.49	**23.83**
750	38.86	**57.92**	21.65	**31.79**
1000	45.71	**63.45**	25.73	**32.82**
2500	63.55	**64.97**	35.18	**36.02**
8420	74.46	-	41.69	-

Table 5: JGA for different scenarios of available training data for the two reference models. The columns marked "CG4T" report the results after applying the proposed method to extend the number of training dialogs to achieve $n = 8420$ with synthetic data. The columns marked "as is" report results without data augmentation. The last row shows the result when using the full training data. Thus, CG4T is not applicable. Better marked in bold for each setting and n, respectively.

7 Conclusion

In this work, we studied whether it is practicable to synthesize dialogs based on annotations to augment the collected ground-truth data for training a TOD system. To this end, we focused on four research questions regarding the feasibility (RQ 1), the effect of CBS during decoding (RQ 2), the performance improvement when using the synthetic dialogues to train a dialog system (RQ 3), and the relation between available data and the effect of the method (RQ 4).

We saw that even with small amounts of dialog, we can train a generator that creates utterances from annotations using a sequence-to-sequence strategy.

While the constrained beam search had slightly adverse effects on the language generation capabilities, it provided significant improvements to the task-completion, i.e., adhering to the annotation.

Augmenting the training data with the synthetic dialogues relevantly increased the performance of the dialog system as measured by the JGA metric.

The smaller the number of available conversations, the greater the effect of the CG4T approach. Past a scale of roughly 2500 collected ground-truth dialogs, we would discourage augmenting the training data in this way since the improvements are too small for the increased effort. Our research showed at multiple stages the importance of having annotations of the highest quality when using the proposed approach.

Limitations

While offering multiple advantages discussed above, our method also has some limitations and drawbacks.

First, since CG4T relies on training a generator model, it inevitably requires additional effort and computing time. One could also argue that this requires more specific knowledge (e.g., programming) than simply prompting a LLM such as ChatGPT to generate dialogs via an API.

Second, as demonstrated by our experiments, the proposed approach is only sensible up to a certain scale of existing data, and it does take at least some data to train the generator.

Third, the approach is heavily dependent on the annotation. As shown on multiple occasions in this work, if the annotation is lacking information, the synthetic utterance will naturally not contain it either. Therefore, to synthesize the dialogs that will be used for training, one has to have access to high-quality annotations.

Additionally, the approach needs to have the *blueprints* to the dialog in the form of annotations. If they do not exist in a real-world scenario, they have to be generated in advance. We argue that this is also feasible with traditional algorithms and heuristics.

Lastly, our experiments are limited to the MultiWOZ dataset. While it is reasonable to assume that the general behavior will be similar for conversations from other distributions, we did not perform experiments on this.

References

Namo Bang, Jeehyun Lee, and Myoung-Wan Koo. 2023. Task-optimized adapters for an end-to-end task-oriented dialogue system. *arXiv preprint arXiv:2305.02468*.

Paweł Budzianowski, Tsung-Hsien Wen, Bo-Hsiang Tseng, Iñigo Casanueva, Stefan Ultes, Osman Ramadan, and Milica Gašić. 2018. MultiWOZ - a large-scale multi-domain Wizard-of-Oz dataset for task-oriented dialogue modelling. In *Proceedings of the 2018 Conference on Empirical Methods in Natural Language Processing*, pages 5016–5026, Brussels, Belgium. Association for Computational Linguistics.

Maximillian Chen, Alexandros Papangelis, Chenyang Tao, Seokhwan Kim, Andy Rosenbaum, Yang Liu, Zhou Yu, and Dilek Hakkani-Tur. 2023. PLACES: Prompting language models for social conversation synthesis. In *Findings of the Association for Computational Linguistics: EACL 2023*, pages 844–868, Dubrovnik, Croatia. Association for Computational Linguistics.

Qinyuan Cheng, Linyang Li, Guofeng Quan, Feng Gao, Xiaofeng Mou, and Xipeng Qiu. 2022. Is MultiWOZ a solved task? an interactive TOD evaluation framework with user simulator. In *Findings of the Association for Computational Linguistics: EMNLP 2022*, pages 1248–1259, Abu Dhabi, United Arab Emirates. Association for Computational Linguistics.

Paul F Christiano, Jan Leike, Tom Brown, Miljan Martic, Shane Legg, and Dario Amodei. 2017. Deep reinforcement learning from human preferences. *Advances in neural information processing systems*, 30:4299–4307.

Mihail Eric, Rahul Goel, Shachi Paul, Abhishek Sethi, Sanchit Agarwal, Shuyang Gao, Adarsh Kumar, Anuj Goyal, Peter Ku, and Dilek Hakkani-Tur. 2020. MultiWOZ 2.1: A consolidated multi-domain dialogue dataset with state corrections and state tracking baselines. In *Proceedings of the Twelfth Language Resources and Evaluation Conference*, pages 422–428, Marseille, France. European Language Resources Association.

Matan Eyal, Asaf Amrami, Hillel Taub-Tabib, and Yoav Goldberg. 2021. Bootstrapping relation extractors using syntactic search by examples. In *Proceedings of the 16th Conference of the European Chapter of the Association for Computational Linguistics: Main Volume*, pages 1491–1503, Online. Association for Computational Linguistics.

P. Guiraud. 1958. *Problèmes et Méthodes de La Statistique Linguistique*. Dodrecht: D. Reidel.

Wanwei He, Yinpei Dai, Min Yang, Jian Sun, Fei Huang, Luo Si, and Yongbin Li. 2022. Space-3: Unified dialog model pre-training for task-oriented dialog understanding and generation. *arXiv preprint arXiv:2209.06664*.

J. F. Kelley. 1984. An iterative design methodology for user-friendly natural language office information applications. *ACM Transactions on Information Systems*, 2(1):26–41.

Nitish Shirish Keskar, Bryan McCann, Lav R Varshney, Caiming Xiong, and Richard Socher. 2019. Ctrl: A conditional transformer language model for controllable generation. *arXiv preprint arXiv:1909.05858*.

Chan Woo Kim. 2022. Guiding Text Generation with Constrained Beam Search in Transformers. [Online; posted 11-March-2022].

Hyunwoo Kim, Jack Hessel, Liwei Jiang, Ximing Lu, Youngjae Yu, Pei Zhou, Ronan Le Bras, Malihe Alikhani, Gunhee Kim, Maarten Sap, et al. 2022. Soda: Million-scale dialogue distillation with social commonsense contextualization. *arXiv preprint arXiv:2212.10465*.

Sungdong Kim, Sohee Yang, Gyuwan Kim, and Sang-Woo Lee. 2020. Efficient Dialogue State Tracking by Selectively Overwriting Memory. In *Proceedings of the 58th Annual Meeting of the Association for Computational Linguistics*, pages 567–582, Online. Association for Computational Linguistics.

Mike Lewis, Yinhan Liu, Naman Goyal, Marjan Ghazvininejad, Abdelrahman Mohamed, Omer Levy, Veselin Stoyanov, and Luke Zettlemoyer. 2020. BART: Denoising sequence-to-sequence pre-training for natural language generation, translation, and comprehension. In *Proceedings of the 58th Annual Meeting of the Association for Computational Linguistics*, pages 7871–7880, Online. Association for Computational Linguistics.

Philip M McCarthy and Scott Jarvis. 2010. Mtld, vocd-d, and hd-d: A validation study of sophisticated approaches to lexical diversity assessment. *Behavior research methods*, 42(2):381–392.

Chiaki Miyazaki. 2023. Dialogue generation conditional on predefined stories: Preliminary results. *IEEE access : practical innovations, open solutions*, 11:85589–85599.

Elnaz Nouri and Ehsan Hosseini-Asl. 2018. Toward scalable neural dialogue state tracking model. *arXiv preprint arXiv:1812.00899*.

OpenAI. 2022. OpenAI: Introducing ChatGPT. [Online; posted 30-November-2022].

Long Ouyang, Jeffrey Wu, Xu Jiang, Diogo Almeida, Carroll Wainwright, Pamela Mishkin, Chong Zhang, Sandhini Agarwal, Katarina Slama, Alex Ray, John Schulman, Jacob Hilton, Fraser Kelton, Luke Miller, Maddie Simens, Amanda Askell, Peter Welinder, Paul F Christiano, Jan Leike, and Ryan Lowe. 2022. Training language models to follow instructions with human feedback. In *Advances in Neural Information Processing Systems*, volume 35, pages 27730–27744. Curran Associates, Inc.

Zheng Tang and Mihai Surdeanu. 2023. Bootstrapping neural relation and explanation classifiers. In *Proceedings of the 61st Annual Meeting of the Association for Computational Linguistics (Volume 2: Short Papers)*, pages 48–56, Toronto, Canada. Association for Computational Linguistics.

Thomas Wolf, Lysandre Debut, Victor Sanh, Julien Chaumond, Clement Delangue, Anthony Moi, Pierric Cistac, Tim Rault, Remi Louf, Morgan Funtowicz, Joe Davison, Sam Shleifer, Patrick von Platen, Clara Ma, Yacine Jernite, Julien Plu, Canwen Xu, Teven Le Scao, Sylvain Gugger, Mariama Drame, Quentin Lhoest, and Alexander Rush. 2020. Transformers: State-of-the-art natural language processing. In *Proceedings of the 2020 Conference on Empirical Methods in Natural Language Processing: System Demonstrations*, pages 38–45, Online. Association for Computational Linguistics.

Fanghua Ye, Jarana Manotumruksa, and Emine Yilmaz. 2022. MultiWOZ 2.4: A Multi-Domain Task-Oriented Dialogue Dataset with Essential Annotation Corrections to Improve State Tracking Evaluation. In *Proceedings of the 23rd Annual Meeting of the Special Interest Group on Discourse and Dialogue*, pages 351–360, Edinburgh, UK. Association for Computational Linguistics.

Fanghua Ye, Jarana Manotumruksa, Qiang Zhang, Shenghui Li, and Emine Yilmaz. 2021. Slot Self-Attentive Dialogue State Tracking. In *Proceedings of the Web Conference 2021*, WWW '21, pages 1598–1608, New York, NY, USA. Association for Computing Machinery.

Hanqing Zhang, Haolin Song, Shaoyu Li, Ming Zhou, and Dawei Song. 2022. A survey of controllable text generation using transformer-based pre-trained language models. *arXiv preprint arXiv:2201.05337*.

Tianyi Zhang, Varsha Kishore, Felix Wu, Kilian Q Weinberger, and Yoav Artzi. 2019. Bertscore: Evaluating text generation with bert. *arXiv preprint arXiv:1904.09675*.

Jeffrey Zhao, Raghav Gupta, Yuan Cao, Dian Yu, Mingqiu Wang, Harrison Lee, Abhinav Rastogi, Izhak Shafran, and Yonghui Wu. 2022. Description-driven task-oriented dialog modeling. *arXiv preprint arXiv:2201.08904*.

Chunting Zhou, Pengfei Liu, Puxin Xu, Srini Iyer, Jiao Sun, Yuning Mao, Xuezhe Ma, Avia Efrat, Ping Yu, Lili Yu, et al. 2023. Lima: Less is more for alignment. *arXiv preprint arXiv:2305.11206*.

A Example ground-truth Dialog

User: i need to take a train out of cambridge , i will be leaving town on wednesday .
Bot: there are 5 trains out of cambridge on wednesday . do you have a departure time in mind ?
User: i would like to go to peterborough and leave after 12:45 , i have to attend a meeting beforehand .
Bot: tr1879 leaves at 13:06 on wednesday . will that work for you ?
User: what is the price of the fair and could you tell me what is the arrival time into peterborough ?
Bot: the price is 16.50 pounds and the train will arrive in peterborough by 13:56 wednesday . would you like me to book a ticket for you ?
User: yes , 1 ticket please , can i also get the reference number ?.
Bot: i booked you 1 seat on tr1879 departing cambridge for peterborough on wednesday at 13:06 , reference: xu1qlhvw . can i help further today ?
User: i am also looking for a museum in centre . could you give me the address , postcode and phone number of 1 ?
Bot: the broughton house gallery is located at 98 king street , postcode cb11ln . their phone number is 01223314960 . is there anything else you need ?
User: that s all i need right now . thanks , you have been very helpful !

Figure 6: The ground-truth to the synthesized dialog in Fig. 5. Speaker roles are added in bold to improve readability.

A Hybrid of Rule-based and Transformer-based Approaches for Relation Extraction in Biodiversity Literature

Roselyn Gabud[a,b,*], **Portia Lapitan**[c], **Vladimir Mariano**[d], **Eduardo Mendoza**[b,e]
Nelson Pampolina[c], **Maria Art Antonette Clariño**[b], **Riza Batista-Navarro**[b,f]

[a]Department of Computer Science, University of the Philippines Diliman
[b]Institute of Computer Science, University of the Philippines Los Baños
[c]Department of Forest Biological Sciences, University of the Philippines Los Baños
[d]YSEALI Academy, Fulbright University Vietnam
[e]Max Planck Institute of Biochemistry, Munich, Germany
[f]University of Manchester, United Kingdom
*rsgabud@up.edu.ph

Abstract

Relation extraction (RE) is one of the tasks behind many relevant natural language processing (NLP) applications. Exploiting the information hidden in millions of scholarly articles by leveraging NLP, specifically RE, systems could benefit studies in specialized domains, e.g. biomedicine and biodiversity. Although deep learning (DL)-based methods have shown state-of-the-art performance in many NLP tasks including RE, DL for domain-specific RE systems has been hindered by the lack of expert-labeled datasets which are typically required to train such methods. In this paper, we take advantage of the zero-shot (i.e., not requiring any labeled data) capability of pattern-based methods for RE using a rule-based approach, combined with templates for natural language inference (NLI) transformer models. We present our hybrid method for RE that exploits the advantages of both methods, i.e., interpretability of rules and transferability of transformers. Evaluated on a corpus of biodiversity literature with annotated relations, our hybrid method demonstrated an improvement of up to 15 percentage points in recall and best performance over solely rule-based and transformer-based methods with F1-scores ranging from 89.61% to 96.75% for reproductive condition - temporal expression relations, and ranging from 85.39% to 89.90% for habitat - geographic location relations.

1 Introduction

Relation extraction (RE) is a Natural Language Processing (NLP) task that is concerned with the identification of binary semantic relationships between entities or concepts in text. RE predicts whether a relationship holds between two entities (or concepts), based on the context of the sentence. Many approaches to RE take as input a sentence together with pre-extracted named entities (within the sentence), and identify relations between those entities using heuristics or machine learning-based approaches (Detroja et al., 2023). For example, in the sentence *"Semangkok Forest Reserve is a designated hill dipterocarp forest conservation area located in Selangor state about 60 km north of Kuala Lumpur, while Pasoh Forest Reserve, is a designated lowland dipterocarp forest conservation area in Negeri Sembilan about 60 km east - southeast of Kuala Lumpur, Peninsular Malaysia"*,[1] an RE system should be able to identify the relationship of the geographic location entity "Semangkok Forest Reserve" with the habitat entity "hill dipterocarp forest", but no relation between "Semangkok Forest Reserve" and "lowland dipterocarp forest". This type of information is helpful in associating information on habitats with geographic distribution of species.

Extracting information from text is better guided by domain knowledge of the targeted use case (Chiticariu et al., 2013; Waltl et al., 2018; Wu et al., 2022). For example, in the biodiversity domain, methods for extracting a plant species' *geographic location* with related *habitat* information, and *reproductive condition* (i.e., reproductive status) with related *temporal expression* that exist in biodiver-

[1]Source: Tani, N., et al. (2016). Selective logging simulations and male fecundity variation support customisation of management regimes for specific groups of dipterocarp species in Peninsular Malaysia. Journal of Tropical Forest Science, p370.

Proceedings of the 2nd Workshop in Pattern-based Approaches to NLP in the Age of Deep Learning , pages 103–113

sity texts, are better crafted with the involvement of domain experts. Rule-based methods lend themselves well to domain-specific RE tasks (Aljamel et al., 2015; Peng et al., 2016; Wang et al., 2022). Aside from being highly interpretable, such methods define a set of rules manually created by domain experts and capture syntactic patterns that are associated with different types of relations observed in a corpus (Ravikumar et al., 2017; Korger and Baumeister, 2021; Xu et al., 2022). Advancements in machine learning (ML) and, more recently, deep learning (DL), have led to state-of-the-art performance in RE. ML and DL-based models learn features from data giving them strong generalization ability, adaptability, and scalability. However, the performance of ML- and DL-based methods relies on the availability of domain-specific annotated datasets; this assumption is not always viable for many specialised domains such as biodiversity, law or finance (Thomas and Sivanesan, 2022).

In this paper, we integrate the advantages of both rule-based and DL-based RE methods by developing a zero-shot hybrid RE approach. Our main contribution is a novel hybrid RE method that is underpinned by a two-step approach. In the first step, we hand-crafted rules that capture syntactic patterns, which were implemented based on regular expressions (regexes). The second step leverages a state-of-the-art transformer model, Text-to-Text Transfer Transformer or T5 (Raffel et al., 2020), for natural language inference (NLI). We created premise-hypothesis templates as input for the T5-based NLI model, to determine if a relation holds between a given pair of entities. Our method presents the following advantages over other RE methods: (1) improved performance over solely rule-based or DL-based methods; (2) reduced computational bottleneck since a substantial proportion of the relations are extracted using the more computationally efficient rule-based method; and (3) reduced labeling cost associated with dataset or corpus annotation.

We applied our method on documents drawn from the body of literature on biodiversity – a relatively under-resourced domain – focusing on two types of relations: (1) plant species' reproductive conditions and their related temporal expressions, and (2) habitats and their related geographic locations. Harvesting these details from biodiversity literature will enable data-driven discovery of plant species' reproductive patterns and habitats. This, in turn, will aid in more informed plans for reforestation and restoration of land.

In the remainder of this paper, we first provide a review of prior work related to our study (Section 2). This is followed by our problem formulation (Section 3) and a description of the dataset we developed and used in our experiments (Section 4). Then, we present details of the zero-shot hybrid RE approach that we developed (Section 5), and the results of evaluating the hybrid model (Section 6). We then analyze our results (Section 7) before providing a summary of our findings and directions for future work in Section 8.

2 Related Work

Existing RE methods can be categorized into two broad types: traditional and DL-based methods. Traditional methods use either rules or machine learning techniques (e.g., those based on statistical classifiers trained on hand-crafted features) to extract a set of predefined relations from a corpus (Detroja et al., 2023). Rule-based methods define rules, which are a set of hand-crafted extraction patterns typically created by domain experts (Agichtein and Gravano, 2000; Fundel et al., 2007; Zhang et al., 2009; Nguyen et al., 2015). These rules are based on manually identified syntactic patterns that are associated with different types of relations, as observed in a corpus. Rules have the advantage of being highly interpretable: they can be easily understood by humans, which makes them a good choice for tasks where it is important to explain the reasoning behind the system's output. However, rule-based methods have two main limitations: they can be time-consuming to create and they are domain-dependent (e.g., a rule-based system that is designed to identify relations in medical text may not necessarily be able to identify relations in financial text). Meanwhile, ML techniques for RE are based on the supervised training of a classification model on a dataset whereby relations have been manually annotated. There are feature-based methods (Miller et al., 2000; Kambhatla, 2004) that use selected syntactic and semantic features as the bases of similarity in training a classification model. There are also kernel-based methods (Zelenko et al., 2002; Culotta and Sorensen, 2004) that use kernel functions to determine similarity between two relation instance representations, together with a support vector machine (SVM) model as a classifier. Although ML-based RE methods gained superiority in the past in terms of performance, their performance is greatly dependent on the set of selected features or the choice of kernel functions. As they are trained in a supervised manner, ML models also require labeled data which can be costly.

DL methods that have emerged more recently have been shown to outperform traditional methods for RE. These DL models learn higher-order, abstract feature representations from sentences that make them more generalizable, adaptable to new domains, and scalable. With the emergence of DL, models that employ neural architectures such as convolutional neural networks (CNNs) (Liu et al., 2013; dos Santos et al., 2015), recurrent neural networks (RNN) (Vu et al., 2016; Zhang and Wang, 2015), graph convolutional networks (GCN) (Zhu et al., 2019), attention-based neural networks (Wang et al., 2016; Xiao and Liu, 2016), and transformer-based language models (Vaswani et al., 2017; Le Guillarme and Thuiller, 2022) have been utilized for RE tasks. However, similar to traditional ML models, training or fine-tuning DL models for downstream applications such as RE also requires labeled data (Zhao et al., 2023).

In recent years, *zero-shot* transformer-based approaches to information extraction requiring no labeled data have become popular (Liu et al., 2020; Du and Cardie, 2021; Cheng et al., 2021; Li et al., 2022). For instance, Levy et al. (2017) reduced RE to the problem of answering simple reading comprehension questions. They mapped each relation type *R(x, y)* to at least one parameterized natural-language question q_x whose answer is *y*. For example, the relation *educated_at(x, y)* can be mapped to *"Where did x study?"* and *"Which university did x graduate from?"*. The success of these types of RE methods is primarily due to the significant developments in and availability of transformer-based pre-trained language models (PLMs) (Devlin et al., 2019; Liu et al., 2019; Raffel et al., 2020). PLMs were pre-trained on large-scale corpora using unsupervised learning objectives such as masked language modeling, and were then fine-tuned for downstream tasks, such as question answering (QA) and natural language inference (NLI), using relatively smaller amounts of task- or domain specific labeled data (Devlin et al., 2019). Zero-shot transformer-based approaches to RE are based on the careful, systematic construction of inputs for PLMs, which then elicit a model prediction (i.e., a label) that can be mapped to a decision on whether a certain type of relation holds. Zero-shot methods significantly reduce the labeling cost associated with RE because only a small amount of labeled data is required, i.e., test samples for evaluating the model.

In this work, we developed a zero-shot approach to RE that is the first of its kind to be applied in the biodiversity domain. Our zero-shot methods for RE are based on rules and transformer models that – when combined – demonstrate superior performance, in comparison to the use of rules or transformers alone.

3 Problem Formulation

Given an input sentence I that is a sequence of tokens $[t_0, t_1, ..., t_n]$, a source entity $E_S = [t_i, ..., t_j]$ and a target entity $E_T = [t_u, ..., t_v]$, we treat the RE task as a binary classification task, whereby the input is the triple (I, E_S, E_T), and the output is $y \in \{0, 1\}$ where 1 indicates that a relationship from the source entity to the target entity $(E_S \rightarrow E_T)$ exists, otherwise 0. In this work, we focus on the two relation types described below.

The `has_time` relation: This holds between a reproductive condition mention and a temporal expression, i.e., "*reproductive condition* `has_time` *temporal expression*", whereby the reproductive condition mention is considered to be the source and the temporal expression serves as the target.

The `has_location` relation: This holds between a habitat mention and a geographic location, i.e., "*habitat* `has_location` *geographic location*", whereby the habitat mention is considered to be the source and the geographic location is the target.

4 Dataset

To support the development of approaches to the above-mentioned problem, we utilized a corpus that is a subset[2] of the gold standard corpus for named entity recognition (NER) that was presented in the work of Gabud et al. (2019) and was designed in accordance to the annotation scheme used in the COPIOUS project (Nguyen et al., 2019). It contains information relevant to the occurrence and reproductive patterns of a tropical tree family, *Dipterocarpaceae* (dipterocarps). The corpus is

[2]Due to resource constraints, we made the decision at the beginning of the study to have only a limited number of documents manually annotated.

comprised of 151 manually selected one- to two-paragraph documents from online environmental science and ecology journal repositories, e.g., Journal of Tropical Ecology, Journal of Ecology, etc. For this RE work, we are particularly interested in the annotations of the following named entity (NE) types: habitat, geographic location, temporal expression, and reproductive condition. The descriptions and examples of these NE types are shown in Table 1. We selected sentences that contain at least one occurrence of an entity pair, i.e., either a pair of habitat and geographic location mentions, or a pair of reproductive condition and temporal expression mentions. We then produced relation annotations by creating data instances, each of which is in the form (I, E_S, E_T, y), where I is the input sentence, E_S is the source entity, E_T is the target entity, and y is the relation label which is set to 1 if a binary relation between the source and target entities hold, otherwise y is set to 0. As mentioned in the previous section, we decided to focus on two types of relations: `has_time` (which holds between a reproductive condition mention and a temporal expression), and `has_location` (which holds between a habitat mention and a geographic location). Table 2 shows the two data instances belonging to the `has_location` relation type, that were created from the following example sentence that contains one habitat and two geographic location entities: *"The main observation site was conserved forest at Dongmakhai (18deg 20' 03"N, 102deg 30' 5"E, 190m a.s.l.)."*

Concept	Description and Example
Habitat	Environments in which organisms live. e.g., *lowland mixed dipterocarp forests*
Geographic Location	Any identifiable point or area in the planet, ranging from continents, major bodies of water, named landforms, countries, etc. e.g., *Sabah*
Reproductive Condition	Indicators of the specimens' reproductive behaviour. e.g., *mast fruiting*
Temporal Expression	Spans of text pertaining to points in time. e.g., *mid-August*

Table 1: Descriptions and examples of our biodiversity entity types of interest.

Two annotators manually provided the label y for each data instance (I, E_S, E_T, y). Our more senior annotator, a Biology degree holder, labeled all the instances in the entire dataset, while a junior annotator, a Computer Science student, provided labels for 30% of the dataset only. They carried out the annotation task independently. We calculated the agreement between our two annotators in terms of F1-score, and obtained an overall agreement of 95.87%. The agreement for the `has_time` relation type is 94.36%, while that for the `has_location` type is 97.37%. We resolved the disagreements by involving a third annotator who is a co-author of this work. The instances with disagreements were re-evaluated and re-labeled by the third annotator. We randomly split our dataset into 70% training set, 10% development set, and 20% test set. Table 3 shows the number of instances for each relation type.

Habitat	Geo. Location
conserved forest	*Dongmakhai*
conserved forest	*18deg 20' 03"N , 102deg 30' 5"E*

Table 2: Example data instances of the `has_location` relation type based on the sentence, *"The main observation site was conserved forest at Dongmakhai (18deg 20' 03"N, 102deg 30' 5"E, 190m a.s.l.)."*

Relation Type	train	dev	test
`has_time`	843	173	388
`has_location`	252	34	127

Table 3: Frequency of instances for each relation type in our training (train), development (dev) and test sets.

5 Methods

In this section, we present our methods for extracting (1) related reproductive condition and temporal expressions (`has_time`), and (2) related habitat and geographic location mentions (`has_location`).

5.1 Regular Expression-based Rules

We created rules based on syntactic patterns (i.e., word order) that were observed in sentences, and implemented pattern-matching using regular expressions (regexes) to extract related biodiversity entities. Given an input sentence, I, that is a sequence of tokens $[t_0, t_1, ..., t_n]$, we firstly categorized every token t_i according to the following

Token type	Symbol	Description	Entity type
source	S	a token that belongs to a named entity type identified as a source category	reproductive condition or habitat
target	T	a token that belongs to a named entity type identified as a target category	temporal expression or geographic location
delimiter	d	a token that is a separator in an enumeration	comma or semicolon
other	o	any token that is neither a part of a named entity nor a delimiter	

Table 4: Types of tokens we designed for the regular expression-based rules.

types: *source*, *target*, *delimiter*, and *other* as shown in Table 4. We define *source* as a token that belongs to a named entity identified as a source entity type, i.e., either reproductive condition (for `has_time` relations) or habitat (for `has_location` relations). Meanwhile, *target* is a token that belongs to a named entity considered to be a target entity type, i.e., temporal expression (for `has_time` relations) or geographic location (for `has_location` relations). *Delimiter* is a token that acts as a separator in an enumeration, i.e., a comma or semicolon. Any token that is neither a part of a named entity nor a delimiter is categorized as *other*. We convert each token t_i into a character representation of the token's type. Hence, we convert a sentence into a string of characters, wherein each character is either `S` (source), `T` (target), `d` (delimeter), or `o` (other). We use this sequence of token types as input to our regex method implemented using Python's regular expression module, `re`. To extract relations, we created the following regex rules:

1. `[S]+(o)?(To|Td|T)+` – *source* token that may or may not be followed by one *other* token, then followed by one or more *target* tokens that may or may not be delimited by any token, and
2. `(?<!S)(To|Td|T)*T(o)?[S]+` – one or more *target* tokens that may or may not be delimited by any token that is not immediately preceded by a *source* token, and followed by a *source* token that may or may not be preceded by one *other* token.

The entity spans (i.e., source and target tokens) that match the patterns above are perceived to be related, and are given the value 1 for y. Figure 1 shows a sample sentence with a text span that matches regex rule 1 above.

5.2 Transformer-based Models

We cast our RE problem as a natural language inference (NLI) problem that we address using a transformer-based model. NLI is the task of determining whether a *hypothesis* is true (`entailment`), false (`contradiction`), or unverifiable (`neutral`) given a *premise* which corresponds to some known knowledge about the subject. We selected the Text-to-Text Transfer Transformer (T5) (Raffel et al., 2020) as our model. Underpinned by a transformer encoder-decoder architecture (Vaswani et al., 2017), T5 casts various NLP tasks (e.g., machine translation, text classification, question answering) as a sequence-to-sequence learning problem, therefore producing outputs via text generation. NLI is one of the downstream NLP tasks that T5 was already fine-tuned on. We used the T5-large model[3] specifically, with 770 million parameters. Given an input sentence I and two entities E_S and E_T for which we wish to determine whether a relation holds,[4] we systematically generate a premise-hypothesis pair which serves as input to the NLI model. Specifically, the input sentence I is taken as the premise, while the hypothesis is created by populating either of the following sentence templates with E_1 and E_2:

- *The <habitat> was in <geographic location>.*
- *The <reproductive condition> event happened on <temporal expression>.*

[3] Available at `https://huggingface.co/t5-large`

[4] The two entities are considered only if one of them is a reproductive condition mention (E_S) and the other is a temporal expression (E_T), or if one of them is a habitat mention (E_S) and the other is a geographic location (E_T). This, respectively, means that we are aiming to determine if a `has_time` or `has_location` relation possibly holds between them.

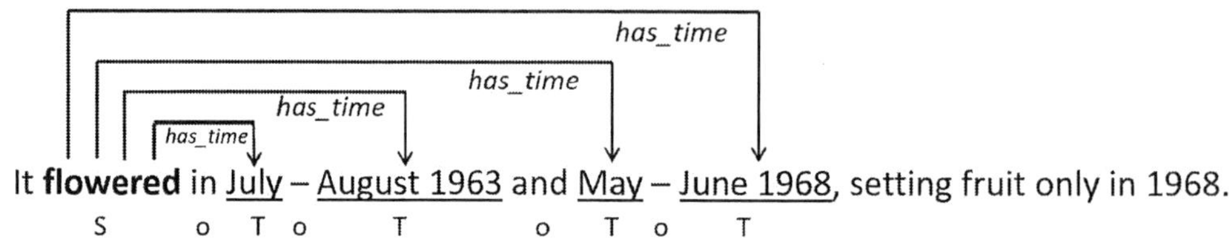

Figure 1: Example sentence with entity pairs that matched the rule `[S]+(o)?(To|Td|T)+`, where S corresponds to reproductive condition (in bold) which is the *source* entity, T corresponds to temporal expression (underlined) which is the *target* entity and o refers to *other* tokens. Source of example sentence: Medway, L. (1972). Phenology of a tropical rain forest in Malaya. Biological Journal of the Linnean Society, 4(2), p128.

Table 5 provides some example inputs for the T5-based NLI model, and its expected outputs. Due to variations in noun forms or verb tenses, the automatically generated hypothesis may not necessarily be grammatically correct; for instance, the example for the `has_time` relation in Table 5 would be more correct if it reads *"The fruiting event happened on August 1963"*. Nevertheless, we did not carry out any engineering on our templates to handle such variations, as we expected the transformers-based NLI model to be robust to such grammatical errors.

For our purposes, we say that a relationship between two entities exists if the model's predicted class is `entailment`, otherwise the entities are considered to be unrelated.

5.3 Hybrid Approach: Rules and Transformers

In order to improve performance and reduce required computational resources, we designed a two-step solution to our RE problem. Here, we combined our rule-based syntactic pattern matching and transformer-based approaches. The first step is to extract relations using our regex rules. These are the regular expressions we designed to extract consecutive entities in a sentence. The instances that were not identified as not pertaining to any relations using the first step, are fed into the second step. In this step, our transformer-based model is applied on the remaining instances. This step produces a set of related entities using less computational resources compared to running the transformer-based model on the entire dataset.

We investigated the incorporation of an enhancement to our hybrid approach: the use of compound entities in filling in the hypothesis templates instead of using single entity mentions, where applicable. We designed rules to identify multiple, consecutive entities in a given sentence that belong to the same entity type and thus comprise a compound entity $E_{compound}$. The regular expression that was designed to extract $E_{compound}$ is `(Et|E){2,}`, where `E` is a named entity of a specific type, and `t` is any token. $E_{compound}$ consists of consecutive entities belonging to the same entity type `E`, which may or may not be delimited by a token (`t`). For example, given the sentence *"It flowered in July - August 1963 and May - June 1968, setting fruit only on 1968."*, the reproductive condition is expressed by the mention *"flowered"* and the compound temporal expression is *"July - August 1963 and May - June 1968"*. Instead of populating a hypothesis template for every temporal expression, we formulated only one hypothesis: *"The flowered event happened on July - August 1963 and May - June 1968."*

6 Evaluation and Results

In this paper, we designed rules based on our training set. We tested and refined these rules on a held-out development (dev) set, and evaluated their performance using the test set. Table 6 presents the performance of our rule-based, transformer-based, and hybrid RE methods in terms of precision, recall and F1-score.

We applied the regular expression rules we created to extract related entities in a given sentence. This approach resulted in 100% precision for both relation types. This means that our regex-based rules can reliably identify positive samples, i.e., correct relations. However, this approach obtains poor recall, i.e., 33.91% and 36.96% for `has_time` and `has_location` relations, respectively, implying that our rules fail to identify many correct relations. This results in the lowest F1-scores (50.64% and 53.97%, respectively) among the methods we investigated. Even using a simple co-occurrence approach obtains much higher F1-scores: 94.57%

Relation Type	Hypothesis Template	Examples		
		Premise	Hypothesis	NLI Output
`has_location`	The <**habitat**> was in <**geographic location**>.	*Bukit Sai and Lesong belong to the lowland dipterocarp forest types with D. aromatica being the predominant species.*	*The **lowland dipterocarp forest** was in **Bukit Sai**.*	`entailment`
`has_time`	The <**reproductive condition**> event happened on <**temporal expression**>.	*It flowered in July - August 1963 and May - June 1968 , setting fruit only in 1968.*	*The **fruit** event happened on **August 1963**.*	`contradiction`

Table 5: Examples of populated hypothesis templates for generating inputs (premise-hypothesis pairs) for the NLI model, together with the corresponding expected outputs by the NLI model. A relation holds between two given entities (in bold) only if the NLI model predicts `entailment` as the output label. Source of the first input sentence (premise): Lee, S. L. (2000). Mating system parameters of Dryobalanops aromatica Gaertn. f.(Dipterocarpaceae) in three different forest types and a seed orchard. Heredity, 85(4), p339, and Medway, L. (1972). Phenology of a tropical rain forest in Malaya. Biological Journal of the Linnean Society, 4(2), p128.

for `has_time` and 84.02% for `has_location` relations.

To evaluate our transformer-based approach, we applied our chosen T5 model on the NLI task, building upon the Huggingface library[5]. Our evaluation on the test set yielded F1-scores higher than our rule-based method. For the `has_location` relation type, our transformer method produced an F1-score of 84.75%, which is slightly higher than that of the co-occurrence-based method (84.02%). However, the transformer-based method was outperformed by the co-occurrence-based one by 7.59 percentage points (86.98% vs 94.57% in terms of F1-score).

It is noticeable that combining our rule-based approach with the transformer model to form a hybrid approach improved the F1-score for the `has_time` relation type from 86.98% to 89.61%, and from 84.75% to 85.39% for the `has_location` relation type. Apart from improved performance, our hybrid approach is also more efficient, in that it requires the application of the more computationally expensive transformer models only on instances that were not classified by the rule-based approach as pertaining to relations.

We further improved our hybrid approach by using compound entities identified using regex rules in generating premise-hypothesis pairs for the transformer model, instead of separate single entities. We evaluated this method (referred to as 'hybrid + compound entities' in Table 6) on our test set and we observed that it obtained the highest F1-scores among all our investigated methods. Specifically, it led to an F1-score of 96.75% for `has_time` relations, and 89.90% for `has_location` relations.

7 Discussion

Our rule-based method is the most precise among all the methods we developed in this study. However, it is also the method that yielded the lowest recall, missing to identify more than half of true relations in the test set. The rule-based approach is suitable for applications that cannot compromise on precision, e.g., systems that support clinical decisions or automatic curation of databases. Its main drawback, however, is its reliance on syntactic similarity only, i.e., solely on patterns found within sentences. Thus, it is not robust to noisy data; any deviation from the expected sentence structure that is captured by the rules, would affect the performance of the method.

Among the methods presented in this paper, our transformer-based method is the most straightforward to implement. It is based on the population of natural-language hypothesis templates with named

[5]Available at `https://github.com/huggingface/transformers`

RE Approach	has_time			has_location		
	P	**R**	**F1**	**P**	**R**	**F1**
Co-occurrence	89.69%	100.00%	94.57%	72.44%	100.00%	84.02%
Regex-based rules	100.00%	33.91%	50.64%	100.00%	36.96%	53.97%
Transformer (T5)	97.16%	78.74%	86.98%	88.24%	81.52%	84.75%
Hybrid	97.31%	83.05%	89.61%	88.37%	82.61%	85.39%
Hybrid + compound entities	95.26%	98.28%	**96.75%**	83.96%	96.74%	**89.90%**

Table 6: Precision (P), Recall (R), and F1-score (F1) of our RE Methods on the test set for has_time and has_location relations.

entities, which are then fed to the NLI model (together with their corresponding premise). The transformer model paired with our hypothesis templates for RE provided us with F1-scores higher than those obtained by our rule-based method.

Our hybrid approach combines the strengths of the rule-based method (i.e., high precision) and the transformer-based model (i.e., high recall). This approach increased the recall for has_time relations by 4.28 percentage points and the recall for has_location relations by 1.09 percentage points, respectively. Error analysis of a small sample of instances from the development dataset showed that the hybrid method failed to identify relations that involve entities in an enumeration. For example, in the sentence *"Ashton et al (1988) record the extent of mass flowerings in peninsular Malaysia and Borneo for the period 1950 - 1983 based on state forest department records (table 5)"*,[6] the hybrid approach failed to determine that there is a relationship between *"mass flowerings"* and *"1983"*. Thus, as an enhancement to the hybrid method, we created regex rules to identify compound entities in sentences, as described in Section 5.3. Where they exist, these compound entities were used in populating the hypothesis templates, instead of individual named entities. With the incorporation of this step, the recall of the hybrid model was improved by 14-15 percentage points (i.e., 98.28% vs 83.05% for the has_time and 96.74% vs 82.61% for the has_location relations). This improved version of the hybrid approach ('hybrid + compound entities') provided us with the best F1-scores for both relation types (96.75% for has_time and 89.90% for has_location), among all the approaches we developed. These results demonstrate the role that rule-based methods can still play in complementing state-of-the-art DL approaches, i.e., transformers, enabling us to obtain optimal performance in RE.

[6]Source: Appanah, S. (1993). Mass flowering of dipterocarp forests in the aseasonal tropics. Journal of Biosciences, 18, p463.

8 Conclusions and Future Work

In this paper, we present our unsupervised relation extraction methods to extract relationships pertaining to habitats and reproductive conditions of plant species as described in text. These methods include: (1) regular expression-based rules; (2) transformer-based models for NLI; (3) a hybrid approach combining our rules and transformer model; and (4) an improved hybrid approach that captures compound entities. Our rule-based method undepinned by regexes obtained the highest precision but lowest recall. Meanwhile, our transformer-based method, which is based on the systematic generation of premise-hypothesis pairs as input for a T5-based NLI model, resulted in F1-score values higher than those produced by the regex rules. The strengths of the rule- and transformer-based methods are combined in our hybrid approach. With the incorporation of compound entities in the generation of NLI inputs, our hybrid approach produced the best performance, with F1-scores of 96.75% for the has_time relation type, and 89.90% for the has_location relation type. Our work shows that even without a large labeled training dataset, it is viable to extract – with satisfactory performance – relations between entities from biodiversity literature. This also shows that the combination of rules or pattern-based methods with state-of-the-art transformer models can lead to an improvement in the performance of RE, compared with a method that is solely based on transformers.

For our future work, we plan to compare our

hybrid approach with state-of-the-art zero-shot relation extraction methods, e.g., those proposed by Tran et al. (2022) and Najafi and Fyshe (2023), evaluating it on other datasets such as FewRel (Han et al., 2018) and WikiZSL (Chen and Li, 2021) which were drawn from the general domain. Furthermore, we will explore using other transformer-based models and formulating RE in terms of other downstream tasks, e.g., question answering. We also intend to integrate our hybrid approach into an application, i.e., an information extraction pipeline that can automate the curation of information from literature to populate a biodiversity-focused database.

Limitations

For this work, we focused on the requirements of a biodiversity-focused project, which is concerned with extracting information about the distribution and reproductive patterns of species in the *Dipterocarpaceae* (dipterocarps) family. We have evaluated the performance of our RE methods only on the dataset described above, and not on a wider range of datasets. The main reason for this is the lack of other datasets (drawn from the biodiversity domain) that are concerned with similar relation types. It is also worth noting that our RE methods are able to extract intra-sentential relations only, i.e., relations between entities within the same sentence.

Ethics Statement

For this work, we used an already existing dataset drawn from the biodiversity domain, that does not pose any data protection issues given that the documents comprising the corpus are all publicly available. All annotators volunteered to carry out the annotation task. They were trained and were explicitly informed that their work will be utilized in this study. Institutional ethical approval was not required as no personal data was collected, and the data that was being annotated did not contain any sensitive information.

Acknowledgements

We thank our annotators for their valuable work in annotating our RE dataset.

References

Eugene Agichtein and Luis Gravano. 2000. Snowball: extracting relations from large plain-text collections. In *Proceedings of the fifth ACM conference on Digital libraries*, DL '00, pages 85–94, New York, NY, USA. Association for Computing Machinery.

Abduladem Aljamel, Taha Osman, and Giovanni Acampora. 2015. Domain-Specific Relation Extraction - Using Distant Supervision Machine Learning:. In *Proceedings of the 7th International Joint Conference on Knowledge Discovery, Knowledge Engineering and Knowledge Management*, pages 92–103, Lisbon, Portugal. SCITEPRESS - Science and and Technology Publications.

Chih-Yao Chen and Cheng-Te Li. 2021. ZS-BERT: Towards zero-shot relation extraction with attribute representation learning. In *Proceedings of the 2021 Conference of the North American Chapter of the Association for Computational Linguistics: Human Language Technologies*, pages 3470–3479, Online. Association for Computational Linguistics.

Jiayang Cheng, Haiyun Jiang, Deqing Yang, and Yanghua Xiao. 2021. A Question-answering Based Framework for Relation Extraction Validation. ArXiv:2104.02934 [cs].

Laura Chiticariu, Yunyao Li, and Frederick R. Reiss. 2013. Rule-Based Information Extraction is Dead! Long Live Rule-Based Information Extraction Systems! In *Proceedings of the 2013 Conference on Empirical Methods in Natural Language Processing*, pages 827–832, Seattle, Washington, USA. Association for Computational Linguistics.

Aron Culotta and Jeffrey Sorensen. 2004. Dependency Tree Kernels for Relation Extraction. In *Proceedings of the 42nd Annual Meeting of the Association for Computational Linguistics (ACL-04)*, pages 423–429, Barcelona, Spain.

Kartik Detroja, C. K. Bhensdadia, and Brijesh S. Bhatt. 2023. A survey on Relation Extraction. *Intelligent Systems with Applications*, 19:200244.

Jacob Devlin, Ming-Wei Chang, Kenton Lee, and Kristina Toutanova. 2019. BERT: Pre-training of Deep Bidirectional Transformers for Language Understanding. In *Proceedings of the 2019 Conference of the North American Chapter of the Association for Computational Linguistics: Human Language Technologies, Volume 1 (Long and Short Papers)*, pages 4171–4186, Minneapolis, Minnesota. Association for Computational Linguistics.

Cícero dos Santos, Bing Xiang, and Bowen Zhou. 2015. Classifying Relations by Ranking with Convolutional Neural Networks. In *Proceedings of the 53rd Annual Meeting of the Association for Computational Linguistics and the 7th International Joint Conference on Natural Language Processing (Volume 1: Long Papers)*, pages 626–634, Beijing, China. Association for Computational Linguistics.

Xinya Du and Claire Cardie. 2021. Event Extraction by Answering (Almost) Natural Questions. ArXiv:2004.13625 [cs].

Katrin Fundel, Robert Küffner, and Ralf Zimmer. 2007. RelEx—Relation extraction using dependency parse trees. *Bioinformatics*, 23(3):365–371.

R. S. Gabud, R. T. Batista-Navarro, V. Y. Mariano, E. R. Mendoza, and S. L. Yap. 2019. Literature mining on dipterocarps: towards better informed natural regeneration and reforestation in Luzon, Philippines. *The Technical Journal of Philippine Ecosystems and National Resources*.

Xu Han, Hao Zhu, Pengfei Yu, Ziyun Wang, Yuan Yao, Zhiyuan Liu, and Maosong Sun. 2018. FewRel: A Large-Scale Supervised Few-Shot Relation Classification Dataset with State-of-the-Art Evaluation. In *Proceedings of the 2018 Conference on Empirical Methods in Natural Language Processing*, pages 4803–4809, Brussels, Belgium. Association for Computational Linguistics.

N. Kambhatla. 2004. Combining Lexical, Syntactic, and Semantic Features with Maximum Entropy Models for Information Extraction.

Andreas Korger and Joachim Baumeister. 2021. Rule-based Semantic Relation Extraction in Regulatory Documents.

Nicolas Le Guillarme and Wilfried Thuiller. 2022. TaxoNERD: Deep neural models for the recognition of taxonomic entities in the ecological and evolutionary literature. *Methods in Ecology and Evolution*, 13(3):625–641. _eprint: https://onlinelibrary.wiley.com/doi/pdf/10.1111/2041-210X.13778.

Omer Levy, Minjoon Seo, Eunsol Choi, and Luke Zettlemoyer. 2017. Zero-Shot Relation Extraction via Reading Comprehension. ArXiv:1706.04115 [cs].

Xiaoya Li, Jingrong Feng, Yuxian Meng, Qinghong Han, Fei Wu, and Jiwei Li. 2022. A Unified MRC Framework for Named Entity Recognition. ArXiv:1910.11476 [cs].

ChunYang Liu, WenBo Sun, WenHan Chao, and WanXiang Che. 2013. Convolution Neural Network for Relation Extraction. In *Advanced Data Mining and Applications*, Lecture Notes in Computer Science, pages 231–242, Berlin, Heidelberg. Springer.

Jian Liu, Yubo Chen, Kang Liu, Wei Bi, and Xiaojiang Liu. 2020. Event Extraction as Machine Reading Comprehension. In *Proceedings of the 2020 Conference on Empirical Methods in Natural Language Processing (EMNLP)*, pages 1641–1651, Online. Association for Computational Linguistics.

Yinhan Liu, Myle Ott, Naman Goyal, Jingfei Du, Mandar Joshi, Danqi Chen, Omer Levy, Mike Lewis, Luke Zettlemoyer, and Veselin Stoyanov. 2019. RoBERTa: A Robustly Optimized BERT Pretraining Approach. ArXiv:1907.11692 [cs].

Scott Miller, Heidi Fox, Lance Ramshaw, and Ralph Weischedel. 2000. A Novel Use of Statistical Parsing to Extract Information from Text. In *1st Meeting of the North American Chapter of the Association for Computational Linguistics*.

Saeed Najafi and Alona Fyshe. 2023. Weakly-supervised questions for zero-shot relation extraction. In *Proceedings of the 17th Conference of the European Chapter of the Association for Computational Linguistics*, pages 3075–3087, Dubrovnik, Croatia. Association for Computational Linguistics.

Nhung T.H. Nguyen, Roselyn S. Gabud, and Sophia Ananiadou. 2019. COPIOUS: A gold standard corpus of named entities towards extracting species occurrence from biodiversity literature. *Biodiversity Data Journal*, (7):e29626.

Nhung TH Nguyen, Makoto Miwa, Yoshimasa Tsuruoka, Takashi Chikayama, and Satoshi Tojo. 2015. Wide-coverage relation extraction from MEDLINE using deep syntax. *BMC Bioinformatics*, 16(1):107.

Yifan Peng, Chih-Hsuan Wei, and Zhiyong Lu. 2016. Improving chemical disease relation extraction with rich features and weakly labeled data. *Journal of Cheminformatics*, 8(1):53.

Colin Raffel, Noam Shazeer, Adam Roberts, Katherine Lee, Sharan Narang, Michael Matena, Yanqi Zhou, Wei Li, and Peter J. Liu. 2020. Exploring the Limits of Transfer Learning with a Unified Text-to-Text Transformer. ArXiv:1910.10683 [cs, stat].

K.E. Ravikumar, Majid Rastegar-Mojarad, and Hongfang Liu. 2017. BELMiner: adapting a rule-based relation extraction system to extract biological expression language statements from bio-medical literature evidence sentences. *Database*, 2017:baw156.

Anu Thomas and Sangeetha Sivanesan. 2022. An adaptable, high-performance relation extraction system for complex sentences. *Knowledge-Based Systems*, 251:108956.

Van-Hien Tran, Hiroki Ouchi, Taro Watanabe, and Yuji Matsumoto. 2022. Improving discriminative learning for zero-shot relation extraction. In *Proceedings of the 1st Workshop on Semiparametric Methods in NLP: Decoupling Logic from Knowledge*, pages 1–6, Dublin, Ireland and Online. Association for Computational Linguistics.

Ashish Vaswani, Noam Shazeer, Niki Parmar, Jakob Uszkoreit, Llion Jones, Aidan N Gomez, Łukasz Kaiser, and Illia Polosukhin. 2017. Attention is All you Need. In *Advances in Neural Information Processing Systems*, volume 30. Curran Associates, Inc.

Thang Vu, Heike Adel, Pankaj Gupta, and Hinrich Schütze. 2016. Combining Recurrent and Convolutional Neural Networks for Relation Classification.

Bernhard Waltl, Georg Bonczek, and Florian Matthes. 2018. Rule-based Information Extraction: Advantages, Limitations, and Perspectives. *Jusletter IT*, (4).

Linlin Wang, Zhu Cao, Gerard de Melo, and Zhiyuan Liu. 2016. Relation Classification via Multi-Level Attention CNNs. pages 1298–1307.

Xinzhi Wang, Jiahao Li, Ze Zheng, Yudong Chang, and Min Zhu. 2022. Entity and relation extraction with rule-guided dictionary as domain knowledge. *Frontiers of Engineering Management*, 9(4):610–622.

Lang-Tao Wu, Jia-Rui Lin, Shuo Leng, Jiu-Lin Li, and Zhen-Zhong Hu. 2022. Rule-based information extraction for mechanical-electrical-plumbing-specific semantic web. *Automation in Construction*, 135:104108.

Minguang Xiao and Cong Liu. 2016. Semantic Relation Classification via Hierarchical Recurrent Neural Network with Attention. In *Proceedings of COLING 2016, the 26th International Conference on Computational Linguistics: Technical Papers*, pages 1254–1263, Osaka, Japan. The COLING 2016 Organizing Committee.

Na Xu, Hong Chang, Bai Xiao, Bo Zhang, Jie Li, and Tiantian Gu. 2022. Relation Extraction of Domain Knowledge Entities for Safety Risk Management in Metro Construction Projects. *Buildings*, 12(10):1633. Number: 10 Publisher: Multidisciplinary Digital Publishing Institute.

Dmitry Zelenko, Chinatsu Aone, and Anthony Richardella. 2002. Kernel methods for relation extraction. In *Proceedings of the ACL-02 conference on Empirical methods in natural language processing - Volume 10*, EMNLP '02, pages 71–78, USA. Association for Computational Linguistics.

Chunju Zhang, Xueying Zhang, Wenming Jiang, Qijun Shen, and Shanqi Zhang. 2009. Rule-Based Extraction of Spatial Relations in Natural Language Text. In *2009 International Conference on Computational Intelligence and Software Engineering*, pages 1–4.

Dongxu Zhang and Dong Wang. 2015. Relation Classification via Recurrent Neural Network. ArXiv:1508.01006 [cs].

Youwen Zhao, Xiangbo Yuan, Ye Yuan, Shaoxiong Deng, and Jun Quan. 2023. Relation extraction: advancements through deep learning and entity-related features. *Social Network Analysis and Mining*, 13(1):92.

Hao Zhu, Yankai Lin, Zhiyuan Liu, Jie Fu, Tat-Seng Chua, and Maosong Sun. 2019. Graph Neural Networks with Generated Parameters for Relation Extraction. In *Proceedings of the 57th Annual Meeting of the Association for Computational Linguistics*, pages 1331–1339, Florence, Italy. Association for Computational Linguistics.

Author Index

Abdar, Omid, 54

Batista-Navarro, Riza, 103
Belz, Anya, 25

Cassidy, Lauren, 25
Chen, Derek, 43
Cheng, Liang, 75
Chiu, Justin, 43
Clariño, Maria Art Antonette, 103

Dasiopoulou, Stamatia, 25
Davis, Brian, 25
Dong, Annie, 54

Feng, Yue, 20
Forbus, Kenneth, 54
Fried, Daniel, 43

Gabud, Roselyn, 103
Goetz, Jack, 54
Gu, Jiasheng, 64

Han, Zhen, 20
Hosseini, Mohammad Javad, 75

Lapitan, Portia, 103
Lim, Stanley, 6
Ludwig, Bernd, 92

Mariano, Vladimir, 103
Mendoza, Eduardo, 103
Mille, Simon, 25
Mohamed, Ahmed, 54

Nan, Zifan, 64
Neves Ribeiro, Danilo, 54

Pampolina, Nelson, 103
Parikh, Ankur, 1
Peng, Nanyun, 6
Peng, Zhiyuan, 64

Rajpoot, Pawan, 1
Ross, Mike, 54
Rush, Alexander, 43

Schäfer, Ulrich, 92
Shen, Xipeng, 64
Steedman, Mark, 75
Steindl, Sebastian, 92
Sun, Mingming, 20

Uí Dhonnchadha, Elaine, 25

Vaduguru, Saujas, 43

Xu, Dongkuan, 64

Yin, Da, 6

Zhao, Wenting, 43

Association for Computational Linguistics
209 N. Eighth Street
Stroudsburg, Pennsylvania 18360

ISBN 978-1-7138-8606-8

9 781713 886068

proceedings.com